A D

A Dysfunctional Success

Success

The Wreckless Eric Manual by

Eric Goulden

First Published in Great Britain in 2003 by
The Do-Not Press Limited
16 The Woodlands
London SE13 6TY
www.thedonotpress.com
email: eric@thedonotpress.com

ISBN 1 904 316 18 2

British Library Cataloguing in Publication Data. A
catalogue record for this book is available from the
British Library.

1 3 5 7 9 10 8 6 4 2

Printed and bound in Great Britain

Thanks to Karen Hibberd, Kathie Jenkins, Luci Goulden, Tony Judge, Andre Barreau, Johnny Green, Deborah Lowen and Suzanne Duncanson

For Wreckless Frank & Wreckless Dorothy

Sussex by the Sea

IT'S DIFFICULT TO KNOW WHERE to start, so I think I'll begin at the beginning and see how I get on…

I was born in Newhaven, Sussex, on May 18th, 1954, in the living room of a rented terraced house – 22 Railway Road – opposite the railway station. My dad was a draughtsman, working for the Parker Pen Company that was just a little bit further down the road.

I've often thought that my birth would make a good beginning for a rock opera or a musical. I was born at twenty past five on a Tuesday afternoon. While I was being delivered (*an unfortunate turn of phrase – 'delivered' – it gives the impression that I came in a van, when in fact I was coaxed out of my mother by a no-nonsense local midwife*) my dad was in the garden playing football with my three-year-old sister. Moments after the happy event, the factory siren sounded and he stood at the front gate, holding my sister in his arms. As his workmates filed past en route for the railway station and town centre he said, over and over again, 'It's a boy, it's a boy…'

Of course, it's all very well beginning at the beginning but I can't really remember much. I was only a baby after all. I can only remember things in bits and pieces – it's as though it slowly dawned on me that I was alive. I remember the garden, a creamy white knitted blanket and earthworms.

The boy next door was called Colin. He lived with his grandparents. He was a bit older than me. One afternoon he tipped earth over me and went off to play with the fat kid, John, who lived next door to him on the other side. John was a bit slow – he wore thick glasses. He wasn't all there – whatever that meant.

Colin had a red pedal car. I always wanted to have a go in it but I don't think I ever did. We used to play in the alleyway at the back of the houses. Colin, John, me and my sister. There might have been some other girls too but I wasn't that interested in girls so I can't remember. We wee-weed up the wall, but the girls couldn't do that. Then we weren't allowed to play in the alleyway because there was a tramp living in the empty house.

They sat me on the draining board and I saw trains going past through the kitchen window. Steam trains and trains without steam that were just passenger carriages with no engine. At night I heard the sound of shunting in the goods yard. I knew what that sound was because I'd seen it in the day. There was a bridge over the river with a railway track in the middle of the road. The train came out of a gate – a great big black locomotive led by a man with a red flag. It went through some big corrugated iron gates at the other side of the bridge behind the bus shelter.

Shopping with my mum. They gave me biscuits and tried to make me smile but I never would. I just sat there in my pushchair making car noises. There was a big trap-door in the middle of the floor. The man in the shop wore a white coat and sometimes he disappeared through the trapdoor into the floor.

I gave myself a haircut just like daddy at the hair-dressers, covered with a blanket and chatting as I snipped. They didn't know where I'd got the scissors from.

I pulled the radio down on top of my head. It was mended with Sellotape and glue.

We moved house when I was nearly four – to a bungalow in Peacehaven. Bungalow meant no stairs, nowhere to play at buses.

No more Colin.

I listened to the radio – the Home Service, *Listen With Mother*:

'Are you sitting comfortably?'

'No.'

'Then we'll begin...'

Other times I watched the television – *Watch With Mother*.

Monday was *Picture Book* – boring.

Tuesday was *Andy Pandy* – better, he wore a stripy one-piece thing but I never knew what it was all about.

Wednesday was *Bill & Ben* – 'Bill and Ben, Bill and Ben, Flowerpot men.' They climbed out of flowerpots, one each side of the Weed, when the gardener went to have his dinner. Then they mucked about for ten minutes until the Weed said 'Weeeeed', which meant that the gardener was coming back. I was very worried in case they didn't get back into the flowerpots in time. But they always did. Bye-bye Bill, bye-bye Ben.

Thursday was *Rag, Tag & Bobtail* – I couldn't begin to understand it but it didn't matter.

And the week ended with the *Woodentops* – '...Sam that worked on the farm and the BIGGEST SPOTTY DOG YOU EVER DID SEE!' That was my favourite. I could have stayed home forever.

I had a red bus. It was a big red plastic one with a friction motor. I loved my red bus. I took a psychotic dislike to it. I screamed and threw it down the step on to the kitchen floor in the old house. Frustration and fury. After several such episodes they hid it. It resurfaced when my mum was clearing out a cupboard. I was delighted. 'Ooh, there's my red bus.' It hit the kitchen floor, 'I Hate It…'.

My sister went to a convent school in Rottingdean. Soon I went there too. The place was run by nuns. My sister was in the big class but I was in the kindergarten. The nuns were all very frightening, apart from the round, friendly Sister Mary Pauline and Sister Jan Elizabeth who was only frightening when she was cross, and she was only cross when she caught us talking about bottoms and other rude things.

I didn't like going to school. It was always winter and they made me sit in the dining room and eat everything on the plate even though I hated semolina and it was playtime outside.

We had to go with Mrs Freeman, the dentist's wife.

The Freemans lived on the South Coast Road in a big house that was also the dentist's surgery. They had identical twin sons, Roy and Neil, who were the same age as my sister. Mrs Freeman took us all to the convent in a light blue Austin Cambridge estate. She called us 'chaps' – I think that was because she came from New Zealand. I didn't want to go and my mum had to drag me along the South Coast Road screaming and crying – through rain, wind, snot and tears. I wasn't always a happy child.

Sister Jan Elizabeth started teaching me to draw numbers and letters and one day she said she was going to teach me to read, and suddenly I could.

And suddenly I was seven, and then I was eight.

I couldn't really understand why we went to a Catholic

school. Our family wasn't Catholic – we were Church of England. I found the Catholic business confusing. All the Hail Marys and statues of Our Lady and rosary beads, and the school chapel with the china thing in the wall full of cotton wool and holy water, and crossing yourself and going down on one knee. We had to learn the catechism. I didn't know what it was but it started: 'What is God?' and the whole class said 'God is love!' And then the questions got more complicated and so did the answers.

As well as being Church of England agnostic, my family, both sides of it, were also northern working class. They came from the surrounding areas of Manchester, particularly Oldham. My mother's parents managed to save enough money and bought a newsagents shop.

Life in the newsagency business was hell on earth – cramped accommodation, early mornings, frayed tempers, customers. But it was a start, and by the end of the 1940s they were able to sell up and move south. They bought another newsagents in Shoreham-on-Sea, Sussex, and the whole family moved down to help run it.

My dad's family stayed in the North.

Until I was nine or so I was only aware of my dad's mother as a vague concept known as Grandma in Oldham. Then I went up there for a week with my dad. My mother and my sister stayed somewhere else. I don't think there was a row about it but my mother had always made her feelings quite plain – Grandma in Oldham was a troublemaker. I couldn't wait to meet her – she got such a bad press that she had to be worth seeing.

We had an old 1930s Morris Ten. It used to belong to a master carpenter who'd converted it from a van into a 'shooting brake' by adding windows and rebuilding the whole back in seasoned timber. I was slightly ashamed of it – to me it was a poor approximation of a Morris 1000 Estate. In fact it was a really cool looking Woody, but surfing wasn't popular in England back in 1963. The front seats had been replaced with modern vinyl tip-up ones, and the original front seats, bucket seats they were called, were bolted together, covered with a blanket, and shoved in the back. The vehicle literally weighed a ton. It had big, flaring mudguards at the front, with the headlights stuck on top like backward facing bosoms.

The windscreen wipers came down from the top of the screen and were driven by a big electric motor mounted inside the cab, or if that failed you could work them by hand, using the lever provided. The indicators were those illuminated orange arrows that fold out of the sides of the door posts. They weren't very reliable – if they came out at all they tended to get stuck, and you had to bang the door post to make them go back in again, so it was best to do hand signals as well. It was a family car in the truest sense – the whole family was involved – pulling the lever to make the wipers work, checking the indicators, and either banging the door post or performing hand signals, according to what was required. Other than that it was entirely unsuitable.

We had an accident in it once, coming back from a family outing to Bodiam Castle. The spokes in one of the back wheels had rusted through. They were no longer holding the wheel together. The world went topsy-turvy, there was a big crash and the thing was lying on its side with us in it. A nice man arrived in a Bedford Dormobile, opened the driver's door like a hatch, looked down at us and asked if we were all all right. Then we were lifted out to safety. We sat at the side of the road until the ambulance came. My mum was concerned that people would think we were gypsies. Shock, I suppose. We were lucky to be alive – by some miracle none of us were hurt, except my mum who had cuts all up her left arm from the broken glass.

It was pretty sensational – the old Morris lying on its side like that. A policeman threw earth over the road to soak up the oil, then a bunch of strong men set to and pushed the thing upright where it did the best it could, lame in one back wheel. It came back to us a week later with new glass in the windows and all the dents knocked out. The spokes had been repaired too. Which was just as well because we were going to Oldham in it.

I was sworn to secrecy about the accident because it might worry Grandma, it might *set her off.*

It took an awful long time to get to Oldham. The Woody/Brake/Morris Thing did a top speed of forty miles an hour and was really only happy cruising at fifteen. It took two days, and we had to stay in a bed and breakfast in Kenilworth. We had an itinerary, specially prepared by the RAC. Why we couldn't be in the AA like all the other boys' dads I just don't know. We even met an AA patrolman somewhere en route. My dad seemed to know him and they had one of those boring conversations that seem to last for hours when you're a kid.

Why did we have to be in the RAC? Dinky did a really good AA patrolman on a motorbike with sidecar, just like the one we'd met in the lay-by, but they didn't do an RAC vehicle. I don't think Corgi did either, though Matchbox might have done.

When we got to Oldham it was just like *Coronation Street*, which was just like they said it would be. Grandma in Oldham was a bit of a disappointment. She lived on her own in a gloomy terraced house with a front door that opened straight off the pavement – 68 Orme Street. The streets where I came from didn't have names like 'Orme'. There was something infinitely depressing about the word 'Orme'.

Grandma in Oldham was a widow. Her husband, Walter, died not long after I was born. Unkind relatives said she nagged him to death. They said she wore him out with her hypochondria. Over the next few years I grew to – I can't say hate, because I don't believe in hatred, I can't think of anyone that I actually hate – but to loathe and despise Grandma in Oldham. For now, however, she was a mere disappointment.

I don't really remember much about that stay in Oldham. My cousins all had adenoidal mouths and big teeth. Grandma took us to a cemetery as a treat. She was a very morbid woman. We had to go into a crypt. There were a lot of panels, which were actually drawers with names and dates on them. One of them said '*Walter Goulden*' followed by a date. The one next to it was blank. Grandma smiled, 'That's where they'll put me when I die.' It was only a small drawer and I wondered how they'd get her in there.

When we got home I told my mum all about it. She was incensed. 'Imagine,' she said, 'showing that to a nine-year-old.'

After that, visits from Grandma in Oldham became a regular event, or *occurrence* as she would say. She came to stay on the flimsiest excuse. One year she came to measure the teapot because she was knitting us a tea cosy. Holidays came in two measurements: Just The Ten Days, and The Full Fortnight. Grandma stayed for the Full Fortnight.

When she'd gone home the resentments all came out and the rows started – she'd driven my mother mad while my dad escaped to work. He didn't know the half of it – the old besom always made trouble. She sat in the kitchen all day, chain-smoking Park Drive filter tips. She smoked and smoked and smoked, and as she smoked she talked and talked and talked. Grandma in Oldham had two major obsessions – death and anything to do with going to the toilet.

While my mum tried to get the lunch ready Grandma would recount the tale of some lingering illness that resulted in hideous death and a funeral:

'...when we got to the cemetery all the Co-op Bakery bread vans were lined up, and as the procession passed through the gates they all sounded their horns and flashed their lights'.

'Why did they do that, Grandma?'

'Oh, it was the girl that iced the cakes – she died.'

My dad always came home for lunch. He washed his hands and face, sat down and ate, went in the bathroom and brushed his hair. He came back and drank a cup of tea out of the saucer, because it was too hot. By this time he was late for work because lunch hadn't been quite ready because Grandma in Oldham wouldn't shut the fuck up and my mum couldn't think straight. Then he'd roar off in his Volkswagen beetle. Back to work in a bad mood. I was always there because Grandma invariably came to stay during the school holidays.

It seemed to me that any time I walked into a room she'd be in the middle of saying, 'and then he died...', and my mum would be making polite listening noises, 'Oh', and 'Oh, really?' and 'Mmm, aha', trying to keep the lid on the mounting tension that erupted from time to time with a hissing *'Christ!'* or *'Bugger!'* addressed to the inside of the oven.

Grandma in Oldham was at her worst in the mornings. Her arrival was heralded by the flushing of the toilet.

Then the shape of Grandma would appear behind the frosted glass panels of the kitchen door. She'd take forever to turn the handle and open it. You could hear the springs in the lock moaning in sympathy. And there she was – wearing a dark blue pac-a-mac over a blue brushed-nylon nightdress, topped off with a hairnet. It was as though Death itself had just walked into the kitchen. She always wore the pac-a-mac because a dressing gown would have taken up valuable space in her suitcase. The suitcase was huge – heavy with floral print summer frocks, pink and blue Trivera two-piece combinations, denture glue, and for all we knew, her own tombstone.

'Morning,' she bleated – never *'Good morning'* – that would have been too positive. Being a well brought up boy, I'd spring up, put the kettle on and offer her a cup of tea. She lived on tea – drained it down by the pot-load. Cold, stewed or two hours old – any condition, it didn't matter. The Oldham contingent were all the same in that. They'd burst through doors, all teeth, gums and lips and go, 'TEA?'

But Grandma didn't always want tea first thing – particularly if she'd had A Bad Night. A bony, arthritic hand would descend on my shoulder and Death would say, 'Don't worry about me, love, your grandma's feeling a little bit hazy this morning.' She'd put a tremble into the word 'hazy', and swoon ever so slightly.

One morning she staggered into the middle of breakfast and announced that she'd just left half her insides down the toilet. She kept a mental tally of who was *'on the toilet'* at any one time – never the tasteful *'in'*, always the more graphic *'on'*. 'Have you seen my dad?' I'd ask. 'He's on the toilet,' she'd reply triumphantly.

She'd sit down, light up the first Park Drive of the day,

and cough all over the breakfast table. And then we were off – one death would lead to another, interspersed with little gaps for appreciation of the distant flushings of the toilet *('that'll be our Doreen…')*, and then she'd be on to the pensioners' club, of which she was Entertainments Secretary – 'Last week we had a penis – he was very good'.

She was also a staunch supporter of the Conservative Party. The Oldham Conservative Association presented her with an engraved silver cigarette lighter in appreciation of twenty-five years' loyal service. The local paper took a photo of her wearing a two-piece and a string of pearls, smiling with all her dentures, and holding up the lighter. She died of heart disease bought about by smoking.

My dad was a Conservative too. He probably joined the RAC because of the blue and white badge – the black and yellow AA badge would have spoken to his subconscious of flaccid Liberalism. He left school at the age of fourteen and became an apprentice toolmaker. He worked his way through the engineering business from the shop floor upwards. He worked for the Parker Pen Company for thirty-seven years. As I got older I began to meet blokes that had worked for him. They held him in god-like esteem. He was legendary – he was the manager who came downstairs, took off his suit jacket, donned a set of overalls, and sorted the problem out in a no-nonsense Yorkshireman sort of way. He was a dark and moody Pennine man, the stuff of TV serials. I was actually very proud of him. But I could tell that these blokes thought he was slightly ridiculous, and I was thankful that they couldn't quite believe I was his son.

He could be the most joyless human being in the

world. He held the view that Christmas and birthday presents should always be something useful, like a scarf, a torch, or a couple of pairs of socks. His manners were impeccable. A friend of my mum's was most impressed when he declined an invitation to go for a drink with them one evening because he'd been painting a window frame and he'd got paint on his hands. The real reason was that he didn't like her, but he was a real gentleman.

I don't think he liked anyone that much, except for me and my sister and, most of the time, my mum. He didn't have any friends. He was badly infected by the Protestant Work Ethic and all the deep joylessness and self-denial that comes along with it. As I got older I sometimes caught glimpses of the real man trying to get out. After my sister and I had left home my mum took things in hand – they moved to Brighton and she forced him to take holidays – they went to Greece and the difference in him was astounding.

I wish he'd learnt to enjoy life earlier on, but he was a workaholic. Outside of work he lived in a world of his own. He didn't have any hobbies, just work. When he came home he fell asleep in an armchair. While we had dinner, or 'tea' as it was called, he listened to the news on the Home Service. Any attempt at conversation was met with a glaring 'Sshhh!'.

But it wasn't all deep joylessness by any means and in 1963 my parents bought a record player. It was a milestone in my life – a Bush record player in two-tone grey vinyl finish, with a white speaker grill across the front. The controls were recessed underneath: *on/off/volume, treble, bass*. The interior contained an ice-blue Garrard turntable, and a smell of wood glue and electricity. The inside of the lid said B U S H in white plastic letters. It came from the electrical shop at the bottom of our avenue on the South Coast Road.

The shop was called Haydyn Williams. That kind of shop hardly exists now. It sold steam irons, television sets, kettles, electric blankets, transistor radios, torches and batteries to make the torches and transistors work. In 1964 the window display included the first LP by PJ Proby – *I Am PJ Proby* on the Liberty label, with PJ Proby on the front cover in his night-shirt against a red velvet curtain. I coveted that record, but all I could afford were singles at six shillings and eightpence each, and the occasional EP – extended play – two tracks on each side. At eleven shillings it seemed like quite good value but they were never quite as loud, and a lot of them wore out quickly. The EPs I find now at car boot sales are generally completely shagged – sad looking bits of smooth, dark grey plastic with a label saying what used to be on them.

The record player was placed on the table in the corner of the lounge, next to the electrical socket. When not in use it had to be switched off and unplugged from the mains at all times, and the man who delivered it warned my parents that it would be extremely foolhardy to plug it into the shaver socket and use it in the bathroom. (When I thought about that later it seemed to me that listening to music while you were having a bath was a really good idea.) But I couldn't imagine doing that in our bathroom. We had a white bathroom suite and brown Marley tiles on the floor. It wasn't a very sexy bathroom. The window faced north and in windy weather the draught from the fanlight made the Polyglaze flap backwards and forwards. Polyglaze was a cheap '60s double-glazing substitute. It was basically just sheets of plastic stuck to the window frames with double-sided tape. It was very popular but it didn't work.

I didn't know much about music. It had always been there on the periphery. Sometimes it was happy – the soundtrack to the summer holidays. ('Six weeks this time!') My sister and I made tents in the back garden by draping old sheets over the clothes line and weighing the sides down with stones from the rockery.

The rockery was a desperate affair – an ant-infested bank topped off with a hedge, dividing our garden from next door's. There was a lot of rubble left over after they'd built our bungalow, lumps of concrete with bits of brick sticking out of them, that sort of thing. And these were inset into the bank with spaces for some plants to wither and die in.

We sat in the tent, which was very hot and smelled strongly of the shed. A contralto voice sang: *'I want an old-fashioned house and an old-fashioned fence and an old-fashioned millionaire'*.

My mum rushed out into the garden to tell us that Ringo Starr had got married. Another Beatle down. But that was later on when I knew about music.

Sitting on the floor in the old house in Newhaven, black and white TV (they were all black and white then) with the shiny brown casing – unnatural wood finish. 'Over the points, over the points, the Six Five Special's coming down the line, the Six Five Special running right on time...' Rushing down the black and white railway line in shades of grey, and then the train – the front of the train – rushing towards the living room and I shut my eyes in terror as it cleared the TV screen. Then I sat on my mum's knee while a group who'd just been kissed by a girl sang, 'We're never gonna wash for a week'. I asked my mum why – 'Because they're very silly young men' she said. They looked quite old to me – they may have been Bill Haley and the Comets.

When my dad left for work the horrible radio was tuned to the Light Programme. *Housewives' Choice*. The theme music was ideal for winding the mangle that sat on top of the Hotpoint washing machine. That was Mondays.

Monday was Washing Day.

The washing machine was wheeled out and filled up with sheets, washing powder and water. There were a lot of rubber hoses. They popped off the ends of the taps, spraying water everywhere. The washing machine jitter-bugged wilfully across the kitchen taking the big grey hose with it so that soapy water was pumped out all over the floor instead of into the sink. And all the time the theme from *Housewives' Choice* jangled cheerfully away.

In the afternoon it was Victor Sylvester, his Orchestra, and the vacuum cleaner – a combination that held me on the edge of tears.

We made a special trip to Brighton to buy some records. Hanningtons department store. The assistant put the record on a turntable behind the counter and directed us to a listening booth with dark brown woodwork and white pegboard walls. The sound came from a speaker up near the ceiling.

They didn't have Telstar, and the Shadows' guitars sounded like they were full of water, so I chose Globetrotter by the Tornadoes. It sounded magical in the booth. It was the sound that the listening booth made, and when I got it home it became the sound of our record player.

My sister chose *A Children's Introduction to a World of GOOD MUSIC*. A deep, crackling voice introduced the instruments of the orchestra in their separate sections. They each played the first line of Twinkle Twinkle Little Star up to 'how I wonder what you ARE'.

By the time the voice had got through the bassoon and the oboe and started on the triangle, it was all becoming a bit tedious, but fascinating nonetheless. Then *the Whole, Mighty Orchestra* got together and performed The March Of the Toys – Toyland.

One record led to another and pretty soon we had a collection. My mum gave my dad *The Shadows' Greatest Hits*, a mono copy on the Columbia label. I've still got it: Apache, 36-24-36, Stars Fell On Stockton, Wonderful Land, The Savage, Man Of Mystery, with musical direction and orchestral accompaniment by Norrie Paramor.

My parents subscribed to the Readers Digest Record Club, the source of many a dreary record. Strauss Waltzes, Brahms Hungarian Dances and Beethoven's Fourth Symphony played by a budget orchestra. Twenty minutes squashed onto a seven-inch record and packaged in a gaudy sleeve, *laminated with "Clarifoil"*. Nobody listened to them – they just sat there in the red wire record rack, reminding us that life was somehow better than it used to be.

Listening to music didn't come naturally to my parents. Not the classical stuff anyway. My dad became a great Kathy Kirby fan, which made a lot more sense than all that Record Club shit. As the record sleeve said, she was *a young, curvaceous, effervescent blonde*, and he liked that sort of thing. Not that he had a roving eye or anything like that.

Kathy Kirby had that pseudo Latin-American thing that was popular at parties. We didn't have parties but sometimes we'd go to one at someone else's house.

Peacehaven in the '60s. 'Through' lounges and hire-purchase furniture. Cheese and pineapple on cocktail sticks, bowls of salted peanuts, cheese straws, cocktail sausages. The grown-ups rifled their children's record collections and pushed the settee back against the wall to facilitate dancing. The Shadows, Chubby Checker, Joe Loss & His Orchestra, The Teddy Bear's Picnic, Goodness Gracious Me...

Grannies waving their arms stiffly in the air and saying, 'Ooh, we do like the pops!' Dads flinging off suit jackets, revealing bri-nylon drip-dry shirts, perspiring and doing that botty-wiggling dance that mums find so seductive and kids finds so embarrassing. Everybody having a great time – except the kids, sitting grim-faced on the sidelines.

I'm sure there was a healthy wife-swapping scene too – car keys in the middle of the floor and all that. But there was no way that my parents could have broken into that scene – even if they'd wanted to – not with the old Morris Eight. You needed a Vauxhall Victor or a Hillman Minx for that sort of thing. And anyway we didn't have a through lounge, and the furniture was all bought and paid for, quality G-Plan.

I came home from school and watched *Blue Peter*. It was boring. I never wanted to make any of the junk that Valerie Singleton knocked up, I somehow knew it wouldn't come out the same. 'You'll need a cardboard tube...' (what she meant was a toilet roll, but you weren't allowed to say that on the television because it was rude), '...a washing-up liquid bottle, which you'll have to cut... like... this – these modelling knives are rather sharp so ask mummy or daddy to help you. To save time I've got one I made before the programme...' I couldn't get my parents to help – my dad came home and fell asleep, and my mum was completely impractical – she once sustained a near-fatal electric shock stripping wallpaper. And anyway, I didn't want to make a useful decorative thing that you could hang inside a wardrobe. *Blue Peter* was for children in another dimension. There was a parallel universe that only existed in the pages of *Boy's World* and *Meccano Magazine*. I couldn't break into it.

I had Spam Fritters for tea and watched *Day by Day*, the Southern TV regional news programme. The Beatles were on. They played From Me To You. Suddenly the whole world was Beatles: Beatle scrapbooks, Beatle wallpaper, Beatle bubblegum cards with pictures of John, Paul, George and Ringo in wacky bathing costumes – having fun in go-karts – George in leather at the Cavern – John hates having a haircut – Paul in a thoughtful moment – the Ed Sullivan show – Carnegie Hall. The triumphant return to Liverpool – they'd conquered America. Four lads that shook the world. There'd never been anything quite like this before. Everybody loved The Beatles.

They played at the Hippodrome in Brighton. I wrote them a letter telling them how much I liked their records and invited them round for tea in the afternoon before the concert. I had a bit of a bad day at school but I knew it was going to be all right because when I got home John, Paul, George and Ringo would all be sitting in the lounge having a cup of tea and waiting for me to arrive. I didn't say anything but I felt slightly let down.

They put a piece of wood across the arms of the barber's chair to make it high enough for boys to have their hair cut. Mr MacNeish cut my dad's hair, then he cut mine. I wanted a Beatle haircut but I got what I was given. Yeah yeah yeah.

The racing finished, and they turned over to the Light

Programme and I heard the latest Beatles' single, I Want To Hold Your Hand. Had they blown it this time?

I hoped not because Mr MacNeish was halfway through his version of a Beatle cut.

PJ Proby sang Hold Me. My sister bought it. She liked the ballads – Gene Pitney, I'm Gonna Be Strong. She had a poster of Tommy Quickly from Fabulous 208 magazine. She also had a poster of the Rolling Stones. She'd labelled them all – Blondie, Curly, Toothy, Charlie and The Other One. I was three years younger but I was beginning to understand that she'd somehow missed the point.

Tommy Quickly didn't really bother me one way or the other. The Rolling Stones did. They appeared on *Sunday Night At The London Palladium*. I'd never seen them before and I thought Brian Jones was a girl. Groups never sounded like the records on the telly – the sound was always rough, ill-balanced and dangerously out of tune. My dad got up and turned the television off.

'That's not entertainment,' he said.

My sister and her friends liked Cliff Richard – they all went to see Summer Holiday at the pictures. She could do the Shake, the Twist, the Hully Gully and the Slop but I'm sure she didn't feel what I felt when I heard The Who. 'I've got a feeling inside – can't explain...'

Dizzy in the head and I feel blue
Things you said well maybe they're true
I'm getting funny dreams again and again
I know what it means but—

I can't explain.

I'd seen them all, even if it was only on the telly. Little Richard, Rufus Thomas, Sounds Incorporated, Manfred Mann, 5 – 4 – 3 – 2 – 1.

Aha it was the Manfreds...

PJ Proby burst through a paper hoop and sang Together on *Ready Steady Go*. The Yardbirds, The Kinks, The Hollies, The Pretty Things.

The Animals:

Cathy MacGowan: 'Why are you called the Animals?'

Eric Burden: 'Basically because we look like animals.'

They did too. But they could as well have been called the Fabulous Shapes and Sizes in their matching Beatle suits – little Eric Burden, a grinning Hilton Valentine and the enormous Chas Chandler busting out between his buttons and holding a tiny Fender bass.

Baby let me take you home da dah...

I wanted jeans. But jeans were common. Newhaven boys wore jeans. Newhaven boys didn't talk properly – they didn't pronounce their Ts when they said words like better, butter, bitter and batter. They said words like 'bugger' in public as well when they thought they could get away with. And they dropped their aitches as in 'addock, 'ang-up, 'atred, 'Ollies, 'Erman's 'Ermits, and the 'Ooh. They did these things because they were common. I knew better than that because I lived in Peacehaven. The trouble was I was born in Newhaven. I was a Newhaven boy. You can take the boy out of Newhaven, but don't ever take the piss.

When Newhaven boys got older they grew quiffs and sideburns and hung around the chip shop wearing drainpipe trousers, leather jackets and winkle-pickers. They rode Triumph motorcycles and got girls into trouble. I knew all this because these objects of my hero worship were in my dad's technical drawing class at the Newhaven Evening Institute.

I wasn't sure what drainpipe trousers were, but I had

an idea they were like the ones Paul McCartney wore on the cover of Twist And Shout, and I was sure that his were black ones with green stitching and zips on the back pocket. Life would have been perfect if only I could have worn a pair of those, and some cuban-heeled Chelsea boots as advertised in Fabulous 208.

My dad was dependent on a drug called Prednisone, which was a form of steroid. The condition for which it had been prescribed had long since cleared up but they couldn't get him off it. Prednisone came in large oblong silver tins. They were everywhere in our house. My dad kept his collection of screws in two of them. Not that he ever did any carpentry – well, I suppose he did once – he built my sister a desk out of chipboard and hardboard on a seasoned pine frame. It took ages because he made a Proper Job of it. It was screwed together, not nailed, and given not just one, but two coats of woodstain, even on the rough side of the hardboard that was on the inside, where my sister's legs went. It was lovingly polished with Ronuk floor wax and topped off with a thick layer of green plastic lino, held on with double-sided Scotch tape.

I had my sister's old desk. It was a ramshackle affair – I tore the lid off it, filled the thing with an arrangement of Prednisone tins and clobbered the hell out of them with my mums thickest knitting needles. I was in a Dave Clark Five fantasy – Glad All Over, Bits and Pieces – *arm in pieces bitsan pieces…* it was my mantra. I sang *Oh Won't You Stay Jussta Lill Bit Longer*, and *Just One Look That's All It Tookayeah Just One Look* by the Hollies, and *Sweets For My Sweet Sugar For Ma Harney* by The Searchers, smashing the Prednisone tins with the shards of plastic knitting needles. When they came and told me to shut up I took to miming with my sister's tennis racket.

I listened to The Beatles No 1 EP – *I Saw Her Standing There / Misery / Anna / Chains* – incessantly, all afternoon, every afternoon for days and weeks on end. The same with the PJ Proby EP – *Zing! Went The Strings Of My Heart / Linda Lu / Answer Me / Stagger Lee*. I had the volume, treble, and bass turned up to the end of the white space past 10, and I listened to the fade-out with my ear pressed to the speaker grill because I wanted to know what happened next – PJ sang *'you're gonna oh oh break my heaaaaart…'* and then he was gone. (A few years ago I found a stereo copy, a different mix, not anywhere near as good as the mono mix, but about three seconds longer, and I was able to get beyond the fade of my childhood. It was a disappointing and almost unpleasant experience.)

When my dad came home from work I had to make sure that the controls on the record player were all turned down to a sensible level. Between 4 and 5 was about right, and I always felt that it was better if the record player was switched off. I didn't think we were supposed to enjoy it too much. Its real purpose was so that we could all learn French from a Linguaphone course.

Linguaphone came in a serviceable vinyl-covered carrying case with clips. It was a collection of seven-inch singles that played at 33$\frac{1}{3}$rpm (a bizarre idea – singles played at 45rpm). There was a grammar and vocabulary book, and a book with the lessons in it, and a lot of pen and ink illustrations of French life. There were thirty-two lessons. I can't imagine that anybody ever got past lesson six, it was so boring.

The main speaker on the records was a man with a deep electrical voice. He said 'LE…' (big space) 'PLAFOND' (big space so that you could repeat it), 'LA…' (wait for it) 'TABLE…' ('taarble') 'LE…' (I'd start to come adrift... and the word) 'POISSON' (would slap me back to attention). Then his mate came in. The recording engineer had a difficult job here – how to make two boring people sound sufficiently different that they could have a conversation. The mate had a higher voice. Less electronic, more nasal. He said: "quandjeparlevitevousnemecomprenezpas – MAIS... q u a n d j e p a r l e l e n t e m e n t vous me comprenez tres bien!'

It tended to stay in its box. You could take self-improvement a little too far. I remember once seeing a library book lying around in our house entitled *Teach Yourself Serbo Croat*. It was worth a try, but for a ten-day package holiday in Yugoslavia it was perhaps a little excessive.

I acquired a tin banjo. It was red and yellow with four nylon strings and a lot of sharp edges. It was made in Taiwan. It wouldn't be allowed today, and not just for the sharp edges. The front of it featured a gaily coloured picture of a grinning native, big white lips, golden earrings, and a Chaka Zulu hairstyle with a bone through it. The neck was a sheet of metal folded into a U-shaped section with indents moulded into it to represent the frets. It was completely unplayable but that didn't matter. Tuning was an unfamiliar concept to me, but I had my own personal system. There were three different sorts of guitar – bass, lead, and rhythm. I'd learnt this from the back cover of the *Twist and Shout* EP.

For lead guitar I tightened the strings as far as they'd go, I loosened them off to slightly less than slack for bass, and for rhythm I had them somewhere in between. I never discussed any of this with anybody else, I just got on with it. I made a guitar strap out of my dad's Tootle cravat (he was not best pleased) and started playing the Devil's Music on this dangerous piece of racist junk.

I decided that I was going to be a pop star. Not so much for the adulation – I wanted to make the noise, wear the clothes and do the moves. I wanted to sing like John Lennon on You Can't Do That, raw with a desperate edge. Other boys wanted to be train drivers, bus conductors and firemen. The girls were all going to be nurses, or house-wives if they were lucky. But I didn't buy into any of that crap – I didn't even want to be something lucrative like an architect. I just wanted to be a pop star and it hadn't even occurred to me that there was money in it.

I decided all this swinging on the garden gate one summer morning when I was nine. I had the good sense to keep all this inside my head. I whispered a warning to myself to keep quiet about it because I knew that people would laugh.

Over the following years they laughed themselves fucking stupid – except the ones who didn't find it funny. 'Castles in the air,' my dad said, weeks before I made my first record. Twelve years previously I'd been mortified when my aunt nudged me conspiratorially and asked if I'd written any good songs recently. My mum must have found an early songwriting attempt lying around in my bedroom and had a good laugh about it with her sister. They didn't mean any harm but I was sensitive.

A boy in my class called Colin Simmonds had a job selling football coupons door to door for Tenovus Cancer. My mum thought he was *such a nice boy*, but I fucking hated him because my bedroom was next to the front door and he came round every Wednesday night and charmed my mum who duly paid up, even though nobody in our family knew how to fill in a football coupon. The next day at school he'd seize upon the moment of maximum humiliation potential, look at me with narrowed eyes and announce:

'I heard you playing your guitar last night.'

Then he'd laugh, a nasty sneering laugh, and look round at his audience for appreciation

'Trying to play your guitar.'

What a laugh! I don't know how the cunt thought up something so humorous. But that was five or six years later, and although it hurt I was at least tough enough to know that I didn't want to be like Colin Simmonds.

Back in 1964 with my Jolly Native Banjo I was becoming aware of exciting new possibilities. The Beat Boom was on. The *TV Times* carried adverts for electric guitars and drum kits that you could buy on hire purchase. The drum kits came in red or gold sparkle finish and the guitars were Flame Red or Sunburst. They looked just like the ones The Shadows were holding on the front of my sister's Cliff Richard EP, *The Young Ones*. They didn't look quite real. They were bright red and you couldn't tell what they were made of. They looked almost edible. I wanted one.

An older boy at the bus stop wore a Beatle jacket with tight trousers and Cuban-heeled boots. He was quite possibly post-pubescently plump and spotty, and he probably looked ridiculous, but to me he was magnificent.

Sometimes the bus was a single-decker Southdown coach, one of the really old ones, and the trick was to get the double front seat next to the driver. That way you got an uninterrupted view of the road ahead, and you could see him working the controls – the big gear stick that wobbled and juddered about when the coach was stationary, and the enormous handbrake that had a silver lever at the top end and grew out of the floor with a set of cogs for roots. And the indicator – a round black thing with a big red plastic knob on top that lit up and flashed red when the driver turned it in whichever direction the bus was going to go next.

It was enough to make you want to become a bus driver.

Sometimes my friend Bobby Chalmers came with me, and sometimes Ronald Beard as well. Ronald had a twitch that he did with both eyes at once. His dad ran the off-licence. When Ronald and/or Bobby came along it was easy – we just commandeered the front of the bus, or rather me and Bobby took the front seat – we stuck Ronald in the seat behind because he was easily pushed around. The Beatle Jacket meanwhile had gone to the back of the bus where he could smoke cigarettes with another older boy who sometimes carried a Real Electric Guitar in a see-through plastic bag.

Except when it was a double-decker. Then the Beatle Jacket and the Real Electric Guitar took the front seats on the top deck, and me and Bobby sat at the back where we had a good view of the electric guitar. The back of the top deck had the added attraction of Shop Assistants – young girls in Dolly Rocker macs with peroxide hair, mini-skirts and beehives. They smoked cigarettes and made a fuss of us. I found all this highly attractive though I hadn't quite figured out why.

I had a crush on Dusty Springfield too.

I don't know about Bobby – he was a magnet for middle-aged homosexuals although we didn't know this at the time. There was a man with large glasses and a fawn raincoat who got on the bus a couple of stops further on, or sometimes he was already on the bus, languishing seductively across one of the back seats. He had an odd name like Tolly or Tosher, something like that. He always wanted Bobby to sit next to him, or sometimes he thought it would be fun if the three of us sat in the long back seat together, but that was usually full of shop assistants.

If Bobby wasn't there he'd invite me to sit next to him by patting the seat, raising his eyebrows and smiling slightly with his lips. But I didn't want to, so I never did.

He started giving us Dinky Cars, new ones in their boxes. Bobby always got a better one than me. I think that happened twice. It was discussed between my mum and Bobby's mum. And then Tolly or Tosher or whatever his name was disappeared. One of the shop assistants had apparently made a complaint.

Another time, during the Easter holidays, we saw a racing cycle outside the newsagents. You didn't see many of those in a place like Peacehaven. While we were inspecting the Derailleur gears, trying to figure out how many it had, the man who owned it came out of the shop. He was wearing a funny pair of stretchy shorts, a shiny orange top and odd-looking rubbery gloves with the fingers cut off. He was very friendly – he told us that the bicycle had ten gears and that he was on a cycling tour.

He asked us if there was somewhere where we could sit and talk, so we took him to a place called The Dip which was a hollow in some waste ground between the South Coast Road and the cliff top.

When we got there he wanted us to play some games together. Not so much me as Bobby, I seemed to be a bit of a spare part really. I should explain that Bobby was plump and juicy looking. I was a bit skinny, and though I'm sure I was the better looking of the two, Bobby was much more succulent than I was.

The man offered to show Bobby how to wrestle. He did this by lying on his back, grappling the wriggling, giggling Bobby to him, and growling like a bear. He didn't want to show me how to do wrestling, just Bobby, which was all right by me because I didn't think I'd like wrestling. It seemed strange, there was something not quite right about it. I insisted it was time we left – we were expected home for lunch. The man said he'd meet us back there in the afternoon – or just Bobby if I couldn't come. I don't know if Bobby talked, but neither of us was allowed out that afternoon.

I changed schools. The convent only took boys until the age of eight and then they started getting rough and chucking the Lego about, so it was girls only after that. My sister stayed put until she passed the Eleven Plus and went to Grammar School. I was moved to a private Catholic school, Xavarian College in Queen's Park, Brighton, run by an order of brothers.

The brothers were like nuns except they were men and they didn't wear the headgear, just little black skullcaps. There were the same statues of Our Lady and before every lesson the same Hail Marys and Our Fathers, which the brothers always seemed to execute with an off-hand on-to-the-toes-of-the-worn-out-black-shoes-and-down-to-the-heels-again   movement   – probably because they said prayers all day every day and they were bored with it.

My parents couldn't really afford to send us to private schools but they somehow managed to because the local state primary schools had a reputation for turning out people who couldn't read and write. People who hadn't been taught how to use the intelligence they'd been born with. The kind of people I met in later life who said things like: 'Oooh, *private school* – I didn't think you was posh.'

Catholic schools were particularly hot on literacy – I

think it was because literate believers would be better served to spread the gospel. I started learning to read and write when I was four. By the age of eight I knew all about verbs, adverbs, nouns, adjectives, conjunctions, similes, metaphors, commas, full stops, apostrophes, and even semi-colons. I didn't feel any pressure, I enjoyed it, and this carried on until I was eleven.

If I'd have chosen to spread the gospel I'd have been fucking good at it. Not that you'd necessarily believe that now – standards have been allowed to slip. Bad grammar, impossible sentence constructions, a disregard for correct punctuation, the use of slang and gratuitous foul language – it's all here, as you may have noticed.

My earliest inspiration as a writer was *The Sussex Express & County Herald*. When I was fifteen or sixteen I used to read it from cover to cover – the banal stories of men who failed to abate smoking chimneys, photo captions that always started with *'some of those…'* as in *'some of those who attended the jumble sale'*, *'some of those who were awarded a prize'*, *'some of those who entered the three-legged race'*…

Of course, I had to add the foul language myself later on. *The Sussex Express & County Herald* was much more upstanding than I am – its writers hadn't spent years playing in British pop groups. Perhaps I should explain that on the European club circuit, British pop groups have always been known for their magnificent use of swear words, particularly the words 'fuck', 'fucking', 'fucker' and 'cunt'. The most sublime use of the word 'fuck' that I've ever heard is the sentence, *'the fucking fucker's fucking fucked'*, in which the word 'fuck' is used as adjective, noun, adverb and verb. The man who uttered this statement was referring to a Ford Cortina.

I went back to have a look at the old school a few years ago. It wasn't there any more and I was surprised to find that the huge area it once occupied had been filled by a small collection of Barratt Homes. They'd left a few vestiges – little bits of walls, the odd folly, perhaps to give the new estate a feeling of history, character – and probably as a navigational aid to help people remember where they live.

I'd been under the misapprehension that I hated that school, but as I clambered around what was left of it, under the eagle eye of the newly formed Neighbourhood Watch, memory returned and I realised that this wasn't the case. Some of it was boring and there were little dramas that seemed enormous and insurmountable at the time – there were bad days, tests, and punishments, and the usual fights, but I wasn't unhappy. Devastating unhappiness came later, in a package with the Eleven Plus.

It was my first big mistake – I can see that now. I was ill on the day of the exam so I had to take it a couple of weeks later – they made provision for boys that were ill. They put me in Brother Edmund's bedroom and I did my Eleven Plus sitting at his desk. It was really easy. I could have cheated if I'd wanted to but it wasn't necessary. And I'm not actually sure how I could have cheated except by turning the page before Brother Edmund came in and told me to. I finished each page in minutes and spent the remaining time conducting a detailed search of Brother Edmund's desk, which revealed absolutely nothing of any interest to me.

When I'd finished, when time was up, it was only three o'clock. Brother Edmund winked at me and I was allowed to go home early. I didn't think any more about it but one day, in a totally unrelated event, the results came and it turned out I'd passed the Eleven Plus. Everybody was very pleased with me – I was one of the *Creme de la Creme* – the top five per cent – and I'd been offered a place at Lewes County Grammar School for Boys.

It was May 1965, around the time of my eleventh birthday. We had to go to an open day. It was pouring with rain and we went in the Volkswagen. I was wearing a blue nylon quilted anorak – they were the new thing at the time. The boys were split up from the parents and we were taken to meet our form masters. I was put in form 1R with Mr Roberts who taught geography.

We were taken on a guided tour of the school. A lot of the other boys already knew each other because they'd come from the same primary schools. I didn't know a soul so I just tagged along behind.

The school was built round two quadrangles. One of them had a white mid-air bunny hutch thing for checking the weather. It had an apparatus in it that drew a couple of lines on a piece of graph paper wrapped round a cylinder – but I didn't know that until the third year because that was when you learnt about Weather, in Geography. That was the only time I ever entered this quadrangle. Mr Roberts opened the hutch so that we could stand around and marvel at the apparatus.

I never went in the other quadrangle – I think that was because it was full of the new physics laboratory.

The quadrangles were lined with corridors with windows all round and sloping roofs made of glass with wire netting in it. When it rained, as it did on the first day I saw it, the effect was extremely depressing – classrooms to one side, rain on the other, cascading liquid overhead, and a browny-grey polished concrete floor underfoot. It was cold too. There were double swing doors to the outside at either end, battered blue paintwork that showed the previous pink paint where it had chipped off. They opened and closed with a violent crash and let a draught in.

We marched along the corridors with Mr Roberts at the helm, me trailing behind in my anorak, past older, bigger, fourth-year boys with Beatle haircuts. (Everybody had a version of a Beatle haircut – even the ones with short back and sides. Brylcream was a thing of the past so they always had a front bit combed down over the forehead that they could shake about and go 'oooh'. Not that those sort of boys ever did.) One of the them, carrying a big bag of books and sporting a haircut straight off the cover of Beatles For Sale said, 'Oh no, are these the new first years – God help us, they get worse every year.'

We looked at the locker rooms where we were going to keep our rugger kit, then we went up to the gym. Mr Roberts said the gym had its own special smell – the smell of sweat.

The first day was awful, though I was never going to admit it. I had a brand new school uniform – shirt, tie, grey V-neck school pullover with little blue trimmings (the school colours) around the V, and a dark blue blazer with the yellow school crest on the pocket.

You wore long trousers at grammar school. My mum bought some grey Terylene and ran them up on the machine. She bought me a pair of Tuf lace-up shoes to go with them. I tried to convince myself that they were like the shoes Bill Wyman had worn when the Stones played The Last Time on *Top Of The Pops* though I knew the Stones didn't wear Tuf lace-ups. But at least mine didn't have animal-track soles – there wasn't a pop group in the world that would wear those. Or the ones with the compass in the heel.

It was September, so I had a woolly school scarf wrapped round my neck, and because it looked as though it might rain I had to take my dark blue school gabardine. (I'd decided ages ago, without really formulating the idea, that the wearing or carrying of a school gabardine was an admission of weakness. You never saw older boys wearing them, or at least only the swotty ones.) I had a new school satchel too, a larger one to accommodate the increased amount of books *that really buckling down to it* was going to generate.

I'd spent the last Saturday before Lewes County Grammar School for Boys playing with my friend Simon at his house in Rottingdean. That had to be the last time – I was never going to play again, because the creme de la crème, the top five per cent, didn't have time for that sort of thing. I was going to knuckle down and buckle down to it. It was going to be tough and it was going to be challenging. I was terrified. At bedtime I fell into a depression. I finally burst into tears and told my mum that I wished I'd never been born. She said, 'This isn't like you.' But it was now.

I tried to put a brave face on but I really didn't like it. I walked over the station footbridge with my satchel over my shoulder and the blue gabardine over my arm. Everything was new. I didn't feel comfortable. There was a gang of older boys at the bottom of the steps by the ticket office. As I began my descent they started up a brutal chant: 'Ooh ooh new boy new boy ooh ooh new boy new boy…'

I felt utterly humiliated. I stood on the platform all on my own. I didn't know anybody.

The teachers seemed to think I was a figure of fun. They were extremely jocular and my lack of height – something I hadn't really noticed until now – provoked much hilarity. We had a different teacher for every lesson. They all had nicknames – but only behind their backs of course, even though they probably had a Ruddy Good Laugh about it in the staff room. The maths teacher was called Mr Knight. His nickname was Nitters. I trailed into the first maths lesson, behind the others as usual, and Nitters said, 'Tell the tiddler to put the wood in the hole.'

He made me sit at the front, where he could 'keep an eye on me' because he could see that I was 'going to be trouble'.

My sister went to the Girls Grammar School. She was a brilliant student – she came top in everything, even the subjects she wasn't any good at.

I must have been a huge disappointment. I'm sure the teachers were excited beyond belief at the advent of another genius. And all they got was me, trying my best to be as grown up as possible.

Lewes County Grammar School was run on the lines of a minor public school. Lewes is the county town of East Sussex. It's a hick market town in a muddy river valley with a castle on the hill. But to half the population it's a centre of cultural excellence, rich in history and full to the brim with the most interesting and informed people in the world.

Some of them are lecturers at Sussex University. Others would like to give that impression – a suggestion of rooms and cloisters – shapeless corduroy bags, tweed jackets with leather patches at the elbows, shirts with soft collars. Add a bow tie, a sprinkling of chalk dust, and a semi-senile air of academic abstraction, and you've got half the teaching staff of Lewes County Grammar School for Boys.

The place was fucking ludicrous. They didn't play football, they played rugby. I say 'they' because I didn't – not if I could help it anyway. It was always mid-November. Standing around on a field of torn-up turf and mud, with a big white H at either end. H for Hellbound, He-man, Homo, Hypocritical, unHappy, Hard-Hearted, Hurtful, Humiliating.

The wind whipped across the field. It was getting dark and the lights were on in the classrooms. The silly oval ball came lolloping over and I got out of the way so that some other, keener boys could dive on it, face first in the mud.

'You're useless. Why don't you go and play tiddly-winks with the spastics at Chailey Heritage.'

I started to walk away. I felt like crying, not because I was useless – but because I just wanted to be somewhere else – anywhere but here. The games master sprinted across the pitch in his tracksuit. (Oh yes, he got to wear a tracksuit while we froze our bollocks off in silly black shorts and blue and black striped Bukta rugby shirts.) He came to a halt in a flurry of shrill whistles -

'GOULDEN! WHERE DO YOU THINK YOU'RE GOING?'

'I'm off to play tiddlywinks with the spastics at Chailey Heritage. Sir.'

Ten laps of the rugby pitch while everyone else had a shower, but at least I missed the wanking. The games master used to stand at the entrance to the shower making sure that every naked boy went through. He didn't mind how long you stayed in there, in amongst the steam and naked pubescent flesh. He must have seen the wanking. He was probably quite pleased about it, because that's what we were aspiring to – Public School Traditions. And if boys couldn't warm up toilet seats for older boys, the least they could do was wank each other off.

I woke up every morning to the sound of the brown and cream Bakelite wireless – the one I'd pulled down on my head. I hated that fucking thing. The seven o'clock news programme presented by Jack de Manio droned away in the kitchen while I got ready for school. When the programme finished it started again – once for the manual workers, and again for the office staff.

The bungalow echoed with cold voices:

'Bathroom's free.'

'It's quarter to eight.'

'Your tea's getting cold.'

'Now Come On!'

There was a routine. My sister seemed to love it as much I detested it. We had to leave the house – and that meant Leave The House, not just Start Thinking About Leaving The House, by 8:15 At The Latest. So my sister gave out regular time checks by the kitchen clock in a stentorian voice that cut through the cold morning air, freezing out Jack de Manio.

'Seven-Forty-Five-And-Counting…'

'Frank, your Shredded Wheat's out.' My mum's voice floated anxiously down the hallway.

'…coming…' (muffled voice from behind the toilet door).

'Seven-Forty-Eight-Precisely…'

I might be putting a sock on by this time. It took me hours to get dressed. It was cold, I was tired and I didn't want to go to school. I'd been putting the same sock on since since seven-thirty-nine and counting, and I wanted to cry. The door burst open – 'Now come on, Eric – shape yourself!'

My mum's job in the mornings was warming up milk for Shredded Wheat until the pan boiled over. Her other duties included making counterpoint time-check announcements, and shouting at me to get a move on. She had to re-light the boiler too, because usually it had gone out in the night.

Suddenly it was eight fifteen and my dad was going to leave whether I was ready or not. I'd just have to go on the bus. I don't know why we didn't just go on the bus anyway. The bus left at about the same time, or later, and we had season tickets provided by East Sussex County Council.

But somehow I'd be ready, and we'd exit in a flurry of shopping instructions, pecks on the cheek and today's *Daily Telegraph*. My mum took out a hanky, licked the corner of it and started scrubbing toothpaste off the side of my mouth in the time-honoured tradition of British mums. But it was better this way – in the old days, when I went to school in Brighton, she once came down to the bus stop and humiliated me with the hanky trick in front of my friends.

We'd rush up the driveway towards the garage. My sister carried a huge leather briefcase, bulging with Extra Homework. She had to carry it under her arm because the handle wouldn't take the weight. My dad had a Gannex coat, just like the one Harold Wilson wore. I don't know why he chose such a blatantly Socialist garment – it was deeply unattractive, man-made, and highly functional. It swished and rustled as he moved around inside it.

The garage had a sliding door. My dad unlocked it

and rolled the three sections into the garage, exposing the waiting Volkswagen. He always grunted, 'Tyres all right your side?' and then we got in. I had to sit in the back because my sister was at the other end of the driveway, opening the gates. She'd leap in at the last minute and we'd be off.

The plastic seat felt cold and hard through my Terylene trousers. We were late so we did fifty miles an hour along the back road past hundreds of bungalows – Wee Nook, Dunroamin', Shangri La, Iona, Homeleigh, Stella Maris, Hilansea...

We hit the A259 South Coast Road at Grassmere Avenue and shot up the hill past Friars Bay Caravan Site doing sixty in third with the engine roaring.

Before long I was doing very badly at school. Everybody was exasperated with me. The teachers told my parents that I stared right through them – it was almost impossible to communicate with me. They thought I might be short-sighted so they took me to an optician. It was my worst nightmare – I had to wear glasses.

Spectacles were a sign of weakness. It was worse than wearing a gabardine. Soppy boys, soft boys, girls and swots wore glasses. Newhaven boys didn't. Pop stars certainly didn't. That is, John Lennon wore them in off-duty moments and one of Peter and Gordon had glasses – I think a member of Herman's Hermits did too, and so did the bass player in The Seekers, but who the hell wanted to look like one of Herman's Hermits? I didn't.

There was no role model. And it would have been useless citing Buddy Holly because I'd never heard of him.

They fitted me up with a pair of horn-rims and the optician tried to convince me that I looked like Michael

Caine. Ridiculous – she must have been living in a fantasy world. In private I thought I looked quite interesting. But I still felt like a complete dork. They kept trying to sell me the idea that only highly intelligent people wore glasses, but I knew better than that – retards wore them too, and the only difference between me and a retard was that I hadn't got one lens blanked out.

I had to go to school wearing them the next day. The teachers had been informed that my problem had been solved so taking them off wasn't an option. It would only get back to my parents and then I'd be in trouble.

I managed to get all the way to the school gates without attracting too much attention, though I did hear some girls giggling at the station. I kept my head down, hung back and hid in the toilet on the train. But when I got there the rest of my class were lined up, waiting to go into the classroom. The glasses were huge by now – they were the biggest thing in the world. I had to walk down the corridor, in front of the whole class, pushing this enormous horn-rimmed glass and plastic structure in front of me. They laughed and laughed and laughed.

I didn't make friends very easily and I spent most days just wanting to go home – well, not really home – because I wasn't doing very well, home was becoming an extension of the hell I was in at school.

It didn't take me long to achieve the ultimate in academic disgrace – I came bottom of the class in music. It was probably more to do with my attitude than any academic inability. I'd like to think that I was too cool to join in with singing 'Green Grow The Rushes Ho!' but the reality is that I was probably too shy and distracted.

My parents sent me to the local church organist and choirmaster for a bit of extra tuition. He lived with his wife in an ascetic bungalow. I was shown into the lounge. It was the sort of home that doesn't have a television and the focal point of the room was an upright piano.

He sat me in front of it and left me to my own devices while he attended to some domestic detail. I'd never really sat in front of a piano before.

My grandmother (the other one, not Grandma in Oldham) was a piano teacher. My sister had had lessons from her – she used to go round there on Saturday mornings. I went with her once. My sister wasn't very good at the piano so I decided to have a go myself. It was the only time my grandmother was ever angry with me. I don't think she wanted me to be musical because my grandfather used to play the tenor sax in a dance band in the 1940s. He got into bad ways – horse racing and womanising. She didn't want me to follow in his footsteps.

I never heard Grandad play the saxophone but years later I met a man who had. It was 1986 and I was in the Len Bright Combo. We played at the Band On The Wall in Manchester and afterwards the promoter said the boss wanted to see me. I had to go down into the cellar of the pub. Beyond the beer kegs and the tubes there was a pool of light – it was like a little sitting room – there was a music stand and next to it a table with a saxophone on it. The boss was a little grey-haired man in a tweed suit. He said the band was really good and paid me the money. I asked if he played the saxophone and told him that my grandfather had been a sax player too. 'He used to play around here after the war,' I said. 'But he gave it up and became a newsagent.' The boss looked at me a bit strangely. Then his eyes lit up and he said, 'Stanley Heap! – the Black Diamonds Dance Band! I used to follow them around. He was very good. That's what got me started.'

My grandad, Stanley Heap. I bet he was good too – he had a mean and moody disposition.

For one short, joy-filled moment I thought I was going to learn to play the piano, but no such luck. When the choirmaster came back I had it all figured out.

'Are the black notes the sharps and flats?' I asked, all interested.

'Well,' came the answer, 'it's not as simple as that.'

He subjected me to a long and bewildering lecture on key signatures. Then he gave me an exercise book with staves in it and we got down to the real business of music – Every Good Boy Deserves Food, Favour, or Fucking-up. He did the best he could and reported back to my parents: 'He's made some progress, but I'm afraid we'll never make a musician of him.'

That didn't stop him from inviting me to an audition to join the church choir. My sister was an enthusiastic member. You had to go along on Saturday morning to rehearse for Sunday, and that's when they held the auditions. I failed with flying colours. I was so nervous in front of all the choir members that I couldn't sing any of the notes as he played them on the organ. All that came out was a vague whimpering noise. They still said I could be in it though – I suppose they thought I couldn't do any harm with a voice like that and I'd help to fill up the choir stalls.

I refused. I got enough religion at school.

We had Chapel for an hour every Friday afternoon after lunch and before Games. The chapel was a monstrous looking building, an architectural disaster built in the 1950s. It was long, narrow and out of proportion.

It was a real show. Five hundred boys briefcases, satchels and duffel bags were stacked up along the wall outside the science laboratories, and then we all passed through the double doors of this hallowed building with its Toytown belltower – peaceful, pious and slightly Quakerish with the smell of furniture polish and pale afternoon sun slanting through the dust. 'Dare Nec Computare', the school motto over the door. I still don't know what it means. We used to joke that it meant 'dare your neck in the computer'.

The masters, in keeping with our unofficial public school status, took it as an opportunity to wear their moth-eaten university don gear – tatty black cloaks, and in the case of the Headmaster and Deputy Head, ermine trimmed and worn with mortar boards complete with tassels. They all sat in the choir stalls opposite the choir, next to the prefects who sat in a specially raised bit where they could keep an eye on the rank and file.

There were hymns and prayers and lay readers and the school choir slaughtered their version of the Nunc Dimittus: 'Lord now letteth thou thy servant depart in peace according to thy word.' But it still wasn't over – there were bible readings, announcements, pronounce-ments, and Here Endeth The First Lesson, and sitting down, and standing up, and kneeling down, and prayers for the poor cunt that achieved a broken neck in a rugby match against Guys Hospital.

I saw it happen. The whole school had to come out and cheer our team on to victory. We stood on the touch line at the edge of the muddy pitch. There was a scrum or a ruck or whatever they call it. One of the Guys Hospital team, a ful-ly grown man with hairy legs and everything, walked all over a pile of grammar school boys in his cleated boots. When he finally ran off with the ball they all picked them-selves up, except for one who stayed down, twitching slightly. He was a few feet away from where I stood.

They had to stop the game. A helicopter was sent from Stoke Mandeville to pick him up. Then the game was resumed on a neighbouring pitch. It was like something out of the Hotspur comic, except that it was real life so our lads didn't go ahead and trounce the opposition – they just lost the game.

We had to share in the Senior Geography master's guilt at having fixed up a match against such older and bigger boys in the first place. It wasn't just his fault, it was our fault as well, and we all had to suffer. We had to raise money to pay for the best treatment available for our fallen hero.

The Senior Geography master was already a star performer in Morning Assembly. He'd been in a Japanese prisoner of war camp. It was cruel to mock him but I used to wish they'd kept the fucker there. He was a monster. He once tried to give the whole school detention for laughing at one of his more elaborate twitches.

He used to start off subtly enough – sitting down, straightening the knot in his tie and performing a few chin-stretching exercises. Then one of his arms would need adjusting and he'd jerk it outwards and fold it back in again. He repeated this two or three times and followed it with a vigorous leg-crossing routine, punctuated with a bit more tie straightening and chin stretching. His face would join in too – eyes blinking on and off at random and the sides of his mouth behaving independently of one other. The poor man must have been through hell.

But he was a positive danger. None of the other masters ever sat next to him, though the odd student teacher made that mistake. He was almost out of control. And with the advent of the broken neck he really came into his own.

He made impassioned speeches in assembly and even

the headmaster started rolling his eyes towards the ceiling. We were far, far from our target. The boy needed oxygen cylinders, a new cushion for his wheelchair and the parents had used up their nest egg. It must be replaced. I came along without a contribution one Monday and when it hadn't materialised by Wednesday I got an hour's detention.

It was him that fixed up the match. I thought it would have been nice if he'd taken early retirement, donated his pension and supplemented that with the contents of his begging bowl. But he carried on. He went to a school rugby match on the coach and afterwards he gave the whole First Fifteen a week's detention for singing lewd and disrespectful songs on the journey home, even though they'd won a trophy of some sort.

Grandma in Oldham came to stay and after she'd gone back there were rows every night. I didn't know what they were about but they came up like a storm when my dad arrived home from work. I used to dread the sound of the Volkswagen. On a bad night it chuntered past my bedroom window on its way to the garage as I did my homework. That meant my dad was staying in, and once the storm got going it would rage and blow until long after bedtime.

Other nights the Volkswagen stopped in the driveway, which meant that he was going out later and there wouldn't be time for a row. He'd have his tea and be off again for a meeting of the Institute of Works Managers, or to Night School where he taught technical drawing. I should have been proud of him – I should have appreciated him because he was doing all this for us, but instead I was beginning to hate him because when he came home the shouting started.

It wasn't his fault and it wasn't my mum's fault either. It's the fault of families – the pressure of family life. I think the family is an essentially dysfunctional unit – all families are the same. Scenes that I thought were peculiar to my family I've since found out are universal. I loved my parents and they loved me – perhaps that was what put us under such pressure.

Rows always started on Sundays. They seemed to go hand in hand with car maintenance. I can remember my mum standing on the concrete driveway on a cold Sunday morning, wearing an apron and one Marigold, clutching a half-peeled potato and gesticulating with a potato peeler, as she berated my dad who was silently dismantling the Volkswagen.

He seemed to do a lot of car maintenance. He had a special contraption involving two crocodile clips, some wire, and a twelve-volt bulb. And with the aid of this and a lot of grunting he adjusted the advance and retard by heaving the fanbelt pulley round until the bulb lit up. I never understood it myself. I would have liked to have joined in, just to be more boyish and son-like, but the reality was that car maintenance was boring – there was never anything for me to do – I just stood there getting cold.

Over Sunday lunch my sister would start talking about Enoch Powell and things would get heated. Or if that didn't do it I'd casually mention the cesspit. You could see the cesspit cover from the dining table and I was very interested in it because every couple of months some men from the East Sussex County Council had to come and empty it. Cesspits were supposed to drain away but these were built on chalk so they overflowed instead. In my mind a cesspit overflow would be akin to a national disaster and we'd all have to set to and clean it up with our toothbrushes – that is, when it was safe for us to leave the house again.

The council men came in a big green tanker equipped with lengths of large metal hose, which they fixed together wearing orange gloves that looked like frankfurters. They attached one end of the hose to the back of the tank, lowered the other into the cesspit, and the contents were sucked into the tank. Then they took it all to the Portobello outflow at Telscombe Cliffs and pumped it out into the sea where it was feasted on by squawking seagulls.

It was a very interesting subject for a twelve-year-old and I'd been fascinated by it since we first moved there. My parents had had enough of it and so had my sister. At some point my sister would storm out in tears and lock herself in her bedroom for an afternoon of homework. After that we usually got onto the subject of how badly I was doing at school.

My abiding memory of being twelve and thirteen is of being more or less constantly on the verge of tears. Everybody wanted me to do well – the pressure was too much. I had all the chances that my parents hadn't had because, as I so often heard, there was a war on when they were young. I felt like screaming. It wasn't my fault. I didn't start it – I wasn't even there.

They wanted something better for us, it's only natural. I didn't want to be an ungrateful little blighter, it's just that I really wasn't sure I wanted what was on offer.

Easter was the worst time. It was like four Sundays in a row – you could discount Easter Saturday even though the shops were open because we'd already had a surrogate Sunday in the shape of Good Friday. It must be better now that the shops are open all the way through – it causes a distraction. In the Easters of my childhood we only had each other, and motor racing on the TV. The weather was always grey and by Easter Monday the tension was unbearable.

Once it got so bad that divorce was threatened and I found myself locked in my parents' bedroom with my mum who was going through the telephone book. She was looking for a divorce solicitor – though where she thought she was going to find one on Easter Monday I don't know. It was a gesture. And I don't know why the door was locked because my dad was busy race-tuning the Volkswagen – we were the last people on earth that he wanted to see at the time.

We caught a bus to Brighton and watched the Mods and Rockers. When we came home everything was fine – it was just another ridiculous family drama. We thought the world of one another really.

Substitute by The Who came out. I thrilled to the sound of it on Wonderful Radio London and it crossed my mind that I'd better make the most of the first week of the holiday. Because I knew something that my parents didn't – I was about to get the worst report of my school career so far. The Headmaster showed it to me before we broke up.

An older boy came into the classroom and announced that the Headmaster wanted to see me in his study. It was a surprise – I had no reason to think he even knew that I existed, but now he was calling for me by name.

He was sitting behind a big desk when I was shown in. He asked me if I knew why he'd sent for me. I didn't, but he couldn't hear what I said so he asked me again. He leaned back in his chair with his head cocked slightly to one side. He was wearing his ceremonial master's robes.

He shouted: 'Speak up when you're answering me!' and his face was like thunder. And then he told me why I was there: I was a disgrace to the school, I was a disgrace to myself. I'd let us all down, and the question he wanted to ask was, 'What was I going to do about it?'

I didn't know what I was going to do about it. I didn't know the rules. And I couldn't think because all the time he was looking at me and the leather sole of one shoe was tapping against the side of the desk, click... click... click... I was almost in tears and I was shaking so much I nearly wet myself.

'WHAT ARE YOU GOING TO DO ABOUT IT???!!!?'

I suddenly knew the answer: 'Get it better.'

'GET IT BETTER WHAT???!!!?'

'Get it better, Sir'

'That's better!' And here he almost smiled. Then he turned to thunder again: 'GET OUT! GET OUT! GET OUT OF MY SIGHT!!!'

I left as quickly as I could, trying to hide my tears from the school secretary. All in a day's work for the Headmaster. Fucking psychopath.

It didn't do any good. I certainly didn't *get it better* – I did my best to make it worse. I didn't mean to but I just didn't know how to *get it better*. From the moment I walked into the place in the morning until I left at quarter to four in the afternoon I was in trouble. There were instructions to be followed that I hadn't listened to, homework to be handed in that I hadn't done, books to remember that I'd forgotten, places to be that I couldn't find, and questions to be answered that I hadn't understood.

'You just don't *lissen*,' they said.

Friday On My Mind – The Easybeats
Matthew & Son – Cat Stevens
Union Jack badges that said 'I'm Backing Britain'

I suppose it was my lack of self-esteem that led my parents to the desperate measure of persuading me to join the Boy Scouts.

I was OK about it in the beginning. I even went along with playing football, though I hated it. I hated games. I was crap at football. In situations where the two biggest, most handsome, best at games and nearest to puberty type of boys were appointed as captains, and went ahead to select teams, it was always me and the fat kid that were left over after all the mates had been chosen and the weeds had been traded for duffers. I didn't like competitive sports and football did nothing for me. It still doesn't. I'm almost ashamed to admit it. I must have got a chromosome missing.

But playing football with a lot of other boy scouts outside the church hall on a Friday evening was a small price to pay for the exciting activities that I'd be joining in as a fully fledged member of the First Peacehaven Scout Troupe, Penguin Patrol.

Building bridges across ravines, felling trees to make a raft, sleeping in a bivouac (whatever that was), and cooking dinners in a billycan over an open fire that I'd lit myself by harnessing the power of the sun's rays through a magnifying glass that my mum had given me for my birthday. It was all there in the boy scout manual, Scouting For Boys.

Scouting For Boys was a fascinating book. It carried step-by-step instructions on shitting in the open air – the construction of a special trench, dug and later filled in with a special trowel. It warned that if a boy had *'thoughts'* he must take a cold bath immediately. It showed you how to pass your darning badge, cooking badge, thrift badge, tree-felling badge, morse code badge and a million other badges, culminating in the Queen's Scout Award for which a trip to Buckingham Palace was in order.

I was going to become a better person. In no time at all my khaki shirt was going to be covered in badges.

Through being in the scouts I met some local boys. I collected quite a gang together and we developed an obsession with an old house. It stood on its own, high up above the Dip (the place where the cyclist had taken me and my friend Bobby Chalmers). Some of the gang maintained that the house was haunted. I said that if it was, perhaps the ghost would answer the door if we knocked on it. But it was more likely that the door would be opened by a very old lady who would ask us what we wanted. And we'd just tell her that we were a bunch of willing boy scouts who were wondering if she needed any jobs doing. She'd shake her head in a dotty sort of way, shut the door and that would be the end of it.

There was no answer. I knocked and knocked and listened for sounds of movement inside but there was nothing so I tried the side door. Still no result. It was obvious that the house was empty. I looked around to see that nobody except the gang was looking, and threw a stone at a small upstairs window. It smashed a pane of glass. That ought to wake up anyone who was in there – maybe alert the old lady that help was at hand.

But there was still no reply.

The back garden petered out into the windswept undergrowth and bushes that grew round the top of the Dip. It was October, firework time. We set up base camp in the bushes, kept the house under observation for a while and considered leaving it and going back to setting off bangers in the concrete entrance of the public library.

But I couldn't leave – I had to get to the bottom of the mystery. The house was trying to tell a story if only anyone would listen. The garden had once been idyllic, but it had gone to seed, and the house was dilapidated, a bit old and sorry for itself. We were going to have to be careful because there was a row of houses at the other side of the Dip, across a field. One of the gang lived over there. He was a bit worried in case his parents caught sight of him. I was surprised by that because he'd usually do anything for a laugh. He was gullible too – I once helped him to come to a decision with regard to pissing on an electric cattle fence – it was his idea, not mine – I just helped him to see it through – with stunning results.

I crawled through the long grass like a commando. The french windows were old and quite rotten with peeling paint. On the inside there were rotting shreds of net curtain. It was the Hammer House of Horror. I scuttled back to the safety of the bushes. One of the other boys crawled through the garden to have a look but he didn't even get as far as the french windows.

So it was down to me. I set off back through the garden again – a bit less carefully this time – we hadn't been caught yet and, after all, there was nobody around because it was Sunday.

The french windows were very easy to prise open. I crawled inside, looked around and grabbed the first available object, a round Crawfords biscuit tin. Back in the safety of the bushes we opened it up and shared out some soft Rich Tea biscuits. I went back in with one of the other boys and we came out with a bottle of Stone's Ginger Wine and a violin case. We washed down the rest of the biscuits with the ginger wine and I had a look at my violin.

There was a boy called Paul. His mother ran the Brownies – I suppose she was Brown Owl. Paul looked a bit like a pig, he had a turned-up nose and misshapen sticky-out ears. He and his mother were both fat. They lived opposite the church hall in a ramshackle house next to the chimney sweep. Paul didn't seem to have a father. He'd been a bit reticent about the whole thing but now he was all for going in and seeing what else we could get. The violin was quite nice but I only wanted to play the guitar or the organ so I sold it to Mark, the boy who once pissed on the electric fence. He gave me five shillings for it.

Suddenly we were all in the house – there were five of us – and I was no longer in control. It was 1967 outside, but in the house it was the 1930s. There were photos and letters and books and trunks full of dressing-up clothes, sheet music, trinkets and a card table on the landing set up for bridge. There were little boxes containing military medals from the first world war, bunting from VE day and stacks of parish magazines from years and years ago. I could tell exactly what the lady who lived there had been like. I didn't know where she was now but that hardly mattered because she was here in spirit. I settled down to find out all about her while destruction raged around me.

We came to our senses, cleared up as best we could, and left. The others had got quite a stash together – the entire contents of the cocktail cabinet, a Spanish guitar, a wind-up gramophone and God knows what else. We hid it all in the bushes and went off to seek amusement elsewhere.

When we came back later that afternoon there was an

older boy and girl. They had found our ill-gotten gains. They seemed quite shocked. They said it looked as though the house had been broken into. They asked us if we'd seen anything, but we hadn't, feigning indifference and setting off fireworks in a hole. They gathered everything together and between them they carried it off. The boy said they were taking it to the Police Station. He should have been in the boy scouts, not us.

The police came round a week later. It was Sunday again. I'd been out on a bike ride with another boy from the gang. We'd been all over the back of Peacehaven, beyond the smallholdings and out onto the downs. We'd spent some time trying, unsuccessfully, to light the stubble in a late-harvested cornfield. When we came back it was starting to get dark.

Around seven o'clock, after tea, the doorbell rang.

My mum said, 'Who the devil could this be on a Sunday night?'

I went with her to answer the door. I was jumpy – I'd almost had a premonition – almost, because I wouldn't allow myself to realise a premonition of something this bad.

'Mrs Goulden? We're from the Newhaven police, we'd like a word with your son.'

I was there like a shot – 'I haven't done anything, what do you want me for?' An admission of guilt straight out of *Z Cars* or *Softly Softly*. *Please let it be the cornfield.*

They came in and sat down. There were two of them, a detective constable and a detective sergeant. The older of the two, the sergeant, was short and tubby with a face like a belligerent bulldog. The other was tall, thin and slightly gingery. They wore raincoats. The bulldog looked at me and asked: 'Where were you last Sunday afternoon?'

I couldn't remember.

He asked me if I'd been playing anywhere near the Dip.

I might have been but I couldn't remember.

'And the house? Did you go anywhere near the house?'

'What house?'

'You know very well what house.'

It was no use, they knew everything and the whole sorry tale unfolded around the hearthrug that my dad had pegged the last time he'd been in hospital.

They'd been to see two of the other boys that afternoon. They'd been onto us for a week now – we were seen. The other boys cited me as the ringleader. Worst of all, the violin that I'd sold for five shillings turned out to be a Stradirvarious. It was worth a fortune. The boy had taken it home and hidden it after we left the house. When his parents found it they got suspicious and the story tumbled out. We hadn't made a good job of covering our tracks.

The police questioned me for about an hour and a half. My mum interjected several times, things like, 'I knew something like this would happen.'

My dad didn't say anything, he just sat and listened intently, occasionally clearing his throat.

The police left. They had two other boys to see and then the evidence would be sifted, the balance would be weighed and prosecutions would be put. In the meantime I was to understand that I was in very serious trouble indeed – I was to be charged with housebreaking, an offence that carried a term of imprisonment.

I cried and cried and cried. It was the end of the

world. I was scared to death and I was terribly ashamed of what we'd done. The old lady was senile – she was in hospital. I kept demanding to know what was going to happen to me, but nobody would tell me. The next day was Monday and I had to go to school as usual.

Having been roundly identified as the ringleader I was pretty well ostracised by the boy scouts. I didn't want to go the following Friday but I had to because I was trying to tow the line. When I got there Piggy Paul and Mark The Fence Pisser made a big play of de-popularising me – not that I was exactly popular in the first place.

Piggy Paul ran around me pointing and shouting: 'Err, err, err, get away from him, get away from him.'

To start with Mark wouldn't even look at me or speak to me, and then he joined in with Paul. I was quite surprised – I hadn't seen them all week, and now that we were in trouble I thought the least we could do was stick together.

I suppose their parents had told them not to have anything to do with me and they were so confused that they couldn't think how to do that without causing a scene. I was a social pariah – I'd got them into trouble.

The Scout Leader, a big misfit that we all called Skipper, wanted a word with me. He took me into the church hall kitchen and shut the door. He stood there on the lino underneath the striplight, big and podgy in his Scout uniform, with bare, ham-like knees:

'About ten days ago…' he started. He didn't really need to finish. If this got out it could bring disgrace on the entire scout troop. I wasn't asked to leave but it didn't take long before I was gone. I stuck it for a while longer but it was obvious that I was never going to fell trees and build bridges.

The most exciting thing we ever did was cycle over to a piece of wasteland on the council estate where they were going to build the new scout hut. We lit a fire and cooked some sausages in tin foil, which we ate in the open air as darkness fell. The best thing that ever happened was when a game of indoor football in the church hall got out of hand and a striplight came down on top of the assistant scout master, an ill-tempered, older man with glasses. He said the F word by mistake.

The old lady was in no fit state to press charges so we were given an official police caution. I had to go down to the police station with my dad on a Sunday morning. I wore my school trousers, a shirt and V-neck pullover, and my school gabardine. As a special treat I was allowed to wear one of my dad's ties. I wanted to wear the black one but he wouldn't let me so I chose a green one that looked like armchair fabric.

It was fairly painless. I was shown into a room with my dad. There was a desk with a detective sitting behind it. He had a big pink face and ginger hair. He was quite old. He studied me with eyes like flint, took in the gabardine and the armchair tie and finally asked me if I knew why I was there.

'Housebreaking, sir.'

'What!!?!'

'Yes, sir.' (I'd been told to call him sir.)

I had to leave the room and stand in the corridor while he had a chat with my dad. After what seemed like ages he called me back in. He said, 'I've talked to your father and I don't think we'll be seeing you in here again. If we do you'll be in real trouble but the best thing you can do now is to try and put it all behind you and concentrate on your studies.' He shook my dad's hand and that was it.

I listened to my transistor radio all the time – Radio London or the other pirate station, Radio Caroline, but increasingly I tuned in to the new government station, Radio One. It wasn't as good but the reception was better. In the evenings, after half past seven, Radio Luxembourg played pop music – really good stuff sometimes but the reception was diabolical, you heard it across a sea of squelch and phasing.

I bought I Can See For Miles by The Who in the record shop in Newhaven on a Saturday afternoon. Then I had to meet my mum who was visiting a friend, a woman she knew in the town. This woman had a son who was older than me. He was a mod – a real-live fighting-on-Brighton-beach mod. We eyed each other in a surly teenage way and he said, 'Got a record? Whatcha got?' I showed him. 'Good choice,' he said and led me into the dining room where there was a Dansette record player. He turned it up louder than I ever dared turn ours up when my parents were in the house and played soul records for me until it was time to go home.

My mum gave me a purple shirt even though I'd done badly at school. It came with a cardboard tag – a picture of a hep cat playing the drums, surrounded by adoring teenage girls. It was exactly the sort of thing.

My ambition was to own a shirt with a button-down collar. I got a dark blue shirt with white cuffs and a white button-down collar – like the one Ray Davies wore when the Kinks played Autumn Almanac on *Top Of The Pops* – except that Ray's shirt was light grey and dark grey because the TV was black and white. But I just knew it was a Beverley shirt, exactly like mine.

The Legend Of Xanadu – Dave Dee Dozy Beaky Mick &
    Tich
Fire Brigade – The Move
Tin Soldier – The Small Faces
Endless cross-country running through freezing cow shit.

I surpassed myself at school – I got a worse report than
anyone could ever have dreamed of. I was nearly expelled
but they put me on report instead – I had a card that I had
to get signed by the teacher at the end of every lesson to
shown that I'd actually been there. I didn't care because
suddenly it was summer. The smell of newly cut grass,
the sound of cricket and distant lawnmowers. Everything
was easy. I was learning to go my own way.

The Jimi Hendrix Experience, Pink Floyd, The Byrds,
    Cream, Led Zeppelin, Spooky Tooth.

Baby Come Back – The Equals
Lazy Sunday Afternoon – The Small Faces
Mony Mony – Tommy James & The Shondells
Fire – The Crazy World Of Arthur Brown
This Wheel's On Fire – Julie Driscoll, Brian Auger &
    The Trinity
Jumping Jack Flash – the last ever Rolling Stones single
    with Brian Jones.

1968 was a great year for pop music. I was fourteen. I
started going to Saturday morning classes at the Art
School in Brighton. My heroes had all been to art school
– Ray Davies, John Lennon, Pete Townshend – so I
wanted to go too. It was obvious. Art School was where
it was happening – you only had to look at art students to
see that.

Grateful Dead, Quicksilver Messenger Service, Jefferson
  Airplane

The Byrds – Sweetheart Of The Rodeo
The Jimi Hendrix Experience – Are You Experienced
Cream – White Room

Hanningtons record department had quite a good selection. It was popular with men in dirty raincoats – they
use to go in there to look at the naked women on the
cover of Electric Ladyland. The record department was
run by a snooty bloke in a suit who wouldn't let you hear
a record unless you were definitely going to buy it. As
most of the records I was interested in hardly got any
airplay, it was a big risk – you had to buy them without
hearing them.

When Richard Branson opened the first Virgin record
shop outside London, he opened it in Brighton, just up
the road from Hanningtons by the Clocktower. You
could listen to anything you wanted all day in there, on
headphones, lying around on beanbags. You could even
smoke dope. It was a sort of progressive music doss
house. Hanningtons record department went into a
Mantovani-laden decline.

I saw Pink Floyd at the Brighton Dome. I'd never seen a
group live before, only on the TV. The *NME* Poll
Winners Concert, where the bands always looked less
well-kempt than in their publicity shots – hair was shag-
gier and clothes slightly ill-fitting. They sounded raucous
and out of tune. It never occurred to me that I could actually go to an event like this – something so fantastic
couldn't possibly happen anywhere near Peacehaven.

I thought it was going to be like the theatre – the lights

would go down, a big red curtain would swish open and the group would start playing. But it wasn't like that at all. There was no curtain and the stage was full of equipment and men with long hair making adjustments to it, carrying guitars and bits of drum kits about and saying, 'Check, one two,' into microphones. It was really casual.

The first band on – the first real professional live band I ever saw – was The Pretty Things. They played four numbers including two from their new rock opera, SF Sorrow. They were incredibly loud.

My uncle played the cornet in a brass band – he once took me to hear them play on Worthing seafront. I was very impressed by the way the bass drum resonated in my chest but this was different again – the whole band hit me in the chest. It was so loud that it hit me with physical force. I was awe-struck.

They had a wall of amplifiers behind them. I didn't know much about that kind of thing but I should think they were Marshall stacks. The sides of the stage were taken up by huge collections of WEM speaker columns, lined up and piled high like a monument.

Phil May wore a red satin kaftan. During the long instrumental sections he strolled around the stage, in and out of the shadows, opening bottles of beer and checking the vibration from the speakers with his hands, like somebody warming themselves in front of an electric fire – I suppose he was checking to see if they were working properly. It was nothing like on the television.

Dick Taylor played an Epiphone semi-acoustic in tobacco sunburst finish, and the organ was a red and black Vox Continental, complete with Z-shaped chrome legs. Towards the end of SF Sorrow the strobe lights came on. They made everything look like a silent film – you couldn't tell what was going on any more. It looked as though the drummer was putting on a fur coat. I thought this was a strange thing to be doing with World War Three going on.

'Er, Twink's been sick,' said Phil.

The organist, John Povey, took over on the drums and they finished off with She Says Good Morning. I was utterly devastated.

Next up was the Third Ear Band who played sinister medieval-sounding music on cello, viola and some ancient English wind instruments.

I was mesmerised and probably quite stoned on secondary dope smoke. The air was thick with it. The Floyd played Careful With That Axe Eugene, Astronome Donome, Interstellar Overdrive, Set The Controls For The Heart Of The Sun, Let There Be More Light, and the whole of Saucerful Of Secrets – all three parts. I couldn't see what was happening on the stage because the light-show was in full force. Giant bubbles rolled across the stage, obliterating the band. I nearly missed the last bus home. I'd never experienced anything like it.

After that I went to every concert I possibly could.

Procol Harum (at least four times because I'd fallen in love with the sound of the Hammond organ)

Stone The Crows (Alex Harvey's brother, Les, on guitar; Maggie Bell on vocals)

Family (in 1969 on the day their third album, *A Song For Me*, came out)

David Bowie alone with a twelve-string guitar, a bubbly hairdo and a corduroy suit. He sang Unwashed And Slightly Dazed, The Man Who Sold The World and his new single: 'Ground Control to Major Tom...'

Doctor John (The Night Tripper)

Love Sculpture (Sabre Dance – Dave Edmunds on guitar through a Watkins Copicat)

The Crazy World Of Arthur Brown supported by
Hawkwind who turned up in place of Shakin'
Stevens & The Sunsets. The audience was an uneasy
mixture of hippies and teds. The teds were disappointed by Hawkwind. I watched from a safe
vantage point halfway up a scaffolding tower behind
the drummer. It was Hawkwind's seventh ever gig.
When the strobe came on their drummer was sick
too.

Jon Hiseman's Colosseum supported by Sandy Denny's
Fotheringay – a mismatch of jazz rock and folk rock
but nobody seemed to mind.

Canned Heat

Wishbone Ash – Twin lead guitars were their thing but
they started with a sitting-down acoustic number. As
the fingerpicking got underway one of the guitar
players looked up through a curtain of hair and blue
lighting and said, 'Good evening, Brighton!' He lifted
the back end of the word *Brighton* so that it turned
into a big, heavily pregnant question with the hint of
a challenge about it. I instantly hated them. The
support act was called Glencoe. I liked them a lot
more. The bass player was Norman Watt-Roy. He
was only two years older than I was.

Derek & The Dominoes – Eric Clapton in what was possibly his last moment of real magnificence, supported
by Brett Marvin & The Thunderbolts with piano
player John Lewis aka Jona Lewie.

The Keef Hartley Band

The Edgar Broughton Band

Keith Relf's Renaissance

Free

The Nice

Audience

Clark Hutchinson

Long John Baldry

Terry Reid

Juicy Lucy

Jackson Heights (Lee Jackson, bass player from the Nice after the Nice split up)

Every Which Way (Brian Davison, drummer from the Nice after the Nice split up)

Matching Mole (Robert Wyatt, drummer from the Soft Machine)

Humble Pie (Steve Marriott from the Small Faces and Peter Frampton, the face of 1968, from the Herd)

John Mayall – saw him countless times, once with Peter Green guesting on guitar. The best was when he had a band with no drummer. The trouble with John Mayall was that he tended to be a bit worthy – he was playing the blues.

I got my first real guitar when I was fourteen, a three-quarter scale Japanese acoustic. Before that I'd had several unsuccessful attempts at making one. They were strung up with fuse wire and were usually unplayable.

My sister was learning folk guitar with the TV series, Hold Down A Chord. The back page of the tutor book had diagrams of all the chord shapes. When she lost interest and went to university I tore the back page off and learned all the chords on it – dominant, sub-dominant, tonic and minor. I didn't know what any of that meant but I could soon do it in all twelve key signatures.

A couple of boys in my class were forming a folk group. They asked me to join. I didn't really want to play folk music but it was a start. Two acoustic guitars and a boy on the electric bass whose dad was a Baptist minister. The boy looked like a Baptist minister too – he even had the haircut – but he was delusional enough to see himself as a Noel Redding figure, a titan of the bass guitar. He tried to persuade me to take up the drums, then the other boy would have to get an electric guitar and we could be a proper rock group.

The other boy really wanted to play folk music and I didn't want to be a drummer so we learned to play Colours by Donovan and fizzled out in the wake of a couple of Gordon Lightfoot and Tom Paxton tunes. The Baptist minister's son got himself a white Hofner Galaxy that looked a bit like Jimi's Strat, the other boy grew up and started playing in folk clubs, and I was the confused kid trying to write songs that bridged the gap between John Mayall's Bluesbreakers and Pink Floyd.

Muddy Waters Willie Dixon Howlin' Wolf John Lee
    Hooker (I'd seen him doing Boom Boom on *Ready
    Steady Go*. Now I had a Chess EP: *Love Blues)*
T-Bone Walker Chuck Berry Elmore James
Strictly Personal – Captain Beefheart & His Magic Band
    (found in the bargain rack in Woolworths)

I got a full-size Eko acoustic guitar and electrified it by sticking the earpieces from a pair of army surplus headphones to the body. I plugged it into a homemade ten-watt amplifier given to me by a local TV repair man that I met at a jazz club. All the heavy-duty musicians were into jazz – it said they were in the *Melody Maker*, so I went to a local jazz club at a pub in Peacehaven called the Gay Highlander.

I had some difficulty reconciling Monty Sunshine & His Jazz Men with Jack Bruce talking about something called *bebop,* and I couldn't imagine how Captain Beefheart could have been influenced by this, but I was prepared to give it a try. I went home confused – my head ringing with trumpets, trombones, clarinets and banjos.

It was a hideous racket but I persevered. A guitar player didn't show up one night so they gave me some chord sheets and sat me at the back where I played chunk chunk chunk chunk chunk chunk chunk all night, with a chord change at the beginning of every bar. Soon I was playing trad jazz at the Pier Hotel opposite the Palace Pier in Brighton.

The Pier Hotel was rough. I saw loads of fights in there. It was what you might call bohemian, which is another way of saying it was full of low-life beatnik scum. It was refurbished in the late '70s and renamed the Buccaneer. Then it turned into the Escape Club. They don't have jazz there any more.

I bought an Ornette Colman record – *The Art Of The Improvisers*. I was gong to buy *Hot Buttered Soul* by Isaac Hayes but they'd sold out so I bought the Ornette Colman album instead. At last I understood. I couldn't begin to play this stuff and I wasn't sure that I wanted to but I started to understand something about freedom in music. I was done with trad jazz.

When I was fifteen the school turned into a mixed comprehensive. Lewes County Grammar School For Boys no longer existed. Neither did the Girls Grammar School or the Secondary Modern. We were all together now under one banner – Priory Comprehensive. I didn't give a damn about comprehensive – what interested me was girls, and suddenly there were loads of them.

At the end of the fourth year the old regime was still in place – apartheid for boys and girls. The train home was divided in half – we had two carriages each – girls in the front, boys in the back. Prefects patrolled the train to make sure there were no transgressions. When the train arrived in Newhaven we were allowed to talk to girls as we walked to the bus stop but once we got there we had to queue separately.

There was a system in place – one week the girls queued at the front, the next week the boys. It didn't make any difference who queued where really because when the bus came that was segregated too – girls down-stairs, boys on top. When it rained the prefects waited in the bus shelter but we had to stand two abreast in the wet. There weren't any members of the public to consider because the bus stop was halfway along a deserted and wind-blasted stretch of road outside the Bevan Funnel reproduction furniture factory. Nobody in their right mind would wait for a bus there.

On the journey to school none of these rules applied – it was beyond the bounds of possibility that we could get sexually aroused at quarter past eight in the morning. But care was taken nonetheless – the girls' summer school uniform, '60s coat dresses with buttons all the way down the front, had to be redesigned because the temptation could prove too much for the boys – we might find our-selves unbuttoning them in an unsegregated moment.

At the beginning of the fifth year this regime was abol-ished. The senior biology master gave us boys a bit of fatherly advice and counselling – he explained how babies were made:

The man supports his weight on his elbows, inserts his erect penis into the lady's vagina and stimulates himself by means of vigorous thrusting movements until he achieves ejaculation. This fertilises the female egg, which hatches out into a baby nine months later. If that happens the man has a responsibility, so he must be very careful.

And that's why, in a darkened field at a pop concert

with the lights flashing and music pulsating, so many young lives are ruined.

It crossed my mind that a man of his age should really know about wearing a johnny. But it sounded fabulous – I could hardly wait, and I'd promise to be careful. I was hoping to try some marijuana too.

Pinball Wizard – The Who
Creedence Clearwater Revival
Jimi Hendrix on the *Lulu Show*

I didn't really care about O levels – as long as I passed enough to go to art school that was all right. School was a big playground full of girls. It was better now.

I ripped a bra advert out of my sister's *Cosmopolitan* magazine – three full colour pictures of three different sized girls shown from the waist to the neck. In the first they were wearing skinny-rib pullovers, the second showed them in Wonderbras and in the third they were totally naked. Three different sizes of bosom. You could apply it to any girl you knew – look at her in the flesh, fully clothed, which was the only way you were ever going to see her unless you got lucky, and then you could rush home and consult the tit chart.

White Light White Heat – The Velvet Underground
Inner City Blues – Marvin Gaye
Let's Stay Together – Al Green

Most of the girls were either going out with or obsessing about some dreamy older boy in the sixth form. But it was always worth a try, and soon there was kissing, then there was French kissing and tentative sorties into the brassiere area – what the manual called heavy petting.

Meanwhile, back at home, I played my guitar from the moment I got in until it was time for bed, with a short break for tea and a quiet interlude while I pretended to do my homework. My mind was made up, I knew what I was into – art school, girls and playing the guitar. One day soon I was going to leave home, lose my virginity, go to art school, join a band, drink lots of alcohol, and take a few drugs too – if I could find any.

I hitched lifts along the seafront to save bus fare. I got a ride in a Rover 90 – brown leather seats and gritty tartan travelling rugs – a real old vicar's car. It smelled of dog. The driver was an older gentleman with a little grey moustache and a clipped military accent. He looked at me as he drove along and then he stopped at a pillar box and asked me to post some letters for him. When I got back in he asked me how old I was, so I told him. Then he patted my leg and said, 'Fancy a rub up?'

I didn't know what to say so I said, 'Only with my girlfriend.' It was the first thing that came into my head and I suppose it was true – I did like that sort of thing but I'd never heard it described like that before. He was persistent. He kept stroking my leg and saying, 'Yes, but surely you like a bit of fun, how about a bit of a rub up?' By now he was in the middle of the bench seat and his fat little legs were having trouble reaching the pedals.

I saw a bus pulling into the stop next to Roedean School. I said, 'Can you let me out here? I've just remembered I need to see somebody who lives here' – even though there weren't any houses, just a girl's public school. He wasn't going to stop at first but then he did. I got out and he leaned over to pull the door shut. He looked at me with gleaming blue eyes and said: 'Pity, 'cause you'd be a bit of fun, you know.'

On the day after my seventeenth birthday I started learn-ing to drive. My mum thought it would give me more self-confidence. Also my dad was going blind. Because of the drugs he had to take, he developed cataracts on both eyes at once. It was a side effect of Prednisone. If I passed my test quite quickly I could drive my dad around until after he'd had the operation.

I started off on a fine spring evening, May 19th 1971, by driving the Volkswagen along a flat road in Saltdean with my dad in the passenger seat. It was quite easy once I'd got the hang of the clutch, and I even got the thing into third gear. I felt all-powerful – I was hooked.

In the first place I hadn't been all that interested. It took me some time to realise what the benefits would be – like staying out long after the last bus had gone. And it was sure to bring increased popularity with girls – I'd be able to date girls that didn't live on the bus route, girls from Alfriston, Lower Dicker and Piddinghoe. And I'd be able to stop off and shag them in the back seat on the way home.

This isn't actually very practical – you could devote a lifetime to perfecting car sex techniques but it really isn't worth it. On a bad night, with an incompatible partner, you're as likely to inadvertently bugger yourself on the gearstick as effect successful copulation – the plastic upholstery sticks to the naked parts, the windows steam up, and some nosey parker from the Neighbourhood Watch comes and peers in at your bottom.

I had some lessons from Mr Griffin but he was horri-ble so I stopped. The trouble with driving instructors in the early '70s was that most of them seemed to be retired policemen. Mr Griffin's problem was that he also looked and behaved like one. He obviously hated the job as much as he hated me. He tried to be nice, but that just made him all the more manic:

'... .clutch Clutch CLUTCH – lift the clutch... and handbrake... HANDBRAKE!!!!! -HANDBRAKE!!!!!! What's the matter with you?'

He glared at me from under big black eyebrows and tore the handbrake out of the floor of the car. In my mind he set about me, lashing me with the frayed end of the cable. But that would be an exaggeration – he probably just ate it.

Mr Hopkins was much nicer – the acceptable face of retired British policemen. He was teaching another boy I knew to drive too, so we formed an alliance and compared notes on his slightly senile behaviour.

I'd be piloting the light blue Hopkins Volkswagen along the seafront towards Brighton with the large, tweedy Mr Hopkins recumbent in the passenger seat.

'It's a lovely day,' he'd declare, in the remains of a Lancastrian accent.

'Yes, it certainly is A Lovely Day,' he'd continue, enlarging on the theme.

Then he'd sit back, twiddle his thumbs for a while, and emit an occasional contented 'ahhh...'

And we'd roll along the seafront in companionable silence, apart from the odd *'aye-diddle-dee...'* that would escape from him.

Sometimes the silence would be broken by an ominous 'POMM!' that would hang in the air, all on its own.

One day he performed an entire symphony. It started very quietly and I thought he was saying something to me that I hadn't quite heard. I said: 'Pardon, did you say something?'

'Oh no – I would never speak to you while you were

driving, because I would not wish to distract you. Now, carry on,' he said with magnanimous gesture.

Our progress was interrupted by further indistinct mutterings, that were getting louder:

<small>tiddly-</small>om-pom-pom ta da-daa tiddly-om-tiddly-om- pom-pom ta da daa Rom Pom BAP bada **ROM POM Tiddly Om Pom Pom Rap** *padaaa!!!!!*

By this time he was beating the crap out of the dashboard in time with the orchestra, and I was having so much trouble not laughing that I put the car into reverse coming off a set of lights and nearly demolished the car behind. Mr Hopkins lapsed into an embarrassed silence as the orchestra packed up and stole away. The best the other boy ever got out of him was a brace of *'tra-la-laas'* and a sudden *'aye yi yi yi like you vairry much!!'* – not bad, but nothing compared with a near accident causing symphony.

In between official lessons I had unofficial ones with my dad. We kept the L plates on the Volkswagen permanently, and every morning I drove him down to the Parker Pen Company. I left the car in the staff car park, walked back up the road to the station and caught the train to Lewes. I didn't mind because I really liked driving.

The only drag about all this was that it meant I got to school on time. As I was only doing two A levels I had a lot of free time. I could have taken a few mornings off, but if I had he might have driven himself. I had to get up to prevent injury and loss of life on the road to Newhaven.

I spent a lot of time hanging out with the girls from the Lower Sixth. I didn't like the girls in my own year.

There was one who reckoned to be related to Virginia Woolf – a literary society had grown up around her. There were a couple of disco chickens and a big homely girl who liked Melanie. There were studious girls, hippy chicks, and the usual collection that were engaged to older blokes called Dave who worked in garages. But the girls in the Lower Sixth had something about them. It was going to be very cool when I passed my driving test and shagged them all, one after another, in the back of the family Volkswagen.

I passed my test first time. The examiner said, 'When I rap my clipboard on the dashboard like this… I want you to effect an emergency stop.' He rapped the dashboard on a street in Hove that had just been spread with loose chippings. My emergency stop was so efficient that he nearly went through the windscreen. He should have been wearing his seatbelt but it wasn't the legal requirement that it is now.

That evening I made my first trip in a car on my own. I drove round to the vicarage and asked one of the vicar's daughters out on a date.

Hull

All the Young Dudes – Mott The Hoople
Drive In Saturday – David Bowie
Virginia Plain – Roxy Music
In A Broken Dream – Python Lee Jackson

I DON'T REMEMBER LEAVING SCHOOL, just School's Out by Alice Cooper. I never said goodbye to anybody. I didn't really want to keep in touch. Somewhere near the end the classroom bully had a final go at me. His friends stood around like members of the Kray Twins gang and watched as he grabbed hold of me and pushed me about. I was taking my school bible to the library. It was a big, heavy thing that had sat in various desks for the last seven years. I hit him over the head with it. He fell to the floor and his friends melted away.

I left home and went to art school in Bristol. It was the thing I wanted to do most in the world but I wasn't very well prepared. I couldn't cook, I had no idea how to handle my finances. I didn't even know how to use a launderette. In my imagination it was going to be a whirl of beautiful girls, casual sex and Sunday after-noons kicking up leaves in the park.

It was a big disappointment. I spent the first term in a student hostel. I started to drink a lot. Then I got a room in a shared flat with two older art students who were heavily into cannabis. One of their friends was a dealer. He came round every night with samples. Most of the time I was as stoned as a pixie on cut-price dope. I did a huge amount of life drawing and got really good at it. But the middle-aged art school models were the only naked women I ever saw. I didn't have much luck with girls that year – I think they were put off by my drunkenness and dirty clothes.

The Foundation or Pre-Diploma course came to an end so I had to apply for a diploma course. I'd decided to do Fine Art. I was too chaotic for much else – graphics, textiles, design, that sort of thing. Anyway, all that was a sell-out, man. I wanted to be bohemian.

I didn't know what I wanted to do really, because I'd never had a clear enough space in my head where I could think it all out. The course of my life was dictated utterly and completely by external influences and pressures. I wanted to go north – get in touch with the northern working-class roots that my parents seemed to have spent my whole childhood running away from.

I found the most northerly art college in the country short of moving into Scotland. I applied to Newcastle upon Tyne Polytechnic (Faculty Of Art & Design) and they sent a letter asking me to go for an interview.

It was a big mistake. I went up by train, lugging my portfolio of drawings, paintings and sketch books. I had to set off the day before because it took a very long time to get to Newcastle. The enormity of its northernness became apparent as I sat on the train. For several hours I shared the compartment with a slightly simple woman in a blue nylon quilted anorak and ski pants. The anorak was zipped up to the neck and she wore those white socks with brown flat-heeled shoes. She was from the north. She was a great conversationalist. We passed a pig farm. 'That's the trouble with pigs,' she commented, 'they tend to roll in their own muck.' So it was true – they were all obsessed with toilets. Shit. All things lavatorial.

The Inter-City Express trundled over the Tyne Bridge and pulled into Newcastle Central Station. I was really in the north now. It was gritty, it was grim, and it was going dark. I came out of the station, took a taxi to an area called Jesmond, and found a cheap bed and breakfast.

The people here were homely, taciturn but warm. The accent was beginning to get on my nerves. It was getting on my nerves because I couldn't understand a fucking word they said. I felt foolish – here I was in my spiritual home, the North Of England, and I couldn't understand a bloody word.

It was a bit better in the pub. There were so many blokes all drinking, smoking, and talking Geordie that you really couldn't hear anything. Whatever rubbish they were saying gathered into a big, thick, fugged-up lump somewhere near the ceiling. The decor wasn't exactly easy on the eye – dartboards, billiard tables, horse brasses, big chairs and adverts for Newcastle Brown – the blue and brown star, like a shit and sky coloured Star of David. It seemed to be everywhere – on the beer mats, on the pumps, on the posters on the walls, even in the pattern on the carpet. They were proud of their Newkey Brown, and at half-past seven with three and a half hours' drinking time left I was halfway down my third pint of the stuff. I couldn't hang around in the B&B with its TV lounge, lacy blue net curtains, and travelling sales reps. I was here to experience the real Newcastle. In the pub.

I got talking to an art student. You could tell he was an art student because he was wearing a bright red jean jacket with a massively thick sketch book hanging out of one of the top pockets. He was a cantankerous and disagreeable sort of person. Taciturn, but without the warm. He had greasy hair and know-it-all spectacles.

They were the sort of spectacles that take on the character of their owner and co-exist with an independent personality in perfect harmony. If the owner looks pleased with himself the lenses twinkle their approval. As the owner airs his knowledge of some subject, the glasses are right there with him, gleaming in agreement.

He was the first person I ever met with knowledgeable spectacles and I really didn't like him. He wanted to know what my references were. I didn't know so he name-dropped a few key Renaissance figures as a punishment. Somehow we got onto the subject of The Beatles, and *Sergeant Pepper's Lonely Hearts Club Band*. Sometimes I wondered if there was a secret manual that I hadn't read. He said it was a seminal work, a work of genius. So I disagreed. It was a weak, pissy load of old bollocks. Which is true in part. Let me explain.

The first time I heard *Sergeant Pepper* was in 1967, lying underneath a table, pissed out of my head in a Barratt Home in Burgess Hill. The sister of a boy in my class was having a party. He'd been allowed to invite one friend so he asked me on the condition that I wore my checked hipsters with the wide white belt, and my purple Beverley shirt with its high teardrop collar. Like the ones The Foundations wore when they did Baby, Now That I've Found You on *Top Of The Pops*.

It was a horrible house, they were a horrible family and it was a hideous party. His sister and her friends were older than us. Their parents went out for the evening and pretty soon most of the lights were off and they were having a full-on snogging session. Except for me and my friend. We were just old enough to be interested in girls, but too young to know what to do about it, so we got drunk on Strongbow Cider. The room spun round in glorious double vision as *Sergeant Pepper* played endlessly on – side one followed by side two followed by side one in continuous rotation. It was the most fabulous thing I'd ever heard in my life.

I never had my own copy of *Sergeant Pepper* because everybody else had it – you could hear it anywhere so I didn't need one. It wasn't until 1974 that I realised there was a serious hole in my collection. By this time I'd forgotten about the greasy, bespectacled arsehole in Newcastle – memories of the only good thing about the party in Burgess Hill came to the fore and I was ready to give it another listen. I got it home, put it on and realised that I was absolutely right – it was a pissy load of old bollocks. And that was my opinion of that record until 1988 when I mentioned it to my friend Andre Barreau who's in the Bootleg Beatles. He said, 'Have you heard it in mono?'

I hadn't thought of that. I went and had a look at my copy – it was stereo. Andre played me the mono version. It's a different mix. It's so radically different that it's another record – it's the record I heard in Burgess Hill.

When it came out in 1967 hardly anybody had stereo. It was the preserve of classical buffs and hi-fi nerds – trombones coming out of the right-hand speaker, violins out of the left, and Vera Lynn in the middle. His Master's Voice – a modern recording miracle. But the pop fan had a Dansette, a Viva Tonesta, or in our case a Bush. One amplifier pumping the sound of the record out of one speaker in a great big mono block.

The Beatles sounded fucking awful in stereo – the instruments came out of one speaker, the singing and guitar solos came out of the other. It was ridiculous, it was supposed to sound like they were in the room with you. It just sounded stupid.

For every million copies of the mono album sold, they probably sold about two thousand stereo copies. So the stereo mix never really got taken that seriously. George Martin remixed the album for stereo with none of the Beatles present. I suppose because George Martin is a classical musician the brass and strings were much more to the fore. The guitars, drums and bass sound really weedy. On the mono version the drums sound like thunder in the breaks, and the guitars are loud, spitting and distorted and the phasing and flanging effects are a lot more extreme. The stereo record sounds like a cheap cover version in comparison.

Mono records were phased out around the end of the '60s and *Sergeant Pepper's Lonely Hearts Club Band* by The Beatles became unavailable – all you could get was the George Martin version. And until the present day, unless you're extremely lucky, and happen to have the odd fifty quid going spare, all you'll find is the stereo edition. So a lot of people who claim it as a seminal work have never actually heard it.

Of course, that fucker in Newcastle back in 1973 probably knew all about the mono version. Paranormal forces would have been working to make sure he did, just to piss me off. As I got more and more drunk, in the course of my Newcastle Brown experiment, he kept saying that when you threw the stuff up it came out green. But he was wasting his time with me, because I hardly ever threw up. I had a cast-iron stomach. Back at the boarding house there was a choice of tea or cocoa. I didn't think they'd noticed that I was drunk.

The Fine Art Department was just as I'd imagined it – modern, gritty and made of concrete. It appeared to be full of large chunks of granite that were being transformed into rough-hewn things of beauty by blokes that looked worryingly like the git from last night. I can't remember seeing any women except maybe a receptionist.

I was shown into an office full of tutors – the interview panel. They were all bunched up on a bench along the length of one wall. They looked quite uncomfortable because there really wasn't enough room. It looked for all the world as if one of them might suddenly be squeezed too far by the pressure of fellow tutors and burst out into the room, leaving the other tutors loose and falling all over the place.

Slightly to one side and in front of them was the head of the department, sitting at a desk. He told me to prop my work up as best I could. The tutoring body stared at me and made remarks under its breath. Sometimes it giggled slightly to itself as if something funny had been passed down the line. But for the most part there was a silence.

'What do you read?'

'Books,' I replied, 'and magazines – in the doctor's surgery,' because, after all, those fuckers hadn't got the monopoly on taciturn. My sketch books were handed round as though they were carrying a contagious disease. I got into a conversation about the future course of my work with a man wearing a cravat. I had a plan to do some large paintings, so I told him all about it. The tutoring body seemed to have nodded off, but the head of the department was feigning benign interest. He looked me up and down and said, 'Why do you want to work so large – is it on account of your, er...' he smirked '...your diminutive stature?' The tutorage sniggered. I reached over the desk and grabbed the bastard by the lapels.

'Are you taking the piss?'

He looked a little worried, but I got the impression that episodes such as this were a part of everyday life here in the Fine Art Department. I gathered up my work and made to leave.

'We'll let you know,' a voice from the tutoring body said. 'Close the door on your way out.'

I received a letter regretting that Newcastle upon Tyne Polytechnic (Faculty Of Art & Design) was unable to offer me a place on its diploma course.

Rock Your Baby – George McCrae
That'll Be The Day – David Essex and Ringo Starr
Make Me Smile (Come Up & See Me) – Cockney Rebel

T Rex, Slade, The Sensational Alex Harvey Band, Kevin
    Coyne, Kevin Ayers, Kilburn & The High Roads

I had to think of somewhere else. One of my tutors suggested Hull. I didn't know anything about the place – I didn't even know where it was.

'What's it like there?' I asked. I didn't want to end up somewhere poncy.

Someone said it had its own telephone company, and the public telephone boxes were painted cream and green. It was a seaport with a huge fishing industry and for a while it even had its own postage stamps. I liked the sound of this but I thought they must be having me on about the telephone company. I couldn't make the giant step inside my own mind that would enable them to plug their system into the pre-BT GPO. I applied for a place so that I could go for an interview and have a look.

I borrowed a five-hundredweight Commer van off a bloke I knew in the pub. It was a piece of shit but I already felt a bond with it because I was using its frayed ex-clutch cable as an E string on my homemade bass. Not that it made a note, but it filled up an otherwise empty space. I'd been buying the strings one at a time, starting with the thinnest, because I couldn't afford a full set. Bass strings were very expensive and I'd only got as far as the A string.

I had to buy a map to figure out where Hull was. It wasn't as far as Newcastle but it was still going to take all day to get there. It was going to be another bed and breakfast experience. I drove and drove and drove, and the van got noisier and noisier. As I roared down the Anlaby Road into Hull, a green warning light with an oil-can motif lit up on the dashboard. I pulled into a garage for petrol. I was served by an old man in a brown dust coat. I told him about the green light, and without uttering a word he opened the bonnet, pulled the dipstick out, and after considering it for a while said, 'I'm not surprised, you've none in.'

He filled it up with motor oil, for which he charged me next to nothing, and gave me directions to the town centre. I liked the place already.

I parked the van in a side street round the corner from the art school and found a very cheap bed and breakfast. After I'd booked the room and paid up, I found out why it was so cheap – I'd be sharing it with an electrician called Dave.

'But it's all right, because Dave's very quiet and he won't be coming in till late – he won't disturb you.'

The room was a twin-bedded hutch with white nylon

sheets. The wall adjoining the next room didn't quite reach the ceiling. The last two feet were obscure glass. When the lights went on next door it illuminated our room too. I hoped that whoever was next door didn't read in bed. I also hoped that Dave wouldn't be a homosexual or a kleptomaniac. Apart from that I was perfectly happy, and intent on fish, chips and Hull Brewery bitter.

In the event Dave wasn't either of those. He came in, said hello, took off his jacket and trousers, climbed into his nylon sheets and went to sleep. He wasn't there when I woke up in the morning. The night was completely uneventful apart from a man next door shouting, 'Shut that light off,' through the partition wall while I was reading in bed.

The dining room had yellowing nets. I swam through a greasy breakfast, accompanied by Park Drive cigarettes and very strong tea in a white mug with brown drips down the side.

The interview was quite civilised. 'It rains all the time in the winter,' they said. 'It gets very cold, and if you get depressed you can't throw yourself in the Queen's Dock because they've just filled it in.' It sounded right up my street. I wasn't at all surprised when I got offered a place. It was meant to be. I was going to the land of fresh fish and real beer.

I felt a few twinges when I left Bristol. I'd gone there determined to love it and found myself hating it. Then the summer term came along, the sun came out, it was time to leave, and everybody started being nice to each other. I loved them all for a minute. I didn't keep in touch with anybody.

I went back to Peacehaven for the summer and got a

job as a fly-press operator in a factory in Newhaven. I
had to leave after a week because of an incident with a
die-cast. It wasn't my fault – the strips were cut on the
piss and they'd only go so far into the machine before
they jammed. So instead of spewing out tape-measure
covers for the Parker Pen Company the machine stood
idle while a man called Terry attacked it with a wooden
mallet. He broke the die. Somebody had to carry the can
so they found me something to do till lunchtime. I'd got
the sack. It was the first time this had ever happened to
me.

It was the perfect conclusion to a shit day, except that I
was out of there with a full pay packet in time for lunch.
Normally, under such circumstances I would have been
straight into a liquid lunch which might have lasted until
the pub shut. But today was a bit special – I had to go and
face my dad because I'd crashed the Volkswagen on the
way to work. It had been really cool – he'd just come out of
hospital again so I had custody of the car. Up until that
morning I'd been a mobile hipster with a job in a factory,
but now I was an unemployed person with a bent bumper.

It wasn't my fault – except it was actually my fault,
and some people might even say it was instant Karma. I
was driving down the hill into Newhaven. There was a
traffic jam, everything was stopping, rolling along a few
car lengths and stopping again. The other side of the road
was quite clear apart from a man on a moped.

He was a classic old git – rubberised mac and one of
those grubby white helmets with a little peak, and a lot of
cracked white leather that came down over the back of
the head and ears, ending up in a chin strap. He was
hurtling up the hill with both wheels in the gutter and the
red and beige Honda was making an appalling noise. It
was a picture of determination.

The front wheel hit a brick, the machine tipped up and launched him into the air. He cruised slowly forwards, helmet first, in horizontal rubberised magnificence until his progress was arrested by a lamp post, which he hit with his head.

Thankfully he was unhurt. He picked himself up and then picked up the moped. Passers-by rushed to help. The whole episode had looked so fucking funny that I couldn't stop laughing.

Perhaps the sneezing fit that followed was brought on by guilt. The traffic was moving again. I looked up in mid-sneeze in time to see the back of the car in front rushing towards me. The crash came right on the end of the sneeze.

And here I was at lunchtime, jobless and alone. My dad was not impressed. And he wanted to know why I was home so early. So I had to tell him I'd got the sack too. I felt as though I'd bought shame on the entire family – me with all the chances in life that they never had, and what did I go and do? I got the sack from a dumb job hacking out nameplates at forty pence an hour.

I went to the Labour Exchange. They gave me a job with much better pay (fifty pence an hour) at Fyffe's banana warehouse in Newhaven. Starting Monday I was going to be a banana grader. I went out and got drunk.

The downside of grading bananas at ten pence more an hour was that banana grading started at seven, whereas nameplating didn't get underway till eight.

Seven o'clock Monday morning rolled around, and by some miracle I'd got myself down to Fyffe's on time. I was optimistic – I tried hard to convince myself that I'd get used to it. Poor fool – I hadn't bargained on overtime.

The foreman was a stout man in his fifties called Mr Hodge. He wore a white overall with lots of lines leading down into the breast pocket where he'd put his ballpoint away without unclicking it first. He had greyish white hair and a mouth that went into a subtle banana shape when he smiled. Mr Hodge came from the West Country – Yeovil or Taunton – somewhere like that. He was a keen darts player.

The bananas were wheeled out of refrigerated rooms in boxes weighing around thirty pounds apiece, stacked up on pallets until they were taller than I was. Each banana grader had a banana grading station in a room dedicated to bananas. A banana grading station consisted of a large set of scales standing on a table made of chipboard on a grey dexion frame, and next to it a sort of sloping table with sides where you could put loose bananas and ones that you weren't sure of. There was also a plastic dustbin, and behind the grader a space big enough for a pallet load of bananas.

Every morning Mr Hodge, who was called Keith when he was in a good mood, stood in the banana room and inspected his troops like a banana republic general:

'Right... tare one and a half pounds...' (here a move towards the nearest set of scales in order to verify the setting) '...twenty-six pounds, best, medium and loose. You know what to do gentlemen – now get to it!'

Keith would then take up his station at one end of the room next to the end of a double-decker conveyer belt, which ran alongside the banana graders. From this vantage point he could keep an eye on the troops while he tore large bunches of bananas into smaller bunches of bananas, popped them on the conveyer belt, and sent them along past us at waist height to his wife stationed at the other end of the conveyer. Mrs Hodge took them off the conveyer, weighed them, stuck a price tag on them, and put them back on the conveyer, this time at ear height and sent them back to hubby.

Mrs Hodge was joined by some other ladies who stationed themselves along the route, on the other side of the conveyer to us, and generally joined in with the banana stickering.

At lunchtime they all went home for the day, except in times when the demand for bananas was abnormally high. Then Keith reverted to Mr Hodge and we did overtime, weighing, grading, and stickering together until seven o'clock in the evening.

I never knew how you were supposed to grade bananas, and I'm pretty sure nobody else did, but we just got on with it. You heaved a box down from above your head, turned round and slammed it on the scales as noisily as you could. Then you took the lid off and inspected the damage. The bananas were usually green, but some were yellow, or yellow with brown spots. I'd usually take these out and reserve them for a box of 'medium', as in medium quality, or sometimes I'd do a personal selection of yellow 'best'. Occasionally I'd take a few bunches of small bananas and make them into a 'medium' box as in medium sized. It depended on my mood. Generally, though, I kept the boxes of medium down to a minimum because nobody else seemed to create that many. We were a team and I didn't want to rock the boat.

Most of the time I just took bananas out until the thing weighed twenty-six pounds, put the lid back on, chalked a B on it and slung it on the graded stack. Except that when it was bananas from the Gold Coast, which it was one afternoon a week, you just used to lift the lid off and pour the contents into the dustbin. Any solid bits you could throw at a colleague while Mr Hodge wasn't looking.

We got an hour for lunch and two ten-minute tea breaks. We had to spend the tea breaks in a tiny room equipped with plastic stacking chairs and a dartboard. Keith took on the rest of the staff at darts while I dozed off on a plastic chair to the sound of 'double tops to win...' thuck, thuck, clung, 'ooh, unlucky...' I hated darts but sometimes if they got stuck into a game the tea break extended to twenty minutes. I liked darts under these circumstances.

I always fell asleep because I seemed to be earning a lot of money, what with the overtime, and I had to go out every night to spend some of it getting pissed in order to blot out the utter tedium of grading bananas. One morning during the tea break I had a nightmare – I opened a box of bananas and the bunches raised themselves up, waggled at me and laughed. I woke up to a scoring dispute.

Mr Hodge got on my nerves. He was so complacent in his stupidity, and I didn't like the two-name trick. If he was in a good mood I'd turn him back into Mr Hodge by calling him Ken by mistake. Sometimes he'd be in a bad mood and I'd misjudge it and call him Ken anyway.

'MR HODGE!' he'd roar. 'And it's Keith, not Ken.'

'Sorry Mr Hedge – er, Hodge, Mr Hedgehog...'

He hated me being an art student. He told me I was a long-haired, pot-smoking waster. He'd read about my sort in the paper. 'You're wasting your life,' he kept saying. Yeah, better to do something worthwhile with it – grade bananas, play darts, read the *Daily Mirror*...

I lasted seven weeks. In my last week I was the longest serving grader, so I had to show the new ones how to do it.

I had to find somewhere to live so I commandeered the Volkswagen and drove up the A1 to Hull. It took some time to get there because the M62 didn't exist. You had to drive through parts of Doncaster and then follow the road out to where England had lost interest. And then you got to Hull.

I drove straight to where the Fine Art Annexe was – Craven Street, off the Holderness Road in East Hull. The interview had been held in the more salubrious Main Building in the city centre so I hadn't seen this place before. What a dump. It was a dilapidated Victorian school building and a collection of concrete and asbestos prefabs. The rest of the street was an abandoned mess of derelict terraced houses. Up near the Holderness Road there was a very greasy fish and chip shop and a public lavatory. The Holderness Road itself transcended all concepts I'd previously imagined of poverty and depression. It was perfect.

There was a music shop on the corner full of heavy-duty band equipment. You could buy a Marshall stack, or a PA system – *'suitable for club use inc. two microphones'* – on hire purchase. I hadn't found this out yet, but there were sufficient working men's clubs in Hull that an artiste could work every night in a different venue for over a year without repeating. The man who ran the shop was barnacled and overweight. Doubtless a member of a group that hadn't enjoyed any success during the '60s beat boom. I bought some guitar strings by way of breaking the ice, and once lines of communication had been opened and established, I batted in with an enquiry about flats.

'They're like rocking-horse shit.'

I wasn't too discouraged by this because I hadn't immediately figured out what it meant. I'd never heard the expression before. Back in town I started the evening's drinking with a bag of fish and chips.

I sat in a pub. A man in a disgusting green suit, red-faced and with a bulbous nose, turned to me and said, ''ere mate, do yer fancy a raucous?' I wasn't sure what a *'raucous'* was, but he elaborated: 'I've got two birds here and my mate's not shown up – they're both gagging for it.' That may have been so, but even I wasn't that desperate. Still, it was an early indication that Hull was a friendly place, and not at all stuck up. I was going to fit right in.

The next day I started flat hunting. I found a place off the Anlaby Road. It was miles from the city centre but I thought it was just right. Two rooms – a bedroom-cum-sitting room, and a kitchen – on the first floor at the back of a family house containing a family. I must have been out of my fucking mind.

It only took about three days of residence to incur the displeasure of my landlady, Valerie. I got the flat by saying I was a very quiet person. I almost believed it myself because I would really have liked to have been a quiet, trouble-free person. It was about half-past eight in the morning, and I was sitting in my kitchen, trying to behave like a normal person having breakfast, even though I had a colossal hangover. There was a knock at the door. Valerie appeared, wearing a quilted housecoat. She had a face like a hatchet.

'For a quiet person you were doing very well for yourself last night.'

I couldn't even put music on during the day without provoking a complaint. One morning when I was getting up after a night of high jinx and romance (she'd said goodbye and let herself out earlier), Valerie's husband Kenneth appeared clutching a bottle of milk.

'I've brought your milk up...' He smiled, simpered, and shuffled his feet. '...There was just one other thing. Er... did you have a young lady to stay the night, only we saw her leaving, and the kids have been asking questions.'

I suppose it was a bedsitting room, only that it had a separate kitchen, and I've always assumed that a bedsitting room wasn't complete without a sink or sink unit, a Baby Belling, and a roll of toilet paper next to the door. It was very cold because it had three outside walls, and almost certainly an un-insulated roof. It was painted in two shades of blue, and contained a ghastly wardrobe and matching chest of drawers that were painted grey and white. These colour combinations only served to enhance the coldness. Heat was provided by a three-bar electric fire built into the original fireplace. There was an electricity meter in a cupboard in the kitchen. It usually ran out when I put the fire on. The fire did nothing to warm the room unless you put all three bars on at once. If the meter didn't run out, the 15-amp bakelite plug that supplied the fire with electricity got very hot, and there was a smell of burning. The carpet had a swirling green pattern that looked as though someone had been sick after eating a compost heap. There was an easy chair with wooden arms, and a coffee table with tea rings in the varnish, which had a look of desperate unwantedness. I found the best way of coping with these depressing surroundings was to not be in them.

The nearest pub was a 1950s Bass Charrington boozer called the Silver Cod. It was not the sort of place that was frequented by art students. I only went in there once. It was lunchtime, after a doctor's appointment. I was depressed and the doctor prescribed Librium. I washed down the first dose with a pint of Bass.

Usually I went to the pub around the corner from the Fine Art Annexe, the Nag's Head. Everybody went there – or I assumed they did because I couldn't envisage lunchtime without a drink. Lunchtime drinking was inexplicably linked in my mind with being warm, and with people being nice to each other. Like Christmas.

The Nag's Head wasn't at all Christmassy. It had formica-topped tables and a linoleum floor. Dirty green wallpaper, maroon vinyl upholstery repaired with gaffa-tape. The lunchtime clientele were mostly women who were now too old to continue working as prostitutes. They argued with one another constantly. They had long running feuds in which two would only speak through a third one, drooling muttered obscenities out of gummy mouths.

I took my dad in there once when he came for a visit. He couldn't find the toilet, and made the mistake of asking one of the hags.

'I'll show you where it is, love.'

'It's all right,' my dad replied, 'I can manage perfectly by myself.'

I don't think East Hull had ever seen such a well-dressed man. He was quite an embarrassment to me, though he didn't seem fazed by any of it.

The art school routine was pretty easy. Nobody seemed to care what you did or where you did it. I started making things with string, chicken wire, old bits of wallpaper and cardboard – stuff I found in the derelict houses that surrounded the Fine Art Annexe. I bought a secondhand bicycle, rode around and took photos of the dereliction and decay.

Huge areas of Hull were being redeveloped. Redeveloped isn't really the right word – demolished is more like it. Everywhere you looked there were terraces of slums crumbling before the iron ball. The rubble was crushed into the ground and rocket-shaped signs were erected that said:

SPACE MADE!

with the name of the contractor underneath, who it was said was a relative of someone on the council. There were large areas of devastation where nobody lived any more, where packs of mongrel dogs, the leftover pets of people who had been moved to a better life on the outskirts, shagged one another in mass canine gangbangs.

But it wasn't all depressing. Everybody went to the pub in the evenings – the Polar Bear, which was an easy-going mix of working men – or let's make that redundant, unemployed, on strike, or working a three-day-week men – and art students.

My flat was miles away from the Polar Bear but I started going out with a girl who lived in a bedsitting room just up the road from it. Unfortunately she was sharing the room with another girl – they had two single beds, two armchairs sat in front of an ancient, spluttering gas fire, a gateleg table, two dining chairs, and a shared wardrobe that I once had to hide in, semi-naked, when the landlady came round one morning to collect the rent. Overnight visitors, especially male overnight visitors, weren't allowed. Contravention of this rule would result in immediate eviction.

Not that I often stayed the night – only when the other girl was away. Fortunately she developed a boyfriend back home in Newcastle. She set off to see him every Friday afternoon and didn't come back until Monday. Before that, we conducted our love life in the unheated communal bathroom and the occasional cupboard. Now we had whole weekends of unbridled, pill-protected sex.

There was an art school band – they were a gang of third-year painting students and they needed a bass player. I'd given up on the homemade bass and bought a real one – a cream-coloured Jedson in the shape of a Fender Telecaster, made in Japan. It was short scale so the strings were really slack and it didn't stay in tune. I got it in a second-hand shop called Polymart, which sold all sorts of other things as well like battery chargers, motorcycle crash helmets and Kenwood blenders, stuff like that.

I saw Ike & Tina Turner's bass player, Lee Miles, playing with Terry Reid and I wanted to play the bass. I saw Free when All Right Now came out and I thought Andy Fraser looked really cool with the curly lead coming out of his bass and going up between his legs to the top of a Marshall stack behind him. I wanted that to be me so I scrabbled all the money I could together and bought the cheapest bass in the shop. It cost me fourteen quid.

I knew that bass players were always in short supply – it was going to be much easier to join a band with a bass guitar. I carefully mentioned the fact that I had a bass guitar and an amplifier to a few people around the art school. It wasn't strictly true, of course, because I didn't have an amplifier. Amplifiers were really expensive. About a week after the rumour had circulated, a third-year student asked if I knew who this bass player in the first year was – apparently he had a bass and an amp and he was really good and they wanted him to join their band and play Bo Diddley numbers and R 'n' B covers.

I told him I didn't know who he was, but I played the bass myself – I'd got a bass and an amp and everything, and I could play quite well and I'd be willing to give it a go if they couldn't find this other bloke. I was in. So I rushed out and combed the junk shops for the cheapest amplifier I could find.

It was a 30-watt Linear Concorde in a sort of bronze cage with two big handles on the top. Someone had built it from a kit. It had valves that glowed blue and red through the mesh. The input was on the back and it wasn't a jack socket like I'd hoped for, instead you plugged it in with a TV aerial connector. It wasn't very loud, producing just enough volume to drive the 10-inch speaker from an old valve radio. Later on, when I got an enormous Selmer Goliath cabinet with an 18-inch speaker, it did little more than throb gently to itself. The vibrating cage was louder than the bass and it looked really silly perched on top of such a big cabinet. It wasn't quite the Andy Fraser effect that I'd been hoping for, but it was a start.

Rehearsals were held in the third-year painting studio on Wednesday afternoons at three o'clock after the pub shut. There was a guitar player called Ozzie, a half-American half-Portuguese singer called Steve Goodfellow who also played really good harmonica and maracas, and a big bloke with a ginger beard on the drums. And me fumbling around on the bass. Mostly we were dead drunk. No one seemed to notice that I couldn't actually play the bass – I think they were thrilled to bits that they'd completed the line-up and, courtesy of the Linear Concorde, they probably couldn't hear me anyway.

We had big plans to play at the art school dances but we never actually did. We got as far as setting up our equipment at one once, but we were too drunk to play so we didn't. The nearest we got to a public performance was when the cleaners came in. They were all hardened Hull ladies and they liked a laugh so they made us play all our stuff while they did the twist and took turns on the microphone. The group fizzled out after Christmas and I started looking round for something else.

I went into Gough & Davy, the big music shop in the middle of town. While I was there I asked the young assistant if I could put an advert on the notice board. He asked me what for and I told him I played the bass. 'Come with me,' he said.

I wasn't sure what was going on; he looked round warily and led me into the stock room, which seemed to be full of hard-looking local lads. I thought I was going to get beaten up. One of them said, 'What yer got 'ere?' and the assistant said, 'This lad plays the bass.'

They'd been looking everywhere for a bass player and preferably one who could sing a bit too. I lied about this. I'd never really done it but I always fancied it and Steve Goodfellow liked me singing Billy Fury songs at jam sessions round at his house. But this wasn't exactly Billy Fury. They were called Dirty Henry and they were working on a two-pronged attack: three twenty-minute sets for the clubs and a hard-rock set for other engagements. 'Other engagements' meant the Trogg Bar on Manchester Street. It was all done out inside with fibreglass and plaster over chickenwire – lots of stalactites and built-in lighting. It filled up every night with Hull lads in high-waisted trousers, platform shoes and feathered haircuts. They came to pull birds, drink lager and pick a fight. There was a stage at one end, and on it there was always a three- or four-piece group doing David Bowie covers and Reeling In The Years by Steely Dan.

Dirty Henry were a bit different to that because their set was going to include Smoke On The Water, Paranoid and Somebody's Gonna Get Their Head Kicked In

Tonight by Fleetwood Mac posing as Earl Vance & The Valients on the B side of Man Of The World.

I had to meet them that night in a church hall in East Hull for an audition. The shop assistant played the drums. He was a bit pro – he had a red premier kit with all the attachments that he bought round himself in a car. There were three guitar players. The leader was a Hull lad called Tom Park. He was a bit older than the others, married with a kid and living in a terraced slum in the shadow of the Reckitt & Coleman factory. And I mean slum – there was a foot of water under the floorboards, the toilet was in the yard, it had no bathroom, no hot water and outside there was a continuous and over-whelming stench of sewage. Tom was unemployed but he was always cheerful and optimistic. He was determined to make a go of the group.

One of the other guitar players was a tall, chubby looking kid called Jerry. He was pale and flabby with a red-hennaed Bowie haircut and a high voice. Tom told me that Jerry's balls had never dropped – apparently he could have had an operation to sort it out but his mum couldn't be bothered with it and he didn't have a dad. Jerry was smartly dressed – he wore brown high-waisted trousers that were the same width as his ample bottom all the way to the turn-ups. The top half of him was clad in an open-necked shirt with a huge collar that stretched from shoulder to shoulder across his grey blazer. He had a really cool Futurama guitar, ice blue with four pick-ups, and when he played he exuded hopelessness. He had a job in a local nightclub, Baileys, which was where the lads and lasses went after the Trogg Bar shut.

The third and final guitar player was a psycho factory worker with a moustache. He was called Tony, which is pronounced *Terny* in Hull. He was almost exactly like

Begbie in *Trainspotting*. As far as I could tell he was only in the group because he had a job, which meant he could afford a Gibson Flying V and an amplifier. He was Tom's brother-in-law. He was rubbish on the guitar. He let me have a go on it while the others were setting up. I'd never played a quality guitar before. It was really easy. I did my John Lee Hooker meets Bo Diddley through Lou Reed in the Velvet Underground. Their heads turned in astonishment and Tom said, 'Fuck-king hell!'

I don't think Tony was very pleased about that but once again I was in, and this time I'd done it on ability rather than mere ownership of a bass guitar. I'd been working on it and even though I still had a long way to go I was getting quite good.

It didn't take long to get without Tony – he muttered something about art students and at the next rehearsal he wasn't there. Neither was his amplifier, which was a shame because Tom had used it, claiming some sort of lead guitarist's prerogative, leaving Tony to plug into the nasty Fal PA system that came with the hall. Jerry was a bit more difficult – he lasted about three or four rehearsals. He had the sheet music to loads of Bowie numbers so it was worth hanging on until we'd learnt them, or at least copied out the chords. He was a nice guy but he just hadn't got it. Fortunately the pressures of his job forced him to leave.

And then we were a three piece – guitar, bass and drums – or we would have been if the drummer hadn't got a better offer. He was gone after two rehearsals. So that left me and Tom and a succession of quickly disillusioned drummers. At one point we had a singer – sorry, a vocalist, but he fancied himself as a professional – he was a member of the VAA, the Variety Artists Association, and we weren't. Not yet anyway, but we were going to be. It was the passport to local success. Once you were in that you could do the working men's clubs.

You had to do three twenty-minute sets in the clubs, interspersed with bingo, a comedian and, if you were lucky, a stripper. There was an accepted format: the first set had to be 'standards' – songs that everybody knew. Lots of sickly stuff and what Hull called *the country-western* – Banks Of The Ohio, I Forgot To Remember To Forget, Save The Last Dance For Me…

The second set was more of a challenge – for this one you had to be up to date. Recent chart hits. There were some awful selections to choose from. One of the most popular was I Won't Let The Show Go On by Leo Sayer, but mercifully we never attempted this one. We did Rebel Rebel, Ballroom Blitz and Tiger Feet by Mud, which really made me want to throw up even though I only had to play the bass on it. I also remember struggling through A Walkin' Miracle by Limmie & The Family Cookin' and We Had Joy We Had Fun We Had Seasons In The Sun. Ultimately it didn't really matter what you played because most of the people weren't listening anyway. As long as you weren't too tuneless. The best advice I ever had was to learn Happy Birthday, The Anniversary Waltz and Congratulations – that would get you through most situations in the Hull pub and club cosmos.

There was no end to the ghastliness that could be achieved with a minimum of effort: You Won't Find Another Fool Like Me by the New Seekers, I'm On The Top *Top* Of The World Looking Down… All this and more filtered through the semi-talent of a semi-semi-pro band, and just when you thought it had reached a pinnacle of unbearableness there was Free And Easy Time at the George on the corner of Walton Street.

There was a resident band, a guitar and bass duo called the Brothers Grimm. Grimm was about right but there was no need to agree with them because they knew that anyway. They did all the popular numbers and, in between songs, they were *funny*.

There was an organist – a lady called Doris – and a compere. He was a burly, northern man in a silver shirt with a gut that overhung the trousers of a shiny suit. Even with the shirt on you could tell that he had a hairy back. A miniature volcano of hair exploded out of his open collar. He was a Tetley Bitter man. He was straight out of the middle row of a Hull Kingston Rovers scrum. He was a teddy bear and when he sang, 'A-baby let me be your lovin' teddy bear…' by Elvis Presley he was one hundred per cent convincing. The ladies loved him. He was low-grade entertainment of the highest order. I wormed my way into his backing band. I didn't last long because I made the mistake of trying to negotiate some kind of fee. He didn't like that. He wished me every success with my continuing career and turned his back. I can't even remember his name now but he was an inspiration to me: 'Collars up, lads, we're going to do another Elvis song…'

Then there was a short break for half a gallon of lager and we'd be back for the next set:

'And now, ladies and gentlemen, it's the time you've all been waiting for – it's Free and Easy Time when we invite you, the lovely lads and lasses in the audience, to Come Up and Give Us A Song!'

It was the same miserable crowd every week. Some fat cow got up and sang Paper Roses. In real life she was a cleaner, but for three minutes once a week she was Marie Osmond, tunelessly wailing, 'Pairper Rerses, pairper rerses…' A big trucker in a tartan coat came over from the lorry park every week to sing Twenty Flight Rock. He was almost quite good. He'd shout, 'Rock cat rock!' at the beginning of the guitar solo and come back in with the third verse about nine and a half bars later. A man in a shiny purple suit and an expensive drip-dry shirt with cuff links sang Runaway by Del Shannon, complete with all the high notes. He smelled of hair-oil preparations and deodorant for men. Word had it that he'd once been a professional.

When all that was over there was just time to acknowledge any birthdays or wedding anniversaries in the audience with a quick blast of Happy Birthday followed by Congratulations, and then it was time to wind up the show with a rock 'n' roll medley starting with Blue Suede Shoes.

'You've been a smashing audience, thanks for coming, have a safe journey home and if you're driving – *Don't Forget To Take The Car!* Thanks very much, ladies and gentlemen, goodnight.'

'Time on your beers, lads and lasses, drink up please, time on your beers...'

Dirty Henry faded away – or maybe I did. I think they changed the name to Pink Leg. Tom and his family were rehoused and he got a job with an early morning start. I was pretty sick of trundling my gear through the streets of Hull late at night. Nobody had any transport so you had to do the best you could. I found a twin pushchair, which I modified to fit my Selmer Goliath cabinet by taking the seat out. I strapped my bass onto the front of the cabinet and the amplifier went in the bit where the twins put their feet. I wheeled it all over Hull in the middle of the night.

I never had any trouble – the only people that ever spoke to me were policemen. They used to pop out of shop doorways and ask me where I was going and what I was up to. I got to know some of them quite well. We had little chats in the middle of the night. One of them asked me if I ever took any drugs.

'Oh, no! It's a mug's game,' I lied.

I'd stopped smoking joints in such a big way after I left Bristol but I was a bugger for amphetamines. I also found that I could get some strange effects by mixing my prescribed antidepressants with cheap sherry. I enlarged on the theme:

'It's really overrated, that sort of thing, I can't see the point.'

'Neither can I,' said the policeman. 'We have to go to classes to learn about it all – they handed round the LSD so that we could try it out.' He made a gesture like someone handing round a packet of Polos. 'It didn't do anything for me, just made me feel a bit happy for a while.'

I smiled. 'Well, I must be off,' I said. 'Keep taking the pills, don't do anything I wouldn't!' He laughed and I trundled off into the fog.

And then it was the summer. Summer 1974. I had girl-friend trouble. I didn't want to see her so I took a walk to the one place I was sure she would never find me. The university. I hated the university – I hated the students with their endless re-enactments of Monty Python sketches, their societies and their prankish games. The university was the last place you'd find me, so that's where I went. I had a couple of drinks in the Union bar but the ambience got on my nerves so I walked out. I strolled down the Cottingham Road, wondering what to do about my love life.

Something that my mum had said a couple of years

previously drifted into my head. I sat down on a bench on one of the grass verges. It was a warm evening and the scent of newly mown grass was in the air with its promise of endless summer nights, romance, new beginnings... The idea slowly took shape:

When I was a young boy my mama said to me, there's only one girl in the world for you and she probably lives in Tahiti...

Yes, she really said that. I'd seen Kevin Ayers three times in the past year and decided that I was going to write songs just like his, full of romance and hot sunshine. Songs like Clarence In Wonderland, Take Me To Tahiti, and Caribbean Moon. So this was a perfect start.

Or maybe she's in the Bahamas where the Caribbean sea is blue...

I wasn't sure where the Caribbean was in relation to the Bahamas but it sounded good and I could already hear the crickets chirping away, the background to my heartache.

Weeping in a tropical moonlit night because nobody's told her 'bout you.

It was like one of those Green Lady paintings – a dusky maiden with a rose in her hair, silhouetted against a turquoise tropical sky; a big moon reflecting on the water, fishing boats and distant huts.

I'd go the whole wide world, I'd go the whole wide world just to find her.

It was a mantra. Maybe the words didn't really make sense, but they did to me (and to a million other people as it later turned out). I sang it in my head all the way home so that I wouldn't forget it.

I'd go the whole wide world, I'd go the whole wide world, find out where they hide her...

Best of all, I figured you could do it with two chords.

Pure, simple Zen expression and just as good as Kevin Ayers.

When I got home she was sitting on the doorstep.

'Where have you been? I've been waiting for hours.'

'I just went for a walk *(I'd go the whole wide world, I'd go the whole wide world…)*'

'Well, can I come in then?'

'Suit yourself *(find out where they hide her…).*'

'You don't care, do you?'

'Of course I do *(…pining away in a heatwave there, hoping that I won't be long).*'

'Well you're certainly not acting as though you do.'

'Shut up, would you – I'm trying to work this out.'

By this time I had my ear up against the unamplified bass guitar trying to hear it. I was sure now that it didn't need a third chord. I think we split up that night but I hardly noticed because I'd just written my best song ever.

You might think it would all be plain sailing after that – I'd written a classic song so surely overnight success was just seconds away. Well, it wasn't. I never thought in terms of success, overnight or any other sort. Success was something that happened to other people, and usually nobody I knew. In fact, I don't think success was even a concept for me at the time. I just didn't think like that.

Whole Wide World was certainly better than my other attempts. I think my worst one at the time started with: *I loaded up the pram 'cause I was heading for a jam with all my friends in the church hall*, and carried on downhill from there. It was a load of fucking rubbish, so why should Whole Wide World be any different? Nobody wanted to play it. They didn't trust it because it only had two chords and that couldn't be right. Also, there was a problem with the chorus – it had a built-in limp. I wasn't bothered about this sort of thing. I'd never learnt to count, so to make the words that I wanted to sing fit, I just popped a couple of extra beats in. I didn't even know I'd done it. It confused everybody who tried to play it – *I'd go the whole wide world just to find her* and then: *I'd go the whole wide world find out where they hide her*, and it was that *find out* that was the problem. Not for me it wasn't – it made total sense to me but it made no sense whatsoever to anybody else.

I was a bit disillusioned. I just seemed to keep coming face to face with my own hopelessness – I was a crap bass player, I couldn't sing, I couldn't write a proper song (not that anybody else could), and my amplifier wasn't loud enough. I went back to Peacehaven for the summer holiday and got a job in a factory as a capstan lathe operator.

I turned out rods that screwed together to make standard lamps for restaurants – something like that, anyway. I never actually saw one put together but that's what the boss told me they were. To me they were just mild steel rods with screw threads. I cut the steel to size and turned them out in their hundreds. The oil and the swarf got in my hair, turned it dark and gave it body. I started to develop a quiff. I was fit and suntanned and I was starting to look like the heroes of my childhood. Apart from having absolutely no interest in motorbikes, I was turning into a Newhaven rocker.

I was drinking like a fish too.

Grandma in Oldham came to stay for the Full Fortnight this time. I did my best to be polite, but I knew that she was only there to cause trouble because that's what always followed a visit from Grandma in Oldham: trouble.

She carried an air of ticking clocks and discoloured

wallpaper around with her. Mostly she just talked about people who'd died, illnesses that had been suffered, operations that had been undergone. Sometimes she addressed some remarks to me, usually a criticism. We tried to be nice to each other but it didn't really work.

A French girl I knew came round one day. Grandma looked her up and down.

'Ooh,' she said, 'French is she?'

And then she leaned forward into the girl's face, did her grinning dentures trick and enunciated clearly and precisely:

'Silver plate.'

The only reaction she got was a look confusion so she tried again:

'SILVER PLATE!'

She turned to me, dentures and spectacles gleaming in the sunshine. 'It's French,' she explained. 'It means pleeeease.'

I began to study her very carefully. She was bigoted, negative, ignorant and hateful. I started a collection of the most stupid things she said – I wrote them down in a notebook. I made large charcoal drawings of various bits of her – the bony hands that I couldn't bear to have touch me, the hairnet holding dark grey hair, permed and frazzled under the dryer in a cheap salon until it looked like a pubic wig. The know-it-all expression, the thunder in her face when she was crossed by somebody who was foolish enough to think that they knew better. The prying, nosey parker, meddlesome looks of delight when she got her way and caused some friction in the process.

Faddy, attention-seeking and difficult: Grandma in Oldham eating baked beans with a spoon, masticating a banana, slurping cold, stewed tea, refusing a lovingly cooked dinner because some small ingredient might set

off her 'troubles'. Grandma in Oldham coughing phlegm
into a hanky and lighting another Park Drive cigarette.
She was hard to love, and sadly, in the end I couldn't
imagine how anybody did.

One Saturday night I went out and got more drunk
than usual. She was still up when I got back. I was having
trouble putting the key in the lock. I could see her
through the obscure glass, coming to open the door. She
was ready for bed, bri-nylon nightie, cardigan, plastic
mac and hairnet. As she opened her mouth to remon-
strate with the wayward grandson, I threw up all over her
pac-a-mac.

She was frosty with me for the remainder of her stay. I
never saw Grandma in Oldham again.

Before I went back to Hull I saw Kilburn and The High
Roads at Hove Town Hall. Everybody in the group
seemed to have something subtly wrong with them. The
drummer was a cool-looking African – on crutches, the
bass player was rather short (and I speak as a not very tall
person myself), the saxophonist looked like a psycho and
the singer, who had a voice that crossed a reedy tenor
with a disgruntled London cabby, also had a gammy leg.
I was sure they'd come from an institution and wouldn't
have been surprised to see them getting out of a Variety
Club minibus. Grubby shirt collars, homemade haircuts,
second-hand clothing and Workers' Playtime – their
glamour was peculiarly English. And musically it
sounded as though the whole thing was going to fall to
bits. It was like a badly made sandwich with the filling
squeezing out at the edges. They had a profound and far-
reaching effect on me.

I suddenly realised that you didn't have to be the most
accomplished musician in the world. What was more

important was a kind of honesty – Kilburn & The High Roads were confirmation that you didn't have to pretend to be an American to play pop music. I went back to Hull determined to try a new approach.

We had a new social secretary at the art school. He was into Art Language, which was all the rage in Hull at the time. Nobody seemed to know what it was all about and the people that were into it weren't forthcoming with any explanation – it was as though they were confused too. They were a supercilious elite, strutting round in Levis, leather bomber jackets and greasy Hush Puppies. They carried little black leather document folders and when they weren't on their way to an important meeting you'd find them sitting in the cafe reading the *Daily Mirror* and enjoying a roll-up.

To show everybody how clever he was, the new social secretary booked a mainstream jazz band to play at the first art school dance of the term. I think it was an Art Language-related statement but he'd got Bebop confused with Mainstream. The disco was bad enough – Harold Melvin & The Blue Notes and Sugar Baby Love by the Rubettes. What we wanted was rhythm 'n' blues and bub-blegum – the Monkees and the Ohio Express cut with James Brown and Bo Diddley. It was a disaster and when the jazz band started everybody left except the Art Language gang.

In the pub I met an ex-painting student called Steve Marshall. He said it was no good, we'd have to form a band to sort the fuckers out. He'd play the drums.

'Have you got a drum kit?' I asked.

'No, but I can make one.'

'Er – can you actually play the drums?'

'Shouldn't be too difficult…'

I was getting used to people not taking these things seriously so I pretty much forgot about it until the following night when Steve came rushing up to me at a party: 'You know that group we're forming, I've found a guitarist 'says he can crank out chords – and he's got an amplifier...'

His name was Stuart Ross. We were all very drunk so agreed to meet the following day and sort out what songs we could play. We made a list:

Drive My Car – The Beatles
Waiting For My Man – The Velvet Underground
Promised Land – Johnny Allen cajun version of Chuck
    Berry song
Down Along The Cove – Bob Dylan
Gimme That Harp Boy – Captain Beefheart
I Saw Her Standing There – The Beatles
Ain't Nothin' But A Houseparty – the J Geils Band
    version of the Showstoppers' hit
In The Midnight Hour – Wilson Pickett
Six Days On The Road – by Dave Dudley but done in the
    style of the Velvet Underground

I don't know where our heads were at. We rehearsed in Stuart's kitchen. I thought he was a miserable git. He thought I was an idiot. We became good friends.

Our first rehearsal wasn't very good. We should have been discouraged but we weren't. Steve arrived with a biscuit tin and two lengths of dowel rod that he intended to use as drum sticks, and I brought along my horrible Jedson bass and a curly lead. Stuart had a Watkins Rapier that he'd painted matt black. It looked the business and so did he with his sub-Peter Tork moptop and leather jacket.

We plugged the guitar and bass into Stuart's Vox AC30. Steve sat down and pulled up the Addis Flip Top rubbish bin to use as a drum. And that was our name – Addis & The Flip Tops – it was already on the front of our drum kit.

We were hopeless. We discarded Drive My Car straight away because without vocals we couldn't tell where we were and nobody wanted to sing. Steve had a go at Hi Heel Sneakers by Tommy Tucker but he couldn't play drums and sing at the same time, and we were worried by the absence of wood clattering on plastic. We managed Shakin' All Over, which I tentatively sang, and that encouraged Stuart to have a go at I Saw Her Standing There.

Steve augmented the kit with a biscuit tin and a poly-styrene drum that he found in the street. It sounded dreadful – the polystyrene went *bock bock bock* but with a little imagination the biscuit tin sounded a bit like the Tamla Motown snare. The bits of dowel kept breaking so we tried using tree branches, the theory being that branches were straight grained so they'd be stronger. This wasn't true – if anything they broke quicker than the dowel. So we clubbed together and bought a set of drum sticks. There was no looking back after that and Steve was soon demolishing a biscuit tin at every session. He acquired a bass drum pedal from somewhere and attached it to a packing case that needed constant repair.

We bullied the social secretary into letting us play at the next art school dance. Our friends were thrilled to bits but everybody else left the hall and crammed into the bar until we'd finished. We did the gig without any vocals. In our own minds we were an almost perfect cross between Doctor Feelgood and Kilburn & The High Roads but without a singer. We did House Party, Shakin'

All Over, Waiting For My Man, I Saw Her Standing There and Gimme That Harp Boy, which was just a riff in E repeated over and over until Stuart shouted, 'That'll do!' and we all stopped.

We badly needed a singer. We almost persuaded a postgraduate teacher training student called Mike Kenny to join. He was a big bloke with long, unruly red hair and a matching beard, metal-framed student glasses with lenses like bottle tops, and a big suede jacket with fringes. We could see that with a few additions from the Famous Army Stores – checked shirt, some of those Lybro work jeans that tapered down to ankle-tight turn-ups, and a pair of Tuf elastic-sided boots – he could become Big Jim McClusky and we could be his backing group. We even made a poster:

BIG JIM McCLUSKY
fights bears, drinks Guinness and sings the blues

And we quickly had the set sorted out too. Most of it was going to be Hey! Bo Diddley – the Quicksilver Messenger Service version, and in between a few lumberjacking tunes – Home On The Range and A Four- Legged Friend, A-Won-der-ful-One-Two-Three-Four-Legged-Friend...
It was going to be an affront of the highest order but Mike Kenny wasn't having any of it, even though he boasts to this day that he was once in a band with me. For an afternoon perhaps.

I sold my Linear Concord and bought a Hohner Orgaphon, an accordion amplifier that I later fitted with jukebox speakers. It was a hell of an improvement. Everything else was either homemade or stolen. We even had the art college PA system. We waited until nobody was about, found a ladder and unbolted the two

Echolette columns from the wall on either side of the stage. There was a lighter patch where they'd been, but nobody noticed. We had the amplifier too, a battered Selmer thing in a rusty metal casing. We painted it gloss yellow with a cheap brush to allay suspicion, and also to make it look worse.

We found the singer of our dreams. I used to go down into the graphics department to chat up girls when I'd had a couple of drinks. That's where I met Alan – a perfect name for the singer in Addis & The Flip Tops – he could be Alan Addis and we could be his Flip Tops. He'd seen us play and he actually thought we were good. He didn't get the joke and that made him all the more perfect. I brought him along to the next rehearsal where he gave his all into a tape recorder microphone. He looked like a scout master but he thought he was Roger Daltrey and every time he punched the air the short lead on the microphone came unplugged from the AC30. He was in – but only for as long as he didn't understand what we were really up to.

He wore pullovers from the army surplus and bought us all a half in the pub. He was very enthusiastic. He wore round National Health glasses that joined in when he had another great idea. He was like a big dog in a small room. He couldn't sing but that didn't really matter. The problem was that none of us could stand him for more than five minutes so we got rid of him and I started singing instead.

The first time I ever sang in public was at the Wellington Club on Beverley Road, supporting Kevin Coyne & Zoot Money. It was an art school dance. The social secretary hated us and treated us like shit. We had to play on the floor in front of the stage using our own PA. But Kevin Coyne said we reminded him of how he'd started off, and him and Zoot Money presented us with a crate of beer.

We developed a repertoire of rock 'n' roll and R 'n' B. We ditched all the pop stuff after a humiliating limp through a Hot Chocolate number – the one that starts 'She was black as the night, Louis was whiter than white…' Stuart did the bit that went, 'No spook in my house, got me?' and it sounded ludicrous – even in the context of Addis & The Flip Tops. The trouble with pop was that it was too complicated – there were unexpected minor chords and sudden transitions into different keys. We just weren't up to it.

We tried to write our own stuff but we didn't get very far. Stuart did one called Doctor Jekyll & Mr Hyde, the result of too much exposure to the new Dylan album, *Blood On The Tracks*. I wrote one called Slap 'n' Tickle, a forgettable piece that was supposed to sound like Kilburn & The High Roads. Stuart came up with The Monster Waltz: *'Down in Bavaria people have locked their doors, shut up the shutters put monster traps down on the floor…'* I thought he was a much better songwriter than I was. We had a go at Whole Wide World but it always ended in consternation because of the extra beats in the chorus.

Most people hated us and we were quite often threatened with violence. We never seemed to play at the same place twice but we had a loyal following of Addis devotees. One of them was an ex-art student hippie called Kevin. He had access to a Renault van so we bullied him into driving our equipment around in it. He didn't mind too much and when the summer came around he sat in his garden and cut out an Addis & The Flip Tops stencil. We sprayed it on everything. Steve nicked a load of Yes T-shirts and we turned them into Addis T-shirts by obliterating the Yes logo with our own. We hated Yes – we hated Genesis, ELP, Gentle Giant, Tangerine Dream, Supertramp, Barclay James Harvest and a whole host of others. We were well ahead of our time, even down to the Yale key that dangled in front of my left eye from a safety pin attached to a black beret.

We played at a garden fete at a school for disturbed children. They wanted us to perform on the lawn in front of the classrooms but the power cable wasn't long enough so we set up in the shrubbery. I played standing in the middle of a rhododendron bush. The kids really liked us – that's what the teachers said. They couldn't thank us enough. Well, of course they couldn't – we were the cheapest group going – they got us for the price of a packet of cigarettes.

The kids threw everything they could find at us. They howled, ripped up the lawn and chucked it at us. They threw the entire contents of a litter bin at us – Walls ice cream wrappers, Lyons Maid wrappers, lolly sticks, half-eaten sandwiches and God knows what – and when it was empty they threw the bin as well. The teachers said it was because they liked us but it would help if we played something they knew. We placated them with our version of Bye Bye Baby.

We played anywhere that we could con people into having us. I don't know how we thought we could get away with it. Quite often we didn't. I learnt to keep a wary eye on the audience. Some thug would point at me, make a throat-cutting gesture and nod towards the door. And later on there'd be a fracas in the car park. Or a psychotic teddy boy would come up and say, 'My mate wants to sing with you.' And it would be made clear to us that 'my mate' was going to sing whether we liked it or not. Then we'd be joined on stage by a budget Elvis lookalike who'd massacre Blue Suede Shoes and perform an energetic series of back flips across the empty dance floor. But everything would be all right and we'd get out alive, in the glow of reflected glory.

I was getting tired of being a student – I'd had three years of it by now and there was another one to go. My parents wanted me to go to teacher training college after I finished. My mum used to say, 'You're a born teacher.' I couldn't think of anything I'd like to do less. In fact, I couldn't think of anything I'd like to do except play music. I didn't think that my lack of ability stood in the way. I didn't think in terms of talent. I wanted to do it – I'd always wanted to do it so that's what I was going to do. I figured that if I played enough I'd get better at it.

In the *NME* we read about a New York club called CBGBs. Groups with names like the Ramones and Television, who had a singing bass player called Richard Hell. I immediately wanted to be Richard Hell because he'd written songs called Love Comes In Spurts and Blank Generation. Apparently Ramones songs were all two minutes long and most of them were about glue-sniffing. I once tried sniffing glue myself and had a hallucination of security guards with dogs in a wallpaper pattern. Apart from that all I got was a headache. But you have to try these things. It must have worked better for the Ramones. There was a picture of them – they looked like a cartoon – tight jeans ripped at the knees, leather jackets, baseball boots and ridiculous moptop haircuts. We never heard any of this stuff at the time – we couldn't get hold of the records. But something was obviously going on.

I had to get out of Hull for a while and think it all out.

I also had to earn some money so I went back home and got a job at Butlins Ocean Hotel in Saltdean.

The stores were run by a man who was also called Eric. He was about sixty and obviously had high blood pressure. Every morning he was very anxious about something called 'breakfastses'. He sweated over a complicated pastel green form and said 'I've got all these *breakfastses* to sort out.' His second in command was an old git called Harry who stood rotting in a corner. They both wore brown dust coats and Harry ate tomatoes which he sprinkled with salt from a cruet stolen from the restaurant. Harry was from the North and only ever uttered one word, which was '*fucknell*'.

Billy Butlin was renowned for employing people with prison records – it was called giving people a second chance. You met all sorts when you worked at Butlins. Me and Butlins were developing quite a history.

I'd started off the previous Christmas working in the coffee bar. I liked the coffee bar so I came back for the Easter break too. The pay was a bit less than you'd get working in a factory but there was a jukebox and the chance of meeting girls.

Actually, the only records worth listening to on the jukebox were Rock Your Baby by George McCrae and Shame Shame Shame by Shirley and Co. Old biddies used to give me fifty-pence pieces to put something on to liven the place up. They were treated to five plays of Rock Your Baby alternating with five of Shirley and Co. Anything that wasn't either of these got bumped off as I cleared the tables round the jukebox.

For years I felt slightly uneasy about liking Rock Your Baby but in 1991 a friend told me he'd seen Joe Strummer back in 1978 in the audience at one of my gigs.

He was surrounded by admiring girls who danced to every groovy punk sound the DJ threw at them. But when Rock Your Baby came on they stopped and looked to Joe for guidance. He gave it a double thumbs up and the girls danced on. I don't think I was very good that night, and the set was interrupted by a fire alarm – everybody had to stand in the street for ten minutes. Sorry Joe. He was a big fan of Reconnez Cherie, which was largely inspired by my Butlins era.

I used to work with a gorgeous teacher training student called Karen. She was a great laugh but unfortunately she was engaged to a straight bloke who was probably called Dave. We used to go out together because Dave was boring. But only on a platonic basis because of the engagement. I caught up with her four years later after a gig at Bradford University. She was living in Bradford with another bloke who was a bit of a headcase or something and luckily had a penchant for staying out all night. I haven't seen her since. I hope she's all right.

I had a thing about one of the Redcoat girls too. I didn't think she'd go for me, even though I was a groovy art student, because I was also a bit of a method actor where work was concerned, and I'd thrown myself into the part of a lowly coffee bar assistant (with a subtle hint of borstal). So I went along to personnel and asked how I could become a Redcoat. An excellent career move – Des O'Connor and Eric Sykes started out as Redcoats, you know. I was laughed out of the personnel office, which I felt was a tribute to my acting skills – a coffee bar runt with a background in petty crime aspiring to the heady world of Redcoating?

The Redcoat Diva and her smarmy Redcoat chums laughed at me as they queued for afternoon tea in the coffee bar. An accident with the milkshake machine sorted that out. I don't know if it was deliberate or not but I just didn't screw it up tight enough and the thing burst open in mid shake, covering me, the coffee bar, customers, Redcoats and all in a force-ten shower of Strawberry Milkshake mix.

The coffee bar was managed by a woman called Pearl. Pearl was no spring chicken. When she got togged up, which she did most evenings, she wore a Regency lady wig and bright blue eye make-up. As she served behind the counter she kept up an endless banter in a broad Sheffield accent – 'I've only got one bloody pair of hands... all in good time... if you don't like it you can bloody well fuck off...' She was fiercely protective of her staff, and if she felt that a customer had overstepped the mark, she strode out from behind the counter and saw them off with whatever utensil came to hand, together with a lot of swearing. Sometimes it all got too much – a customer would make her cry and the hotel manager would have to come round in his dinner jacket and bow tie to sort it out. She was very proud of me over the milkshake incident because she hated the Redcoats – 'Tell 'em all to fuck off, love'.

There was a crappy high-class pastiche about Butlins that I found quite beautiful. The building itself was a magnificent 1930s hotel with a spiralling staircase, ballroom, and loads of original art deco features. But the staff were desperadoes and lunatics. By the mid-'70s Butlins was out of fashion – the clientele was an odd assortment of troublemakers, dirty weekenders and older people that didn't trust *abroad*.

Still, things had to be done properly. Having first checked that my white jacket was spotless – even if it did have frayed edges and a couple of holes in it – Pearl would send me up to the kitchen to collect a catering-sized tin of Luncheon Meat, which I'd parade through the hotel on a silver tray, covered with a white linen cloth.

The coffee bar was done out in true '70s style – a lot of orange, brown and white formica. Tea and coffee were served in white disposable plastic cups in brown plastic cup-holders. The job consisted of clearing tables, emptying the rubbish and washing up cup-holders.

In the evenings I operated the griddle, frying up bacon in front of the customers it was destined for. They were usually drunk. I was quite often in the same condition having spent my break down the road in the Spanish Lady. I considered a half bottle of Captain Morgan's Navy Rum an essential complement to an evening's griddling on time and a half. When a queue developed I used to lecture them about diet, pop music, coastal erosion – anything that came into my head, often insulting individual customers, because my assistant was usually Karen and it made her laugh and whisper things in my ear. New Years Eve 1974 ended with two blokes, both customers, fighting in the coffee bar, Pearl in tears, the manager disarming me of a carving knife with which I was threatening a third bloke, and the fire brigade arriving complete with hosepipes and breathing apparatus to tackle a fire in the staff quarters. We all sang Auld Lang Syne and had a glass of champagne on Billy Butlin.

I was quite surprised when they re-employed me for the Easter session. But when I came back in the summer they could only offer me a job behind the scenes, as a stores porter.

Working in the stores was a drag. It was a four-man operation headed by Blood Pressure Eric and his revolting sidekick, Harry. They needed employees to unload trucks, make tea and go to the betting shop for them. When Eric wasn't sweating over *breakfastses*, and Harry wasn't masticating tomatoes, they were working out a complicated Yankee or generally studying form. Apart from me there was a jack-the-lad apprentice moustache grower – a cross between Ringo Starr and David Essex in That'll Be The Day, but with none of the charm. He wore jeans made from denim that was printed to look like it was patches. I can't remember his name so I think I'll call him Patches.

There was a routine – arrive at about eight thirty or quarter to nine, make excuses for being late, unload a consignment of tea bags, baked beans or luncheon meat and prepare for the Bread Delivery. This was a big deal for some reason and required A Cup Of Tea. By this time, Blood Pressure was getting stuck into *breakfastses* and Harry was devouring his first tomato of the day. Patches would be on red alert for the Bread Delivery – a responsible job that involved ticking off *breads* on a form. Patches had to do that because I was officially useless. So I made the tea.

Everybody had their own cup, which was distinguishable from the others by a chip in the rim or a small paint stain on the base. Harry's cup must never be washed up because it ruined the taste of the tea, Blood Pressure took three sugars, Patches only took a dash of milk but two and a half sugars, and his was the Arsenal mug, which No One Else Must Ever Use. We were a big happy family.

The Big Boss was a genial RAF type with a handlebar moustache. Blood Pressure was scared to death of him – terrified, for some reason, that he might come in and catch us sitting down. So, between assignments, we had to stand up. We even took our tea breaks standing up –

except Blood Pressure, he sat at the desk doing the *break-fastses*. The Big Boss came round a couple of times when no one else was there and we had a chat about this and that. He seemed perfectly reasonable to me, and actually sat down himself. I couldn't see what the problem was.

Apart from standing around developing shop assistants' legs, making tea and carting luncheon meat around, I had to man the uniform store for an hour in the morning and afternoon. The uniform store was fun. It was stacked with outmoded garments – the Golden Age of Butlins on coat hangers. I wiled away many a ten minutes trying on old commisionaires' outfits from the '50s, all gold braid and cockaded hats.

Saturdays and Wednesdays were the best days because they were the laundry days – Patches and I would collect all the dirty sheets and towels, bundle them up, send them down in the lift and load them onto the laundry van. Harry used to help us load the van, which was a good laugh because he couldn't lift the bundles, and if you threw one at him you could sometimes knock him clean over. But the best part was meeting the chambermaids. It wasn't long before I fell for one. I got off with her at the summer Staff Party. But the next day was sheet day, and in a less glamorous setting than the Staff Club, and with the embarrassing Patches in tow, she blanked me.

I was too shy to ask her out. I was crap at asking girls out anyway – one of the first girls I ever asked out laughed and said, 'I don't think so'. I'd never quite got over it even though I was only fourteen at the time. Eventually I managed it. I tried to be cool and not look surprised when she said yes.

We went to see Chris Farlowe and the re-formed Thunderbirds at Hove Town Hall (exactly a year after the Kilburns). Chris Farlowe wasn't very good that night, which was a shame because I'd seen him loads of times with Jon Hiseman's Coliseum and later with Atomic Rooster and he'd been really good. But while Farlowe and the Thunderbirds trudged their way through a turgid version of a ghastly song – Barry Manilow's Mandy, we got it together. None of it mattered, she didn't mind that they were crap – and she was a Who fan too. It seemed that she'd blanked me because she was just as shy I was, but now it was official – we were in love.

We went out every night. I was staying with my parents, over the hill in Peacehaven, and she was sharing a room in the female staff quarters. Being caught in the staff quarters of the opposite sex was punishable by death or something. Morals were a bit strict in 1975. We couldn't exactly pop back to my place so we did most of what you might call our courting under the stars along the under-cliff walk and spent hours kissing goodnight by the front door of the hotel in the light of the Butlins sign.

Long after the last bus had gone I'd walk home over Telscombe Tye. Sometimes it was moonlit, sometimes it was pitch black. By the time I got to bed it was almost time to get up again. I didn't care – I'd never felt more alive. She was called Sue and she'd just left school. She was going to go to art college in Cheltenham.

When we left Butlins we wrote to each other every day. Sometimes she came to see me in Hull.

I'd just moved into a new flat, which was just as well – I couldn't possibly have taken her to the old place, an attic slum on Park Grove that was infested with mice. My friend Paul had come to stay for a couple of weeks at the beginning of the second year while he was looking for a flat. He never moved out. He slept in a sleeping bag on the floor with mice running all over him. As soon as you switched the light off you could hear them. When one of us pulled a bird, which was only ever me, he slept on the floor in the kitchen. It made the rent very cheap – four pounds and twenty-five pence divided into two, and that included gas and electricity.

The new place was much better. It didn't have a bathroom but after the Park Grove slum it was like a luxury flat. The entrance was down an alleyway. Now we had a room each. Paul took the living room, where there was plenty of space to dismantle his motorbike in the warm, and I had the attic. We tried to limit most of the squalor to the kitchen and because the toilet was outside we got quite good at pissing in the sink.

Addis & The Flip Tops was coming adrift. We wanted to do something new, turn it into an English version of the Magic Band. But Steve left to concentrate on his painting and Stuart was about to follow. We decided to knock it on the head.

I got a new band together with a keyboard player called Graham Beck. Graham was in my year at college. He had a cheap 'Insta-Piano' with a split keyboard. He was able to play bass on one half and put the other through all kinds of effects. We never bothered even looking for a bass player. The drummer was a guy called Mike Holden who was known all over Hull as Arthur Smee. In real life Arthur had a good job working for the council. He was in charge of road construction. Away from work he was a belligerent pisshead just like the rest of us. He was short, bald and bespectacled. He always wore a rumpled tweed suit. The first time I saw Arthur he was hoola-hooping at an art school dance, surrounded by girls.

We were going to do my songs. They might not be very good – in fact, most of them weren't, but they were what was going to distinguish us from all the other local groups. Everybody else played cover versions – proficient versions of LA Woman by the Doors, and Reeling In The Years by Steely Dan. I was certain that no group I was in could ever achieve that standard of excellence but I really didn't want to anyway. It just wasn't relevant. It wasn't the truth.

I wanted to write songs that were about my life, not sing a lot of second-hand shit about somebody else that I didn't even know. I wanted my new group to be real and unique. And anyway, being a songwriter gave me kudos – I was a shit bass player, a barely adequate guitarist and a hopeless singer. But in the songwriting field there wasn't much competition because there weren't that many in Hull.

Arthur made us rehearse every night. We couldn't do a gig until we were good enough. He was one hundred per cent belief – a slave-driver, a tyrant. He was exactly what was needed. I had to stop going on stage drunk, from now on I had to play sober or he'd kill me. He applied pressure – we always needed another song by tomorrow night's rehearsal.

Our first gig shocked everybody. Suddenly I could play the guitar and we had an hour-long set of fairly OK songs culminating in Whole Wide World. At the next gig word had got around and all the local groups came to see us. After that we never played anywhere that wasn't full.

We got a residency at the Bull Hotel on Beverley Road next to the public baths. It had an upstairs room with a small stage and a bar. We went to see Bernard, the land-lord, with a proposition: we'd take the door money and he'd have the bar take. He took us up to see the room. It was equipped with a PA system and half the stage was taken up by a magnificent Yamaha electronic organ. Bernard said we could use it if we liked. He gave us a demonstration, a two-fingered assault on When The Saints Go Marching In and, courtesy of the technological advances of the mid-'70s, he was accompanied by an entire marching band and an orchestra that stepped in and out of time and hit all the right bum notes in perfect accord. We had trouble not laughing.

Afterwards he said, 'If you're good – and only if you're good, mind – I can pull a few strings for you.' He looked round, as though checking the empty room for walls that have ears, and lowered his voice conspiratorially: 'If you're good I can get you into the Bass Charrington Inter Pub Talent Competition.' We weren't as impressed as we should have been – his big publican's face loomed into ours and he said, 'Folks have been known to get jobs on liners having won that.'

We played there every Tuesday night right through the spring and early summer of '76. But we never did enter the Bass Charrington Inter Pub Talent Competition. I know we were expected to because one night as we finished playing, a man at the bar turned round to Bernard and said, 'Eee – between them and't ventriloquist I reckon we've gorrit sewn up this year.' I hope they didn't feel too let down – it just wasn't our sort of thing.

I finished college. They gave me a degree – a 2:2. An arrogant graphics student from North London said, 'What's it feel like to get a degree for messing about for three years?' I said, 'It feels like this.' And then I hit him. It was a fitting end somehow. Everybody said I ought to go down to London and get into a real band. I'd been going out with Sue on a long-distance basis for nearly a year now. She didn't want to stick around in the West Country and I could quite understand why she wouldn't want to come and live in Hull so we decided to move to London and get a flat together.

Melody
Road

WE FOUND A ROOM IN a cheap hotel in Earls Court. All I can remember about it is a pink candlewick bedspread. I remember walking down a wide street, big white houses, with Arabs in full Lawrence of Arabia gear sitting on the steps. I'd never seen Arabs before. I was fascinated and slightly disgusted by a kebab shop. I couldn't imagine what shaped animal they'd got it from – or even if you could actually eat it. It could have been furniture polish for all I knew.

We were going to go to all the places we'd heard of – the Marquee, the Nashville, the 100 Club, Dingwalls Dance Hall, the Roundhouse, and even Ronnie Scott's; it was surely going to be an almost nightly thing – but first we had to find somewhere to live. We'd heard Chelsea was nice, so the next morning we got up early and headed over there.

Two or three accommodation agencies later, we could see that Chelsea had been a bit ambitious. We decided to settle on Fulham. In fact, we were already in Fulham because there weren't any accommodation agencies in Chelsea. Eventually we found a place that was shabby enough to take us on – Busy Bees Accommodation Bureau – or something very like it. But there was no way that we were going to get a flat for fifteen to twenty pounds a week. The best they could offer was a double room, own cooking facilities, share bathroom and toilet, sixteen pounds a week; and they sent us off to meet an Indian gentleman in Parsons Green who would show us the room in question.

It was fucking horrible. The walls were all purple, and it was very dark. There was a moth-eaten curtain, a double bed with the usual non-colour candlewick bed-spread, an armchair that looked like a stoat's nest, a large wardrobe, and a table with an encrusted gas ring sitting on it. The only light was a forty-watt bulb in a gilded plaster wall-light with a gold-fringed purple shade halfway up the purple wall next to the bed. We couldn't live like this.

We saw an advert in the *Evening Standard* for an agency in Oxford Street who assured us on the phone that they could fix us up that very same day – just come along, they said. So we did.

They had exactly what we were looking for: a one-bedroomed flat in the middle of Fulham for fifteen pounds a week. All we had to do was pay a returnable fee of the equivalent of one week's rent to enrol with the agency (nothing they could do about that, a legal require-ment – but we'd get it back as soon as we took the flat). We were a bit worried about this, but as they said, there was the flat, waiting for us, and all we had to do was come up with fifteen quid (cash if you've got it – save waiting for the cheque to clear), and they could make an appointment to view. What could we do? We handed over the cash.

Forms were filled in and signed, and then we had to wait with some Australians who seemed to be regulars there. Then it was our turn, and they got on the phone, all smiles, to the landlord. The smile turned to a frown: '…all right… yes…' (grimace) 'oh, what a shame, they would have been ideal. Unfortunately that one's just

gone, but let's see what else we've got...' Nothing suitable. 'Drop back in about the same time tomorrow.'

'Er, can we have our fifteen quid back?'

'Oh, no, that's actually none-refundable – but that is
actually all you pay when we find you something. Best is
to drop back in – or better still, why not phone later in
the week...'

We were beginning to understand that the dream flat
had probably never existed. The phone was permanently
engaged, and that was the last we saw of the fifteen quid.

We had better luck the following morning. We went to
Fulham and walked into the first accommodation agency
we saw where a very sympathetic woman offered us a flat
in Wandsworth. Our only concern was that Wandsworth
was an awfully long way out and twenty pounds a week
was a lot of money.

The landlady was a Polish woman called Mrs Sprogis.
She lived in a huge house on the edge of Wandsworth
Common. Her living room was the size of a car park,
grandiose, exotic plants everywhere. It was overheated,
stuffy, and it stunk of dog. Her husband sat in a chair,
one eye blinking on and off, oblivious to everything.
Stroke victim. A couple of overweight, out-of-condition
dogs roamed around – a fat Alsation and a lapdog like a
mobile slipper. There was a huge mirror over the mantelpiece reflecting the scene back at a giddy angle. Mrs
Sprogis was about sixty-five or seventy. She had bulging
eyes and glasses with thick lenses. She didn't so much
speak as emit a querulous moaning noise, heavy with the
weight of Poland's suffering.

She was soon convinced that we were a nice young
couple, which I suppose we were to an extent. And we
lied about our work prospects to her complete satisfac-

tion. Then she took us down the road to see the flat, explaining on the way that the previous tenants had been a problem. By now she was as sure as I was that this wouldn't be the case with us – I might have been a fairly naive young man, but I'd figured out a long time ago that the only way to get a flat was to pretend you were someone else, and act accordingly.

The flat was huge compared with the kind of thing we were getting used to – the entire ground floor of a four-bedroomed Edwardian house. The front room, which must have been twice the size of the shithole we'd seen in Parsons Green, was divided from a smaller room by three panelled doors that folded back. The smaller room had French windows opening onto a sort of yard that ran alongside the back part of the house, which was littered with empty beer bottles and rusting Party Four cans. The rest of the flat was down a corridor. There was a dining room and beyond that a little kitchen, which was divided up to accommodate a small bathroom. The kitchen led into a tiny conservatory with the old outside toilet leading off that. And then there was a garden with a bay tree and a vine growing along the wall.

'Which bit's ours?' Sue asked. I kicked her into silence in case Mrs Sprogis got the idea of splitting it into two flats and doubling the revenue. But Mrs Sprogis had other things on her mind, wringing her hands and bleating about the state in which the place had been left. It was full of empty beer bottles. We assured her that we could soon clean it up. (We were turning into members of the Famous Five by now.) We went back to her place and sorted out the paperwork.

And that was it – we collected our bags from the hotel, bought a dustpan and brush, and moved into Number One Melody Road. Yes, really – a perfect address for a young man trying to break into the pop business.

And that's exactly what I did – I broke into the pop business. But not that sort of pop. I blagged my way into a job as a Quality Control Inspector at the local Corona Lemonade factory. First, though, I got hold of a copy of a magazine that every ex-art student was supposed to subscribe to – it was probably called 'The Artist' or something, I forget now, but it was full of jobs I'd never heard of for which you needed qualifications that I never knew existed. I applied for a job as a commercial artist. The advert said the job involved paste-up and silk-screen printing. I'd done a bit of screen printing at college, and though I'd never done paste-up I figured it was just mucking about with a lot of cut-out bits and a jar of cow gum – I'd seen it done. I reckoned I could bluff it.

The job was in West Acton. It took ages to get there from Wandsworth. I had to get a bus to East Putney, take the District Line to Earls Court, change onto another bit of the District Line heading towards Paddington and Edgware Road, and change again at Notting Hill Gate for the westbound Central Line (Ealing Broadway branch). When I got off at West Acton it was a bit of a walk. It seemed to me it was half a day's work just to get there. An Indian man interviewed me – well, I say interviewed, but basically all he did was ask if I could start in the morning, which I could. I'd got the job. I told him I'd done four years at art college, got a degree and all that, but he didn't seem interested.

The next morning, by some Herculean effort I got there for eight thirty and they started me on painting little metal figurines with enamel paint alongside a lot of West Indian ladies. I soon realised that this was all anyone did, except the bloke who'd interviewed me – he stuck the labels on the cardboard boxes that the figurines were packed in. It wasn't quite the life I'd imagined as a commercial artist in Swinging London. If I was more than five minutes late I lost an hour's pay. It was badly paid so what with that and the tube fare it took me two hours every day to break even. I stuck it until the end of the week.

I went to the Job Centre at Clapham Junction and asked to be put on the Professional and Executive Register, on account of my degree. As they didn't normally get people applying for this on the strength of a degree in painting and sculpture, they wanted to know what I thought I might be qualified to do. That pulled me up short. They asked me if I had any Special Skills that might have a bearing on my employability. I had to think for a minute before admitting to being able to mix concrete. So, they put me on the Professional and Executive Register as a general labourer. I'd confused the bastards, that was my Special Skill. The Professional and Executive Register was abolished soon after that and you had to take what you were offered.

I went downstairs and had a look at the boards to see if there was anything remotely suitable. It either had to be easy, local and not too many hours, or really well paid. There was a cleaning job in Clapham Junction. I took a note of the job number over to a mousy, bespectacled woman with a twitchy mouth who looked like she was possibly called Barbara. Barbara looked me up and down and read out the job as though I was a contestant on a game show. She wanted me to be completely sure. When we were satisfied that I'd made the right decision, that I knew my own mind, she picked up the phone and dialled the number. Cupping her hand over the mouthpiece so that the other party wouldn't hear, she looked at me and said, 'It's ringing.'

It rang for a long time, long enough for her to cup the mouthpiece again and ask if I'd had any experience of this type of work. 'What, cleaning?' I said. 'Well, I cleaned my teeth this morning...' She decided the phone had been ringing long enough, they'd obviously gone home for the day. 'To be honest, Mr Goulden, I think you're over-qualified for this job – why don't you come back tomorrow?'

We had our first major row. But you couldn't really call it a row, it was more one-sided than that, as in me losing my temper. It was something really stupid – we were putting clothes away in a drawer and Sue slammed it shut really hard because it was full and a bit stiff. I went mental because it could have trapped my hands – if they'd been anywhere near it, which they weren't. The whole thing escalated and I banged my head down on the floor so hard that I almost knocked myself out. We were both screaming and crying, it was horrible. Suddenly I hated myself. As it was happening I had this disembodied feeling – I was adrift over Clapham Common. London was just too big for me. I still feel it when I'm there, it's a bit like claustrophobia, but it's more agoraphobic than that. Drab, grimy suburbs stretching out for miles and miles and miles. Bedsit land – a million miserable exist-ances. London was bigger than I was and I was lost in it.

I found the perfect job – if I could blag my way into it. Quality Control Inspector. The hours looked horrific but it was in Wandsworth and the rate of pay was double what you got for cleaning. I quickly convinced myself that this was me, and got them to fix up an interview.

I was a little over-qualified – five GCSEs would have done it, but I was well prepared. I'd really worked myself into the part. Sure, I'd spent four years at art school, I'd had my fun – even got a degree (a bit sort of off-the-cuff, that bit), but yes, I had had my fun, and now it was time to buckle down and get on with the business of earning a living. I nearly made myself sick – I didn't want to know myself, but I got the job. And none of this 'start tomorrow'. I didn't have to start till the following Monday.

Which gave me the rest of the week to sort out the empty bottles. Most of them were from Young's Brewery, which was just down the road. There was a supermarket trolley in the back garden, which I divested of old Party Four cans and refilled with light-ale bottles. It didn't even make a dent in the collection at the side of the house – and then there was the cellar – full of pint and two-pint bottles. You got more money back on them too. I allowed myself a moment of piety – whoever had lived here must have had a monumental drink problem. On the second trolley-load the man in the Brewery off-sales proposed a deal. He couldn't be bothered with counting bottles any more, so we arrived at a cash settlement of thirty pounds. Not bad – a week and a half's rent, in fact. And then there was the Bass Charrington collection, and three car batteries, which I trundled round to the scrap yard and got fifty pence each for. (At this point you have to remember that beer was only thirteen pence a pint.) Life in SW18 was just about as happy-go-lucky as it could get.

On Monday morning I started at Corona Lemonade. When they said it was in Wandsworth what they really meant was Earlsfield. I had to run down East Hill every morning and catch a bus in Garret Lane. I never once had breakfast before I left – there was barely time for a cup of tea.

The factory manager was a tall, lanky bloke called Philip. He had a well-trimmed beard and light brown hair swept into a fashionable '70s style quiff. He looked like one of those illustrations in a barber's shop window. He would have been about ten years older than me, and I could see it all – the three-piece suite with moss-green Draylon covers, Ford Cortina, lovely wife (with a face like a shrew), two kids, both girls (three and five), Barratt Home, the lounge he wallpapered himself one weekend, cheap holidays abroad. A homespun lad from Devon, he probably liked to play rugby with his strapping mates, but didn't get the chance as often as he'd like these days – family to bring up, pressure of work – and none of this comes cheap, you know – you've got to work for it. Oh, and he'd got the work ethic all right. The subtle pressure – introduce the snout to the proverbial grindstone and apply downward pressure.

Every morning at five-past eight Philip threw the main switch and the conveyer belt juddered into motion. There's something quite beautiful about a bottling plant (as long as you don't have to work in one). It could be an allegory for a perfectly ordered society, or a microcosmic universe, complete within itself.

Corona Lemonade (Duntshill Road, SW18) was a huge great 1970s warehouse type of building. The front of the building had a big roller shutter that opened high and wide enough to allow access for two or three large flatbed trucks at a time. The building was divided into two halves. The lorries loaded and unloaded in the front half, and the bottling was done in the back. The conveyer belt meandered all the way round the factory hall, beginning and ending at the same place. Crates of empty bottles were loaded onto the conveyer belt by a team of casual workers – students and the like. They had to make sure that the tops had all been taken off the bottles, but other than that they didn't have to think at all, just shuttle backwards and forwards chucking crates of empties onto the start of the conveyer and taking crates of brand new lemonade off the end. The two ends of the production line were joined by a subsidiary conveyer belt that sent the empty crates over to the other end, where they were automatically refilled, six bottles in each, ready to be taken off and stacked up on pallets by the itinerant students, who moaned a lot and flexed their muscles.

The empty bottles were automatically lifted out of their crates and fed into the washing machine. The empty crates then went along a subsidiary conveyer belt to the other end of the line where they queued up waiting to be refilled with bottles of pop. The washing machine was about the size of a small two-bedroomed bungalow. It was covered with gantries, ladders, walkways and inspection hatches, and I was in charge of it. It was divided into three sections: a pre-wash that soaked all the labels off and got rid of dead wasps and fag-ends, a main washing tank, and a drying chamber. The bottles went in sticky and disgusting, and came out of the other end gleaming. They made their way, in single file, past two stoical South London ladies who sat sucking boiled sweets and occasionally leaning forward to pick a cracked, broken or otherwise imperfect bottle off the line and dropping it in the bin.

The next stop was the carbonating, filling and capping hub of the bottling universe. The syrup was mixed in enormous vats, upstairs in a laboratory, by a middle-aged man with big glasses and greased-back hair. He was the chemist. Philip, the chemist and myself all wore white lab coats, which gave the proceedings a bit of a B movie, science fiction look. The ladies wore blue polyester housecoats from Primark or Danemak, and the fork lift truck operators wore green boilersuits with *Corona* picked out in yellow on the top pocket. The students just wore what they arrived in. The rest of the casual workforce favoured the sort of pale mauve vests that later featured in the Ian Dury song Blockheads. I don't know what they wore in the winter, because I didn't last that long.

The syrup was prepared according to an exact formula developed by the far-flung department of Corona Lemonade that dealt with such things. A large part of my job was to make sure that there was no deviation from this evidently successful formula. We were making lemonade, limeade, cream soda, strawberryade and a couple of other disgusting preparations that I can't quite bring to mind at the moment, in separate batches at the rate of a hundred gallons every two hours, for eight hours a day, five days a week. It was being shipped out for delivery as fast as we could produce it. We were flooding the country with a carbonated solution of sugar, saccharine, and various chemicals that it was advisable to handle wearing rubber gloves. We often did four hours' overtime – that's another two batches – another two hundred gallons of soft drink stickiness in order to keep pace with the demand. Corona Lemonade must have been doing something right. It doesn't bear thinking about.

The bottles whirled upwards into a carousel where they were filled up, carbonated and capped. The carousel was a mad-looking thing, with pipework coming out of the top of it that went through the ceiling to the vats containing the soft-drink mixture in the laboratory above. More pipes led off to a carbon dioxide tank at the rear of the building. The carousel was topped off by a clear perspex hopper containing virgin bottle tops. Two young Malaysian girls had the job of filling this up from time to time, generally over-seeing the operation and switching the machine off if the bottles were backing-up down the line. They giggled a lot and one of them told me that the other one planned to invite me round for tea. I didn't push it because to all intents and purposes I wasn't a single man and anyway I was in love.

Every half hour I had to take a bottle off the line, clamp it into a centrifuge that was mounted on the wall, and spin it round like a propeller. There was a piercing mechanism with a gauge attached to it in the cap end of the centrifuge. After I'd got the bottle well shaken up, I'd activate the piercer and take a pressure reading in pounds per square inch, which I then entered into a special chart attached to a clipboard. Then I had to do another test with a funny little optical device – specific gravity, sugar content – something like that. I never quite got the hang of that one, but I took the readings and duly logged the details. After that I had to do something complicated with a torque wrench to make sure that the caps were properly screwed on. Too tight, not customer friendly. Too loose, on the other hand, disaster. Flat lemonade, or worse. There were specific guidelines, laid down by the company in pounds per square inch. I entered my findings and left the clipboard lying around so that Management could look at it.

I didn't worry too much about this stuff – I just entered the readings and hoped for the best. If I got behind I made some of them up to save time, and if the figures looked a bit abnormal I took the clipboard and consulted Philip. When I did this I always felt like a bit part player in a company presentation film.

The bottles hurtled out of the carousel and down the

line to the Level Check. The lemonade was paraded past a white perspex screen, illuminated from behind. The screen had two horizontal lines on it and the lemonade level had to be somewhere between the two in order to meet accepted guidelines. This operation was supervised by an older lady called Margaret, whose menopausal twitch was seriously augmented by years of watching bottles juddering past. She practically vibrated. Margaret's other duties included cleaning the canteen so, twice a day, for three quarters of an hour in the morning and afternoon, the levels had to take care of themselves. Litres were probably won and lost, but fuck it, we weren't going to eat our sandwiches in a dirty canteen. And that's all there was to eat – cheese rolls and ham rolls from the Indian shop on the opposite corner. And you could wash that down with tea, coffee, hot chocolate or tomato soup from the vending machine – or a litre of cream soda if you felt like it. Not for me, I was off to the pub. I quite often used to overdo it and come back pissed. In the ten weeks that I worked there I think it was noticed a couple of times. That's right – ten weeks. It may sound pathetic to you, but I'm quite proud of it because those ten weeks are the longest time I've held down a real job in my life.

The noise was fucking horrendous – 15,000 bottles at any one time, clanking, bashing and jiggling along half a mile of meandering metal conveyer – being un-crated, and re-crated, stacked and stacked again, bang, flunk, crash, from eight in the morning till five at night, with an hour for lunch and two ten-minute breaks, and four hours' overtime twice a week. Then they wanted me to come in an hour early. Seven o'clock. I'd get paid an hour's overtime, and there wasn't any choice. Fuck that, you might as well move in. Everyone else seemed to like it except me. The noise was beginning to affect my hearing. When the plant shut down at break times I could feel the silence sucking my brain out of my earholes. It was tedious – checking the gauges on the washer, emptying the sludge out of the de-labelling tank, doing the tests and filling in the data on the clipboard. And a new, exciting idea from head office – a bottle library. I was to take a bottle from every batch, put the date and batch number on the label, then file it away upstairs on a special shelf. Pretty soon there were more bottles than shelf space.

In between performing all these tasks, I hung around outside, smoking cigarettes and drinking coffee from the machine. When it was wet I sat in the label store. And that was another of my jobs – I don't know if anyone remembers, but in the days before barcodes, labels on bottles used to have a set of tiny notches cut out of one side. By holding a certain plastic chart up against the notches, a wealth of information could be read off about the product. There was a special machine in the label store for cutting these notches. I didn't know what I was doing with the machine. I just set it to a plausible looking arrangement of notches and hoped for the best. I don't think it really mattered. I took the wads of labels and loaded them into the automatic labeller between Level Check and Re-crating. Sometimes when I was bored I'd open a pack of labels and start autographing them: *'Best wishes, the Quality Control Inspector'* – *'Cordially yours, the Quality Control Inspector'*, that sort of thing. It gave me a thrill to see the autographed bottles lined up on the shelves in my local off-licence.

One afternoon Philip was supervising the labelling machine, which had been giving a bit of trouble, when something on one of the labels caught his eye. He tried to flip it out, but the machine was too quick and his finger got squashed in the mechanism. It was stuck in there for an hour, and they had to call the fire brigade in with specialist equipment to get him out. It hurt, too. Luckily, by the time it was over, he was past caring why he'd put his finger in there in the first place.

During the summer it wasn't too bad. But halfway through September the mornings started to get colder. It wasn't completely light at seven o'clock in the morning either, and as October approached, the idea of coming home in the dark to a cold flat was becoming a reality. This could end up being the rest of my life if I wasn't careful. It wasn't what I'd had in mind so I gave in my notice.

Philip was very disappointed – it seemed a shame after all the training I'd had – and it turned out they thought I was really good at the job. But if I wasn't happy what could they do?

They could offer me another job – the chemist was going to retire soon. How would I like to work upstairs mixing the lemonade in the big vats? It involved an earlier start, and a certain amount of shift work, but there was a corresponding increase in pay. And I could regard it in the light of a promotion.

They could fuck off with that. After I'd finished paying off my overdraft there wasn't much point in earning a shitload of money bottling lemonade because I spent most of it on beer and Cinzano (our favourite drink at the time). I was drinking to forget. I was in the pub at lunchtime, in a different pub every night, and at weekends I was in the pub all the time except in the afternoons when they were closed – then I sat at home drinking cans of Ind Coope Long Life and large glasses of Cinzano with a dash of Corona lemonade. I thought that was really sophisticated – being able to afford cans of beer and bottles of Cinzano for home consumption. I thought of it as extra-mural drinking. My life outside the soft-drinks industry was one of industrial hard drinking.

I was getting nowhere with the idea of being in a band. I just didn't know how you went about it outside of some institution like an art college. I was such a provincial hick – I wrote an advert on a postcard and put it in a newsagent's window in Clapham Junction:

> Guitarist wants to form or join band –
> anything considered!!

followed by the number of the payphone in the hallway, and quite possibly the address too. I paid for the card to stay up for two weeks. I only got one reply and that was from a bloke who fancied being in a group but didn't play anything. As it turned out he couldn't sing either so I tried walking up and down Ladbroke Grove because a friend of mine in Hull had told me that the streets of Notting Hill were paved with musicians. He was wrong.

We saw The Clash at the Roundhouse. They were supporting the Kursaal Flyers. We went to see the Kursaal Flyers because they came from Southend, which gave them a tenuous Dr Feelgood connection. The Clash were a life-changing experience. Most of the bands I saw around that time were totally harmless, but not The Clash. It was one of their first gigs – September 5th 1976. Keith Levine was still in the band, so there were three guitar players. They were the most confrontational thing I'd ever seen. They looked like stick insects – tight, straight-legged jeans; short, homemade haircuts. Strummer wore a black shirt with *Chuck Berry Is Dead* bleached into the back of it. From the moment they came on there were adverse comments and snide remarks about the regular Sunday At The Roundhouse audience sitting on the floor in their smart '70s apparel:

'I like your jeans – didja get them at the Jean Machine?'

After a few numbers Joe Strummer said, 'I suppose you think you can pay your one pound fifty and just come in here and sit down like it was a fucking TV set… I mean, you could get off your denims in case you wear 'em out.'

Then they played a song that I later found out was called Janie Jones. Their sound was an aggressive cacophony of out-of-tune guitars and ragged vocal chants. I wasn't sure that I liked it but I found it very attractive. They weren't going down at all well, and after a few more numbers Strummer addressed the audience again:

'…well now it's time for audience participation, right? I want you all to tell me what exactly you're doing here.'

Somebody shouted, '…to drink beer.'

There was a silence. You could hear the amplifiers buzzing…

'Well listen,' replied Strummer, 'I don't know what size you are around the waist but I guess it's in advance of thirty-six, so if you want to carry your corpulent body out to the bar and stuff it with a few barrels of whatever you fancy then go ahead.'

I was impressed by that even though I could have done with drinking some beer myself. When seven o'clock rolled round I saw Joe Strummer propping up the bar with a dangerous looking individual who I later realised was Sid Vicious. I would have liked to have talked to Strummer but I was too shy. I almost felt that I should make some pledge of allegiance – there was something going on. I wasn't sure what it was, but this air of dissatisfaction was something I could identify with.

'Get on with it!'

'Get on with what, you big twit – haven't you got any brains at all? All right then, so you might've got five A levels, what do I care? That's just a dirty trick.'

I answered an advert in the *Melody Maker*. The Flying Tigers needed a rhythm guitarist – that could be me, I like tigers. The bloke on the other end of the phone was an American pretending to be a Cockney. He sounded like Dick Van Dyke in Mary Poppins – cor blimey, mate. The number was a kebab shop in Clapham. The American was the singer in the group, and that was where he worked, in the kebab shop.

The Flying Tigers played garage music – the Standells, the Chocolate Watch Band – and threw in a mixture of R 'n' B and Chicago blues – Hoochie Coochie Man by Muddy Waters and Killing Floor by Howling Wolf. The singer was called Mike. He liked the sound of me, said I should come to an audition they were holding on Sunday in Baddersea – I should bring my Axe, and an Amp.

I went there on the bus with my Hohner Orgaphon with the jukebox speakers, and my Top Twenty guitar in a floppy blue plastic case. Their lead guitarist arrived with a brand new Selmer combo in red vinyl finish, and unpacked a Gibson from a professional looking hard case. He had a gingery beard and long blond hair. He was wearing a green velvet jacket with enormous lapels and high-waisted denim flares. I found out later that he was a school teacher in real life. He looked somewhat dismayed when he saw me – my hair was very short, badly cut, and I was wearing an ancient pair of straight Tesco jeans, old plimsoles with no socks, and a blue and white striped long-sleeved T-shirt. I was thin, spotty and very possibly drunk. I said hello and a speaker fell out of the front of my amplifier, as though it was winking at him. I was just what they weren't looking for.

A few weeks before I left Corona I read an article in the *Melody Maker* about this new label called Stiff Records. They'd just put out a single by Nick Lowe: In The Heart Of The City. I heard it on Capitol Radio. It was a minute and a half long. It only had three chords. There was something going on here that wasn't a million miles away from what I was into, so when I left the lemonade factory at the beginning of October I decided to take a tape round to Stiff. They were looking for new talent and for an instant I was sure I was exactly what they needed.

Put that way it sounds as though I made a considered decision and carried it through. But it wasn't quite like that. I left Corona Lemonade on Friday evening with my final pay packet – one week's pay plus a week in hand and a full tax rebate because they'd had me on an emergency tax code for ten weeks. I had money to burn, so the weekend was a fairly drunken affair. On the Saturday night we went to see Eddie & The Hot Rods at the Nashville.

It was OK but the real treat of the evening was the support group, a hopeless bunch of oiks from Croydon called The Damned. They were absolutely useless except for the guitar player who even had to tune the bass player's bass for him in the middle of the set. The singer wore an outfit made up of several different shades of black. He had dyed black hair, greased back in a desperate attempt at Vincent Price, augmented and enhanced by a glass of tomato juice that looked exactly like what it

was – a glass of tomato juice. The front of the bass drum
was splattered with paint and kicked in so that the tattered remains of the front skin quivered in time with the
music. The drummer was revolting – he kept sticking his
tongue out at the audience. It went in and out of his
weaselly, pasty face and he looked like a small, vicious
creature catching insects. They had a backdrop, which
was an old sheet of plastic like the sort of thing a double
mattress might be delivered in. It had 'The Damned'
daubed on it in black paint. When it fell off the wall most
of the audience cheered and it was the biggest applause
they got. Nobody seemed to like them very much and the
feeling appeared to be mutual. Their final insult was a
cover of The Beatles' Help!.

I got up on Monday morning and made a tape of
some of my songs. I'm not sure that I even started out
with the intention of giving it to Stiff Records, I think the
idea gathered momentum as I went on.

I'd never made a tape before. I'd mucked about with a
Grundig tape recorder that belonged to the baker's son
when I was about fifteen. He was learning to play the
drums. We wanted to form a group but we didn't know
how to do it. He had a red sparkle-finish snare drum and
a hi-hat. Later on he got a matching bass drum. I had an
acoustic guitar, which I electrified by sticking the earpieces from a pair of army surplus headphones onto the
body. I amplified it through the gram socket of an old
radio with a lead made out of old light flex. It whistled a
lot and when I ran out of ideas I just tuned the short wave
in and out. I wanted to sound like Spooky Tooth,
Mandrake Paddle Steamer or Blossom Toes. He wanted
to play stuff like Honky Tonk Woman – stuff that he'd
heard at Brighton discotheques. That was the difference
between us – he could get into discotheques underage,

and I couldn't because I looked too young. He wasn't really into music but we were both into girls. He saw drumming as a way of increasing his pulling power.

Anyway, that would have been back in 1969 and since then there had been technological advancements that rendered the Grundig domestic tape recorder obsolete. Cassettes. It's a shame because cassettes sound horrible. They get grubby, the cases shatter and you're left with these silly transparent plastic devices that fill up cardboard boxes. And even if you've written what was on them on the label, you can't read it because the writing fades in the sunshine, and when you try and play them they just warble for a little while and then stop and you have to unwind thousands of yards of tape from the innards of your cassette player. And anything to do with cassettes seems to attract a very individual sort of grit that could possibly be breadcrumbs.

Tape recorders sound much better. They've got comedy value too. I'll always remember two French teachers and the senior German master trying to spool up a tape in assembly. It was a recording sent by the mayor of Blois which was the twin town to Lewes. It was his address to our school. When they finally got it right so that it played forwards and at the right speed, the French address was so distorted that it was unintelligible anyway. The teachers all had to try and look interested and serious because they were sitting in a line on the stage, but I definitely saw the junior physics master, Mr Lee, break into a snigger. For a moment I nearly forgave him for hitting me round the head repeatedly and calling me a stupid, stupid, stupid, stupid boy when I was twelve.

But it's cassettes that concern us here. It was Sue's cassette player. A real '70s thing – brown, beige and cream with big square chunky buttons. The cassette was one that we didn't want to listen to any more – I had to erase the B side before I took it round to Stiff so that they wouldn't think that I either listened to Eric Clapton's Rainbow Concert or worse, that I actually was Eric Clapton's Rainbow Concert. I turned up my amplifier, propped the cassette microphone up somewhere near my mouth and sang my songs into it. I don't think I even listened back. Most of the songs weren't very good, they were a bit throwaway, but two songs definitely survived, Telephoning Home and Whole Wide World. There were a couple that sounded like Dr Feelgood, one or two country numbers with lyrics about being bored and living in England, and two or three where I'd tried for Frank Zappa doing the Kalin Twins and failed.

When I'd finished it was lunchtime so I went to the pub and had three or four pints of Dutch courage. I worked out how to get to the Stiff office, pocketed the cassette, and before I'd thought about it I was emerging from Royal Oak tube station. I imagined that the office, or offices, would be up several flights of stairs with brown linoleum and chipped magnolia woodwork. I'd be very cool about everything and it would all be very businesslike. We'd have a chat and they'd promise to get in touch, even if they didn't mean it.

It wasn't anything like that: 32 Alexander Street turned out to be an old shop containing a large desk with an anorexic girl sitting behind it. Apart from that, I had an impression of an awful lot of people who all seemed to be staring at me through the window. Because they'd seen me I couldn't really walk past and take another run at it so I kicked the door open in an aggressive manner and strode in. The insecurity that triggered the aggressive behaviour did me a favour in this case – I think they interpreted it as genuine punk attitude, which I suppose it was. Genuine punk attitude – the insecure underdog.

A big bloke with shaggy hair and a beard came forward and asked if he could help me. I was a bit fazed by this but I didn't want to show it so I said, 'I'm one of those cunts that brings tapes into record companies.' I supposed I was now – I'd got the bug. On the way there I saw President Records and it had crossed my mind that I could take a tape to them next – they put out Baby Come Back by The Equals so they couldn't be all bad. I wonder what they would have made of me.

The guy with the shaggy hair and beard (who turned out to be Huey Lewis, later of Huey Lewis & The News) directed me towards the anorexic girl. I gave her the cassette and turned to leave. I just wanted to get out of there but she said, 'Don't you want to leave your name and number?' I gave her the number of the payphone in the hall and just about ran out of the place.

I caught a 28 bus all the way home and tried to forget about the stupid and humiliating thing I'd just done. By Wednesday I was really worried – I wanted to hide from the whole world. They must be having a right laugh about me. On Wednesday evening I met Sue from work in the West End. We bought the *NME* to read on the bus home. When we saw an advert for the latest Stiff Records release – New Rose b/w Help by The Damned I felt better – if they could sign that load of old shit they could sign me, or at least not laugh at me quite so much as they'd probably been doing.

The next day I was on the verge of panic, wondering what was going to become of me, when the payphone started ringing. I answered it out of curiosity. It didn't usually ring during the day and if it rang in the evening it was always for upstairs, unless it was Sue's mum. I wasn't speaking to my parents at the time due to a protracted argument about sex outside marriage and my unwillingness to do a teacher training course.

The caller asked for me, which was a bit of a surprise. When I said I was me he said he was Jake Riviera from Stiff Records calling about my tape. I immediately started to apologise. I wanted to explain that they could just use the cassette again rather than going to the trouble of sending it back. But I heard him asking me if I'd like to come to the office as soon as I could to discuss the possibility of making a record. He told me they loved the tape and if I felt OK about it we should record a single as soon as possible. He asked 'What are you doing this afternoon?' 'Fuck all,' I said, '—that is I'll have to check but I think I could manage it.' I didn't want to appear too easy.

I shuttled along there for three o'clock. The anorexic girl said that Jake and his partner, Dave, had been held up but in the meantime I could talk to Nick. Nick was a tall, skinny bloke with a hawk nose. He was wearing a suit so I assumed he worked in the office because I didn't know anybody that wore a suit for any other reason. He said that they'd like to record the song Whole Wide World and if it was all right with me he'd like to produce it. I thought it was strange that the office boy was going to produce my record but I thought I'd better go along with it. Then it dawned on me that he was Nick Lowe, the man behind the fabulous Heart Of The City.

He was enough of a poser to be into pop. I couldn't tell which particular pop producer he was modelling himself on but there was a bit of Phil Spector in there and he thought it was all a big laugh.

He suggested cider from the corner shop and borrowed fifty pence off me so that Suzanne could get two bottles. We were knocking it back when Jake arrived with Dave Robinson in tow. Dave Robinson was his partner in Stiff but his big interest was in managing Graham Parker & The Rumour. He was a big, podgy looking bloke with curly black hair and bleary eyes. He looked like a scrap metal dealer. He was carrying a golf club. He aimed it at my head and took a swing, stopping just short of smashing my brain in. I just looked at him, he was obviously testing me. I wasn't fazed by things like that – if he was going to stove my head in with a golf club there wasn't much I could do about it anyway.

We had a talk, Jake and Dave outlined what Stiff was all about, most of which I knew already – they hadn't got any money and nobody was going to become an overnight success but we could still have a good time. They thrust a guitar into my hands and asked me to play some of my songs, anything that hadn't made it onto the tape. So I did. Then they phoned Pathway Studios and fixed a recording date for the following week.

I had no idea what a recording studio would be like. It's all a lot less mysterious now – everybody knows what a recording studio is, what it looks like, what it does. Loads of people have actually been in one or even converted the spare bedroom into one. But I never had, not then, and nobody else I knew had either. I'd seen a couple of photos of groups 'in the studio' and even seen One Plus One with the Rolling Stones doing Sympathy For The Devil at Olympic Studios in Barnes, except I didn't know it was Olympic Studios at the time.

I had an idea that it was going to be big, like an aircraft hangar, with lots of acoustic tiling, like pegboard on the walls. I was right about the pegboard. Pathway

Studio was in Grosvenor Road, Islington. In fact, Islington would be putting it kindly – it was more like Stoke Newington, which was nearly as far-flung as Wandsworth. I didn't know how to get there on a bus with my trusty Hohner amplifier and Top Twenty guitar, and it was my big day so I got a taxi all the way from Wandsworth. It cost a fortune – like five pounds with the tip. The taxi driver lifted my amp out for me, dropped it on the pavement and said, 'What do they do here, repair these?' Cunt.

There was an alleyway up between the buildings and a door leading into what looked like an outhouse. It was really small inside and it smelled of cigarettes, electricity and sweat. Nick was there already with the engineer, Bazza, a stocky, bespectacled man with a hint of mad professor. Bazza built the desk at Pathway. Later on he converted an old post office van into the Stiff 'China Shop' mobile and produced my third album, *Big Smash*, which is probably the reason why half of you are reading this.

Nick suggested a quick visit to the pub to calm my nerves while Bazza mikéd up the kit. Some recent sleeve notes written by Elvis Costello for a re-release of his first album suggest that he was there too:

Each time I arrived at the Stiff office I had another bunch of tunes to present. At one point it was seriously suggested that I share a debut album with Wreckless Eric, supposedly in the style of the "Chuck meets Bo" release on Chess. I just happened to visit Pathway on the day of Wreckless' first session. While Mr Lowe took him round to the pub to build up his courage, I cut enough new demos to make a nonsense of this idea.

Clever boy. But he's got that wrong – he wasn't there. His gang all thought I was an airhead but I've got a fucking good memory. Elvis – or DP as he was called then – was at the next session. And he didn't *'happen to visit'*, he was finishing off a track called 'Mystery Dance'. I remember him playing me a new song. He looked very pleased with himself and so did his spectacles. But he didn't make any demos and I didn't go to the pub either. There was talk of doing an album called *Wreckless Meets DP*, but it never happened. He was almost unpleasantly ambitious. I don't think I would have enjoyed it.

I wanted to write songs, make records, do gigs and make a living. I never wanted to elevate songwriting to the status of a craft. When people talk about 'well-crafted songs' it makes me cringe. They're the same people who tell you that the song is the important thing – the people (if you remember earlier on) who would listen to *Sergeant Pepper* in stereo and wouldn't mind if the print in this book was out of focus. I'm sure Elvis Costello has a mono copy of *Sergeant Pepper*. One afternoon in a hotel in Leeds during the Stiff Tour, Larry Wallis was running around in a policeman's helmet and everybody was drunk, except for Elvis – he was in Woolworths buying up rare copies of God Save The Queen on the EMI label, which had somehow found their way into a bargain bin. When he came back his glasses were gleaming so hard I thought they'd jump off his face.

That's another Christmas card list I'm off. I'm trying to write about recording Whole Wide World – obviously it's the biggest moment in my life, except I don't believe in biggest moments in my life. It was quite special though. I just wish the bespectacled one hadn't shoved his beak in like that but I've got things back under control now.

Pathway was owned by Arthur Brown's manager – the studio was apparently built on the proceeds of Fire. If that isn't a good start then I don't know what is. It's weird to think that in 1968, just eight years previously, when I was just fifteen, I was mad for the record that financed the studio where I made my first record.

I think Stiff used Pathway principally because it was cheap. It was cheap because it was only eight track. There were plenty of sixteen-track studios but the real grown-up stuff was all done on twenty-four track. But that was OK because Stiff Records were all about cheap – cheap, brash and cheerful. I got some out and played them just now. They still sound wonderful – big, bright and pulsating, especially the ones produced by Nick Lowe. He knew how to get the best out of Pathway – him and Bazza the engineer. Other people have tried since and a lot of them have said the place was rubbish. I went in there myself in the early '80s and came away disappointed. They had new engineers who played by the rules – they used noise gates, noise reduction and modern compressors that were much too subtle. They didn't know how to mike up a drum kit using only four microphones, and they tried to get that '80s 'in your face' bass drum that sounds like somebody flicking a credit card. It's fine in its place but it didn't work coming out of Pathway.

The control room was tiny – there was enough room for two people to sit side by side at the mixing desk and anybody else had to sit behind them on a narrow bench up against the wall. The speakers were built into home-made plywood enclosures that hadn't even been painted. You had to be careful not to bang your head on them coming into the control room. There was a tiny window above the desk through which you could see part of the live room. On the end wall there was a shelf with two or three two-track Revox machines on it. They used these for the tape echo. Whole Wide World had loads of echo on it so the Revox machines were turning all the time.

You might be wondering why I'm telling you all about Pathway. I think it needs documenting because for a very short while it was possibly the hippest recording studio in the country. It was like Muscle Shoals – a complete dump but everybody wanted to record there. Though perhaps not Abba, Wings, Rod Stewart, or Elton John & Kiki Dee, whose Don't Go Breaking My Heart had just been knocked off the number one slot by Pussycat with Mississippi, which was in turn overthrown by Chicago's supremely sickly If You Leave Me Now and superseded by the even more dreadful Under The Moon Of Love by Showaddywaddy – a group who deserve to have a tribute band called *Shoddywaddy* named after them. And it got worse – by the New Year Shoddywaddy had given way to David Soul who in turn relinquished the top slot to Julie Covington, who made February 1977 more depressing that it otherwise might have been with her rendition of the mawkish Don't Cry For Me Argentina, written (of course) by our very own Andrew Lloyd Webber.

Well, really – I sound like Paul Gambaccini, who once told a record plugger that in his opinion I had No Talent Whatsoever and he would definitely not be playing any of my records.

And on the subject of Andrew Lloyd Webber: a few years back that very right-on American indie act, the Indigo Girls, financed a remake of Jesus Christ Superstar. I can't understand why – they gave all their struggling musician friends in Atlanta a bit of a gig and in the process popped some more money into the Lloyd Webber account – not nearly enough to have a whole community's worth of housing in the St Paulli area of Hamburg demolished to make way for a purpose-built theatre showing nothing but Cats every night, but every little helps. I mention this because when I was recording in Pathway I was helping to create this thing called 'Indie' – if I'd known then what it was going to become maybe I wouldn't have bothered.

Steve Goulding from The Rumour played the drums and Nick played the guitar – a Telecaster plugged into the Pathway 15-watt valve amplifier. They had the backing track down in two takes. And while Nick put the bass on I wrote a third verse, which is just as well because this was the verse that prevented Cliff Richard from covering the song – apparently he objected to the line *'caressing her warm brown skin'*, but I wouldn't change it.

After that they put endless tracks of tambourines and handclaps on it, which they bounced together as they went along. The instrumental break was too long so Bazza edited the multi-track tape. I remember Nick saying that the producers of Typically Tropical's hit, Going To Barbados, had been appalled when he and Dave Edmunds suggested editing a multi-track master. I've always thought it was quite normal practice because it happened at my first recording session. I'm pleased it did. Years later, when I lived in France, there wasn't much to do on the long winter evenings so I learned how to edit tape. I'm really good at it now – I've successfully edited two-inch, twenty-four track tapes while recording engineers have stood by shitting themselves.

Back then I wasn't quite so capable. I was probably as pissed as a parrot. To be honest I felt like a spare part most of the time. I didn't really know what was going on. Some time at the end of the '80s I bumped into Nick and we got talking about Whole Wide World. 'It's a great sounding record,' I said. 'I don't know how you did it.' And he said, 'Oh, it was just the Velvet Underground song book. I didn't do anything really, it was all down to you – you sang it.' I was really made up by that because Nick Lowe will always be a hero for me, even though I don't get into the stuff he's doing now so much. At that time I was amazed to find that he was into the Velvet Underground but of course it makes absolute sense – you can hear it in the chord structures on a lot of his early solo stuff. Well, I think you can anyway.

By the time Nick had put the Duane Eddy guitar on the end it was time to call it a day, even though I hadn't put the finished vocal on. We were supposed to have the whole A and B sides finished and mixed in eight hours but Jake came round with some cans of Red Stripe, heard it and decided it was going to be a two-session job. He was really pleased. We all went to the Red Cow in Hammersmith to see The Damned and then Bazza very kindly gave me a lift back to Wandsworth in a dilapidated Morris van.

I went back a few days later to record the vocal and that's when Elvis Costello was there, but he fucked off before I got started. It took quite some time to do the vocal – I wasn't at all confident about my singing ability but Nick knew what he wanted from me. Originally when I went to Stiff I thought that the most I could expect was that they'd give my songs to somebody else to do. But Nick assured me that part of my appeal was my voice, which he thought would sound great coming out of a transistor radio.

Nick was apparently one of the crowd of people, along with The Damned and Huey Lewis, who were cluttering up the office when I went in with my tape. Later he said that he thought I was such a strange person that he went to listen to the tape immediately. Afterwards he hurtled downstairs to get Jake who flipped and said, 'Get hold of this weirdo – where did he go?' It took them three days to find me, when I finally answered the payphone on Thursday morning.

Whole Wide World was by far the best vocal performance I came up with on Stiff. Nick gave me the time to do it – he was very patient, going through it bit by bit. We used a big old Neuman valve microphone and there was no pop shield other than the one covering the actual microphone. Later on, especially when my 'career' was careering down the slippery slope, I became quite used to studios where I had to sing in front of part of a pair of ladies' tights stretched and sewn over a loop of coathanger wire. It's supposed to stop you getting too close to the microphone. It's a stupid idea for the most part. Nick showed me how to almost kiss the microphone – '...where the Caribbean sea is blue,' and the word 'blue' had to be sung so close to mike that it would sound as though I was singing directly into the ear of every girl that heard it. I was going to break their hearts. It was just what I wanted to do.

It was a bit of an anticlimax. I had to start looking around for another job so I signed up with Manpower in the Walworth Road. I went to the Walworth Road place rather than the more up-market Jermyn Street branch because Walworth Road dealt with manual labour and I didn't actually think I was a contender for any other work. I didn't want a job that I'd have to get involved in,

like at Corona Lemonade, because it was obvious to me
that there weren't any jobs that were actually at all interesting, not if all you wanted to do was be a pop singer.

I had little or no confidence and I was going through a
Dickensian phase – I looked like something out of Oliver.
My work prospects were definitely not very good but it
didn't matter because I was soon going to have a record
out. It didn't bother me that we hadn't finished the B side
– I just sort of assumed they'd ring me up and fix a date to
get that sorted out. I didn't want to ring them because I
didn't want to seem pushy.

I can't stand pushiness but sadly it's the way things
are, especially in the music business. It seems to be the
people that make the most noise about themselves that
get somewhere. You've got to be seen to be 'hungry' –
hungry for success. It was worse in the '80s when uncool
was the new cool. I was in the VIP bar at the Limelight
Club one night in 1987 – I'd only got in because I was
with a friend of Shane MacGowan's and we had the mis-
fortune to be out with Shane MacGowan (who stank of
piss, by the way). I was incredibly bored because I didn't
drink any more. I found the Limelight VIP bar very
depressing. It was full of large people filling the air with
talk about themselves. Occasionally I spotted someone
I'd seen on the telly or on a record sleeve, but mostly they
were self-important nobodies. A big groovy guy said to a
fat businessman, 'The band's ready to roll and we want
you to manage us – we're gonna be big, fucking big,'…
Big people with big hair in the big time being big. Fucking
big. I hated the '80s. Before we left I took my chewing
gum out and stuck it on the seat. As we were walking out
I glanced round in time to see Paul Young, dressed in a
sharkskin suit, lowering his arse on to it.

So I saw out November and December of 1976 doing menial jobs through Manpower Services. I worked in a packing department for a couple of days, got a call to get myself down to Arding & Hobbs department store in Clapham Junction where a lorry needed unloading, spent a few days in the basement of the Army & Navy stores in Victoria moving bed bases and assorted furniture items around – at this one I worked with some of the resting thespians from Jermyn Street. They could have been the same people that later made it into the VIP bar at the Limelight – wankers.

I had a few pleasant days at the Oyez stationery company in Long Lane, Bermondsey, where I met a fellow Manpower employee, Steve Smith, who was then the singer and harmonica player in a South London band called S.A.L.T. Later on he surfaced in Bad Manners. We had a terrific time – Steve was one of the few Manpower people with a sense of humour, or a sense of the ridiculous more like. They sent us into an empty and semi-derelict part of the building where there were loads of cardboard boxes containing the confidential files of a lot of former Oyez employees. Our job was to tear them all in half, put them into bin liners and take them out to the rubbish. We spent a lot of time reading them, of course. We'd set aside the most lurid and interesting ones, tear a few up and take a break. Then, reclining on a bin liner or two, I'd read the files out loud accompanied by Stevie's harmonica. What a team – we should have made a record.

I spent some time in the basement of the newly built St Thomas' Hospital near Waterloo. The heating and hot-water pipes had been lagged with asbestos. The world was beginning to realise that asbestos was a health hazard. The electricians wouldn't go down there to perform essential wiring and maintenance work so they called in Manpower and we went down there in nylon boilersuits, headgear and special breathing masks and lagged the pipes again over the asbestos lagging with bandages and quick-drying liquid plaster that had to be painted on to the bandages with a brush – they let me do that bit because I'd been to art school. The boilersuits, headgear and breathing apparatus were taken off us to be destroyed every lunchtime and evening, and we had to sign a disclaimer in case we got cancer in years to come, so they were definitely taking it seriously. So much so, in fact, that we got ten pence an hour over and above the normal Manpower rate. While we were there the Queen came to officially open the building.

When we came back from the pub after lunch the red carpet was down and the hospital staff – everybody from the board of governors to the most presentable representatives of the nursing, portering and cleaning staff – were getting ready to welcome Her Majesty with a big hurrah. But no representative from the Asbestos Rescue Unit – we were ordered to stay in the basement until the Queen had gone home. I suppose they didn't want her catching cancer off us. At least I can say I've had the pleasure of working under the Queen.

Around Christmas time they sent us to the Tannoy factory in Thornton Heath. They were moving everything into one building and our job was to clear out the stores from a sub-basement level building. We had to bring everything up to ground level, load it into a truck, wait for a responsible and qualified person to drive it across the road and unload it all again. We did most of the loading and unloading in driving snow with ice underfoot. Apart from being dangerous, it was a frustrating job because there were loads of components – I knew they were good, but I didn't know quite what was what so I didn't know what to nick. So I didn't nick anything except an old wooden stool, which I took home with me on the bus. Anyone who saw Ian Dury on the first Stiff Tour will have seen that stool. He commandeered it from my house, sat on it to play the drums through my set and used it as a prop in his. It was stolen by a fan on the next tour he did. I'd like it back please – it had a cushion gaffa-taped to it that Sue's mum gave us.

I was getting to know the regular Manpower work-force by now. They were awful. There was a bloke who'd been in the army. He had a little moustache and a pair of spectacles that knew more than he did. I'd worked with him on the Arding & Hobbs campaign, the Army & Navy job, and a lot of other dumb assignments too. He was one of the keen ones – if the job finished early he'd go back to the office to get another one whereas I'd just go to the pub and try and forget about it. Every time we stacked something up on top of something else, or shunted something large into an available space, he'd say, 'Boof! Sorted!' and his glasses would twinkle in agreement. I never knew his name. I just thought of him as the Twat.

There was another one called Tom. Tom came from Plumstead and his obsessions were Real Ale and Socialism. Him and the Twat hated each other, though in a parallel dimension they would have made an excellent set of book ends, or a promising start to a very worth-while collection of toby jugs. Tom was a gangly fuckwit in his late forties with wild grey hair. He also wore glasses, but his glasses weren't intelligent. They just came to work with him on the bus and clung on like a retarded child in a shopping centre. He ranted on about the rights and plight of the working man, and spouted facts about real ale, often referring to a tattered copy of the Camra Real Ale guide, which he carried in a pocket of his gabardine. The first thing he did when he arrived at a job was to ascertain where the nearest real ale pub was and inform everybody else so that we'd be all right at lunchtime.

Tom made the Twat furious. The Twat said Real Ale was stupid – there was no such thing. Though if there was no such thing I can't see how it could have been stupid. But he'd turn to the rest of us, glasses pleading, as he reasoned over and over, 'Ale's ale...' The Twat read the *Sun*. Tom read the *Daily Mirror*. They were just different versions of the same stupid person. Tom came to a bit of a sticky end – an accident in the workplace. In a playful moment, having consumed a quantity of real ale at lunchtime, he bet us all that he could swing out of the back of the truck by holding on to the webbing strap that you use to pull the roller door shut. He was going to do a Tarzan act – show us all who was boss. He was goaded on by the Twat who I'm sure, with his army training, was able to see exactly what was going to happen. It was obvious. Instead of swinging out gracefully and leaping to the ground with one of those idiotic 'Huppla!' exclamations, thus establishing the supremacy of Real Ale and Socialism over Right-Wing Military Imperialism, the roller door descended with him and he landed on his back in a heap of brown dust-coated gangliness and pebble glasses. He looked like an illustration from some comical Victorian book. He was very lucky not to have broken his back. He got up and hobbled through the rest of the afternoon but I could see that he was really hurt. He didn't come in to work the next day. I never saw him again. We made an agreement and everybody said that he'd slipped and fallen – that way he'd get some compensation. He had four kids and we heard that he was going to be off work for a long time.

By February we'd done Tannoy and I was sent to the newly built National Theatre to help out in the maintenance department. That was quite a cushy job for the most part. They'd send me off to a far-flung corner of the building with some plastic rubbish sacks and I'd do a bit of tidying up. It was quite good because I was the only Manpower person there so I didn't have to put up with a lot of morons, thespians and over-willing students. It was almost ideal until they sent me up into one of the cooling towers. If you cross Waterloo Bridge heading north towards Covent Garden you can see the cooling tower in question – it's on the southwest corner, nearest to the bridge. You'll recognise it as a cooling tower because it's got lots of vertical slits running down the sides of it. In February 1977 I was working behind those slits on a daily basis.

I had to clear away all the debris that the builders had left behind. That was a laugh because there was only one way down: I had to chuck it all in the lift that the actors used – paint cans, old cement bags, planks, oil drums, rubble – it all had to go down in the lift. I mingled with a lot of eminent directors, playwrights and actors who shared the lift with me. Some got quite annoyed but most of them treated me with indifference, as though it was the most normal thing in the world to share a lift with a scruffy urchin and a lot of rubbish in between acts two and three of Othello. If anybody spoke to me they were usually patronising. One very important looking gentleman looked down his big nose at me and said: 'You're becoming quite a fixture in this lift, going up and down with your bags of rubbish. Never mind – as long as you're enjoying yourself!' And he and his colleagues ha ha ha'd their way out of the lift. One day I was going to meet these fuckers on equal terms.

I got rid of as much rubbish as I could find and reported back to the maintenance department. They sent me back with a wire brush and told me to clean the rust off all the metalwork on the cooling fins. After a couple of days when I'd done all that, and taken a bag full of rust dust and paint flakes down in the lift, they gave me a paint brush and a big can of yellow paint and told me to paint everything yellow. They didn't even come and inspect the job to see if I done it correctly. I can't really blame them because it was a bit cold up there, what with all the slits. Smashing views, but very draughty.

I don't think the girls in the Manpower office liked me much. Days went by without the payphone ever ringing, and when I rang them all the jobs were gone. Then one night they rang and asked if I'd like a cleaning job at the Tarmac Roadstone depot in Greenwich for a few days. I had to be there at eight in the morning. It was nearly fucking impossible – train to Waterloo from Wandsworth Town, then a hike over to Waterloo East, another train to London Bridge and yet another train to Greenwich. I expect they normally would have given the job to Tom but he was off work with a bad back.

I bet they had a right fucking laugh about this one back at the office. When I got there I cleaned the canteen, which wasn't too bad, then I had to clean the toilets. It was disgusting. It seemed that before I arrived the whole workforce had had a go at using them and missed, and then cleaned themselves up as best they could with pages torn from the *Daily Mirror* which they'd left strewn around the floor. I had to do the best I could and then scrub everything down with a strong solution of Sanilav.

The next day it was the same again. I couldn't take it so I walked out and went home. Except I didn't go straight home – I got off the train at Clapham Junction and went into the Job Centre. I'd fallen a long way since I'd gone in there and scored a job as a quality control inspector. Today I was interested in a vacancy as a table-clearer in a cafeteria. I hoped that none of the Job Centre staff would remember me, but there was little chance of that because I was starting to look like a down-and-out.

The woman called them – 'We have someone interested in your vacancy...' and fixed me up with an interview. She advised me to wear something smart. The cafeteria was in the basement of Swan & Edgars department store at Piccadilly Circus. It's Tower Records now. You can buy a re-release of my first record in the building I worked in when it first came out. I got the job because I was the only candidate that could write their own name on the application form. I started the following day. Not that they were desperate or anything.

It wasn't all gloom and doom, it just mostly was. When the winter set in we realised that the downside of having a lovely big flat with lots of rooms was that we couldn't afford to heat it so we spent all our time in one small room, which we also slept in. We didn't have a TV and there came a point when we couldn't afford to go to the pub any more so we stayed in and huddled round a convector heater – one of those bronzey brown ones with a red light bulb behind a beige grill.

Sometimes, if we could afford the coal, we lit a fire. For a while we burned the worst of Mrs Sprogis' furniture. The previous tenant had shoved a collection of Sprogis wardrobes in the shed and there were some chairs in the cellar. They all went up in flames. Anything that was dry got burnt, but mostly we used the heater. We had the heater, cans of Long Life and playing cards.

Not long after the Whole Wide World recording sessions I went to a gig at the Victoria Theatre: Graham Parker & The Rumour supported by the Tyla Gang and The Damned. The Damned were fantastic and they finished up by demolishing the drumkit. The Tyla Gang were disappointing after the Styrofoam single. For the length of one side of a record you could almost believe that Sean Tyla was a crazed American weirdo. I think he was an ex-policeman in real life – he certainly behaved like one. I met him once in the office. Suzanne said, 'Sean, this is Eric', and the belligerent Sean said, 'Yeah I know it is.' I asked him how he knew: 'Because it's written on your head in ballpoint,' he snapped. It wasn't but he'd probably been checking up.

I can't even remember much about Graham Parker & The Rumour that night. I expect they were very good. I had to meet Nick and Jake in the pub round the corner so that I could get in without paying. John Peel drifted past wearing brightly patched denim flairs. He had lots of long hair even though he was receding. He was probably still at the point where he wasn't going to play any Sex Pistols records on his programme.

A tall character came over to the table and had a word with Jake who said something and pointed to me. The tall character came over and said: 'Hello, Eric, my name's Lee Brilleau. I've heard a lot of good things about you. It's a pleasure to meet you at last.'

I'd just met one of my heroes. I was introduced to Dave Edmunds and I spent some time in the bar with Lee and also Lew Lewis who'd just been kicked out of Eddie & The Hot Rods, which I think is quite an accolade. He'd made a single for Stiff – Caravan Man and Boogie On The Street. It sounded almost like an American record. It was very basic – I think they recorded it on a Revox.

There was an aftershow party, backstage in the artists' bar. I'd never been to anything like that before. It was full of large, self-important people – much like the Limelight Club later on.

Nick Lowe said to me, 'There's someone you ought to meet who you'll probably get on with – Ian Dury.' I was nearly lost for words. I knew he was around. The Kilburns had split up but Ian was managed by Blackhill who had the offices above the Stiff shop. I remember Nick pointing him out one day as he walked past the window looking quite dejected and wearing an old lady's raincoat – quite possibly the same one he later wore on the cover of Stiffs Live Stiffs. He was carrying a couple of plastic bags full of lyrics. Nobody wanted to sign him.

And here he was now, standing in the corner with what looked like a pair of torn French knickers tied round his neck. I managed to blurt out something stupid and embarrassing, the way you do when you meet your hero. Ian always reckoned I told him he was the best lyric-writer in the country and this pleased him very much. As I remember, he thought I was taking the piss and called his minder, Fred, to come and sort me out. He was with a beautiful black girl, Denise Roudette. She convinced him that I was serious and soon we were getting on fine. Fred was Fred Rowe and he wasn't exactly Ian's minder because Ian didn't have the money to pay a minder. But Fred had been the Kilburns' roadie, although in real life he was a professional cat burglar and hard man, and Ian's downstairs neighbour.

They took me back to Wandsworth in Fred's old Commer van. Ian gave me his number and told me to call the next day and arrange to come and see him. I felt very strange and shy about phoning him but I did it, and he asked me to come round to his place, 40 Oval Mansions, after work. Ian's place has been written variously as Cat Shit or Cat Piss mansions, which was how Ian referred to it after he'd got successful and moved out. It wasn't that bad for a flat in what could now be considered as Central London. The area was a bit rough – there were a few muggings but that was nothing unusual for South London, and most of the walls were made of lath and plaster with a bit of horsehair thrown in. You could probably hear what they were doing next door.

I was a bit early so I stopped off at a pub for a quick drink. I needed one anyway, to steady my nerves. The Bill Grundy Show was on the TV, perched on a shelf over the door to the Gents. I sat down with my drink just as he introduced the Sex Pistols. I saw the whole swearing episode. There were a few decrepit individuals dotted around the saloon bar but nobody paid it any attention. I'd never heard the word 'fuck' uttered on TV but I found it curiously unshocking because I heard the word and used it myself on a daily basis.

I went round to Oval Mansions and rang the bell. A sash window was thrown open four floors up and Ian's head appeared. He threw down a Yale key attached to a red handkerchief. I let myself in and climbed up the stairs. He met me at the door. 'Come in and sit down,' he said, 'I'm just finishing something off with Chas.'

I misheard Chas as *chairs* and as I knew he'd been to art school I thought he was maybe doing some sculpture. But when I got in, 'chairs' was Chas Jankel, a man with a Davy Jones haircut, clutching a semi-acoustic Gibson. The room overlooked the Oval Cricket Ground though I probably couldn't see that at the time because it was November and it was dark. There was a table in front of the window spread out with large sheets of paper. Ian sat at the table and Chas occupied the only other chair, so I sat on the edge of the bed and listened as they finished off a new song, Sweet Gene Vincent. Then Chas left for a gig.

Ian questioned me closely about Stiff Records. We talked about songwriting and he wanted to know why I thought he was good. I told him how much I admired him for his Englishness – we weren't American so why should we feel obliged to write American lyrics and sing them in phoney American accents.

I was surprised to find how much Ian was influenced by American culture – Pop Art, rock 'n' roll and jazz, which he synthesised through a provincial English perspective and made his own. You can see the same thing in the painting of Bo Diddley by Ian's friend and mentor, Peter Blake. It's an English experience of Bo Diddley, provincial and slightly second-hand in that it's actually a painting of an image on an LP sleeve.

We became friends and met up regularly. One day Ian said to me, 'I've heard some of your stuff – I went down to Stiff and got them to play it for me.' I must have looked mortified but he smiled and said, 'It's all right – it's nowhere near as bad as I thought it'd be.' A few months later he was working with Norman Watt Roy recording *New Boots & Panties*. Norman remembers Ian telling him about me very early on – 'There's this young geezer called Wreckless Eric, he's a better lyric-writer than I am.' Ian could see my potential but he wasn't going to tell me that. It was his way of looking after me. He worried about my meteoric rise with Stiff, thought it was too much too soon and he was absolutely right. I made all my mistakes in public.

One Saturday we went for an early evening drink in a pub called The Rising Sun, just off the Clapham High Street. We were the only customers and the landlord was quite friendly – sometimes they weren't because we looked a bit of a sight really. We got our drinks and sat down at a table near the bar. I became aware of another customer. He was the kind of person that I thought only existed in comic strips – a self educated. He had horn rimmed glasses, a mop of mousey blonde hair and an armful of library books which he placed on the bar. He tried to engage the landlord in conversation – current affairs topics, that sort of thing, but the landlord wasn't having any of it.

Meanwhile Ian was holding forth. He was telling me how he originally thought of calling the Kilburns Cripple, Nigger, Irish, Polak & Jew. Suddenly the bookworm strutted over to our table looking furious:

'Excuse me – I couldn't help but overhear your offensive remarks about Jews. Are you Jewish? Are you yourself a Jew?'

Ian considered the situation for an instant. Then he snapped his leg-iron into place, stood up and hobbled over to the man. He looked up into his face and said quite calmly, 'No mate, I'm Irish.'

I was nearly filling up with tears. The landlord rushed round from the bar and said, 'Right! That's it – you finish your drink and leave.' For a minute I thought he meant us, but he was pointing at the bookworm. He said, 'I won't have people like that in my pub.'

Afterwards we went to the chip shop so that Ian could get fish and chips to take home for him and Denise. I always had the impression that Ian lived on fish and chips – fish, chips, kebabs and the odd slice of toast. The chip shop man asked us if we were from the circus that was setting up on the Common. Ian thought that was very funny and so did I. It was something that we both remembered years later, shortly before he died.

Denise came to stay at Melody Road while Ian got on with some writing. She installed herself in the front room with her bass guitar and a practise amp. I knew she played the bass and wondered if she'd play with me but I was too shy to ask her. I mentioned this to Ian but he didn't seem keen so I didn't push it. I think Denise wanted to play with me too, and when she came to stay at my place nobody could stop us.

She used to practise all the time. She had a job working in a café restaurant in Clapham. She only worked Sundays but she earned enough from that to live on. I really wished I could get a job like that but for the moment I was stuck with Swan & Edgars. I'd come in from a day's table clearing she'd be hard at it with the bass. We started to play some of my songs. We were both very shy about it – we giggled a lot and I can imagine that we looked around to make sure no one was watching. Denise was insecure about her bass playing ability and I wasn't at all confident about my songs, especially in front of Denise because she'd worked for the Kilburns and was obviously a big inspiration to Ian. I was sure she'd think they were rubbish, but she didn't. We worked on it every night and I spent all day in the cafeteria looking forward to the evening when we could have another go.

Soon, Denise went back to Oval Mansions. I was really sad because I thought the playing might be over, but she kept on coming round and we got more and more stuff together.

One day Ian announced that he was coming over too. He wanted to see what we were up to. I think he thought we were having an affair. He was quite surprised at how much we'd got done. He made us play everything for him and then he made us play it all again. His eyes were shining and, knowing him as I do now, I can see that he was very pleased with us.

He said we needed a drummer and made me get him

an enamel washing-up bowl and a Party Seven can out of
the garden, which he played with a couple of Bic ball-
points. A few days later he was back with drum sticks
and shortly after that Fred rolled up in the Commer van
with a fire-damaged Olympic drum kit, liberated from
the back of a second-hand shop in Bermondsey without
the owner's permission. Suddenly we were almost a real
group.

We set up in the front room, in the bay window. The
thought of any disturbance we might be causing the
neighbours never bothered us. We only ever had one
complaint and that was sometime after eleven o'clock at
night when Ian was helping Denise to 'sit on the bass
drum' by playing it as hard as he could, four to the bar. A
bloke from upstairs knocked on the door and asked if we
could make less noise. Ian was quite put out by the inter-
ruption. 'Tell them we're busy working in here,' he
shouted.

I gave up working at the cafeteria sometime in April '77.
Stiff put out a compilation, *A Bunch Of Stiffs*, with
Whole Wide World on it. The release date was April 1st.
That's right – my first record came out on April Fool's
day. One afternoon, a couple of days before the release,
when I was drudging my way round the cafeteria, I said
to myself: 'Fuck this, I'm a recording artist – what am I
doing here?' So I left my trolley, full of scraps of half-
eaten dinners, and headed off for the office to pick up a
pre-release copy of the album.

I tumbled out into the falling night without even looking at the cover. I hardly dared in case my track had been
excluded at the last moment. But there I was on the inner
cover, stoned, immaculate, in the darkness next to a globe
in Chris Gabrin's studio last November. And next to it:

Wreckless Eric

Go The Whole Wide World

Written by Eric.
An exciting new songwriting
addition to the scene.

Wreckless comes from Hull.
His opening gambit – "I'm one of
those cxnxs that brings tapes
into record companies" – landed
him a lucrative contract.

I didn't even mind that they'd got it wrong and said I came from Hull. At least they'd been listening when I said I was a cunt. I rushed home. Sue was there when I got in and we put the record on. I can hardly describe the strangeness of hearing your first record for the first ever time on a record player. It sounded fantastic, and the louder and the more times we played it the better it sounded. We looked at the cover, scrutinised every inch of it, propped it up on the mantlepiece, played some of the other tracks and came back to mine. We always came back to mine. It was a hit record that I'd known all my life.

It was another anticlimax – where do you go from there? I couldn't keep playing it all night and there was an excitement inside me that I could barely contain. We went out and had a few drinks – that is, I had a few drinks, Sue probably only had a couple.

As I said, I decided to give up work. I tried to get the sack so that I could go on the dole. The cafeteria was too depressing, I never saw any daylight because it was on a mezzanine floor in the basement above menswear. It was a hangout for elderly, faded actresses and middle-aged gay men who kept asking me to meet them after work for a drink – I'm sure I could have made quite a good living as a rent boy and male prostitute.

People who hadn't got the imagination to go and eat somewhere nice came along at lunchtime and ordered half a chicken with boiled rice and overcooked vegetables. I'd spot them from the other end of the cafeteria and lurk by the table while they pecked at what they couldn't bring themselves to eat. When they realised their mistake I'd pounce, carrying off the untouched chicken like a vulture. And that would be my lunch. If they weren't quick enough at giving up on it I'd encourage them by wiping the table for them with one of my disgusting dish-cloths.

I had various strategies for getting the sack. I arrived late every day. I took long lunch breaks and came back drunk. That didn't work – they just stopped my pay for the time I wasn't there. And they were used to drunks – they quite often recruited casual labour from the Charring Cross arches. As long as they looked clean. I was rude to customers and management alike. But they wouldn't sack me. I even tried lighting up a cigarette next to a No Smoking sign in menswear. Smoking anywhere other than the staff canteen meant immediate dismissal so I did it in full view of the security guard. He took the cigarette off me, crushed it out and reported me for trying to get the sack.

One morning the manager asked me why I was late.

'It's none of your fucking business,' I replied.

'I know that you're trying to get the sack,' he said. 'You just want to claim unemployment benefit. But it won't work.'

I did my best to look shocked at the suggestion – 'Unemployment benefit? I've got a private income. I'm only here gathering material for my book.'

There was nothing I could do so I gave up and handed in my notice.

On my last day I spent all afternoon loading up the trolley. It was a big industrial thing with two large open containers, one for tea slops and other fluids, and another for leftover food. It had trays underneath for cups and saucers and plenty of room on top for dinner plates. I usually took it back to the kitchen at regular intervals and unloaded it, but not this afternoon. By four o'clock I could hardly push it and the slightest movement sent cascades of disgusting liquid slopping over the sides. The plates were piled so high that I couldn't see over the top of them.

It was an easy mistake to make, a disaster just waiting to happen. Carefully checking to make sure there was nobody underneath, I misjudged a turn by the stairs. One wheel went over and that was it – the whole lot crashed and clattered down half a flight into menswear – broken china, rancid tea, chicken skin, cabbage, bones, milk, gravy, lemon meringue pie, teaspoons, liver, curry and rice and peas and chips and knives and forks in a lake of oozing liquid… It was a mess.

I had to spend the rest of my shift clearing it up – they said I wouldn't get paid until it was done. But it was worth it. They had to admit that it could have happened to anybody, but why was the trolley so full? As if they couldn't guess.

I signed on and claimed benefit. They paid me eleven pounds a week but I wasn't really any worse off. Table-clearing only paid twenty-eight pounds a week and by the time they'd taken off tax and insurance and I'd paid my fares and had something to eat (or drink) at lunchtime, most of it was gone.

I decided to become a home handyman. It was quite easy, I just put some cards up in newsagents' windows around Wandsworth and waited for the phone to ring. An old lady up the road employed me for two hours every Wednesday morning. I had to mow the lawns, clip the hedge, weed the flowerbeds and do a few other bits and pieces like mending the garden gate and replacing a worn-out curtain rail. I started at ten, did an hour of this sort of thing and then it was time for elevenses. She sat me down in the kitchen and gave me a cup of tea and a slice of lemon drizzle cake and we'd have a chat about this and that.

My number was passed around the old lady mafia. I soon had a string of clients and I'd spend most mornings clipping hedges, weeding, hoeing, oiling hinges, patching up fences and doing the odd bit of painting and decorating. It was a perfect occupation for someone like me. And all the time the benefit was rolling in; I just had to sign for it once a week and worry that they'd catch me out. But they never did.

It was a glorious existence. The famous summer of '77 was gearing up and the days were getting hotter and hotter. Ian and Denise came round most afternoons to rehearse. We were planning a B side.

I didn't generally communicate very well with Stiff – it's was the common music business problem – everybody was too busy. They hadn't got time to talk to you and find out what was going on, what you wanted or what you needed. If you couldn't talk in banner headlines you were fucked. Ian knew this and he became my go-between.

He persuaded them to pay for some demo time in a ramshackle four-track studio near Tower Bridge. We took the results in and played them to Dave Robinson. He thought they were fine – 'very good' were his exact words. I suppose they were OK considering it was only the second time I'd ever been in a recording studio. I remember that meeting well. It was a Saturday afternoon, the only time Dave could fit us into his busy schedule managing Graham Parker & The Rumour. Ian asked if Stiff could see their way to paying me a retainer so that I could concentrate on my songwriting instead of wasting my time doing menial work. He asked for thirty pounds a week. Robinson could hardly look at us. He was unshaven and his eyes were red-rimmed. He looked as though he'd been up all night. He was evasive and one way or another he turned us down with a flip comment. 'Very interesting,' he said.

When *A Bunch Of Stiffs* came out it was a different matter. Whole Wide World was John Peel's first choice, he played it on the Friday after the album came out. I listened in absolute shock. It was reviewed in all the music papers and my track seemed to be the favourite. Ian encouraged me to keep going into the office to remind them of my existence. One sunny morning I was sitting in the famous aircraft seats in the front office. Dave came and sat next to me. He said, 'Whole Wide World seems to be getting a lot of attention, we're thinking of taking it off the album as a single. We'll need a B side – have you got anything?'

'Yes,' I said. 'It's called Semaphore Signals.'

Ian was the obvious choice as a producer. We decided to record it in a four-track studio in Wimbledon called Alvic where Ian was making demos of the songs that eventually appeared on *New Boots & Panties*. But first we had to practise the song at my place until it was perfect.

I got the idea for Semaphore Signals on the top of a 168 bus coming home from work one night along the Wandsworth Road. It was another two-chord job. I wanted it to be like a Who number, like Happy Jack, with explosive instrumental sections. But it came out like me because I can't really do other people.

Denise came up with a strange and wonderful bass line. Every bass player I've worked with since has had trouble with it and yet it sounds so simple.

Ian always said he was the best drummer I ever had. I can't really tell if he was or not. His style was unusual but it worked well. His left arm and leg were very weak because of the polio. His bass drum was strong but he used it sparingly and led with his right hand on the hi-hat. He kept the hi-hat clamped shut and didn't use his left leg at all. He played the snare with his left hand – almost dropping the stick onto it. He had one rack tom, which he only ever hit with his right hand, and no floor tom. He didn't play drum fills like any other drummer – he'd do something odd between the snare and tom or between his collection of huge cymbals. If it hadn't been for the polio he would probably have been a renowned jazz drummer. He used very light sticks but when he wanted to he had a vicious hit that made his playing very loud.

He'd come in, sit down and start playing time. Then he'd chant: 'Hit me with your rhythm stick, hit me, hit me, hit me...' I never imagined it would become a number one hit – a number one conceived at Number One Melody Road.

We recorded Semaphore Signals two days after my birthday, on the 20th May, 1977. We got started early, took all our 'bits', as Denise called them, down there in a Sandy McNab, as Ian called it. We were pretty nervous – at least I was, and Denise looked petrified. It had been a hell of a week. Ian had been domineering, overbearing and given to fits of frustrated anger when we couldn't do what he imagined in his head. Sometimes he got stroppy with me but most of his anger was directed at Denise. Once she left the room and didn't come back. We searched the flat and found her hiding in the cellar. Ian was probably more nervous than we were – he'd never produced a record and I don't think he ever did again. It mattered to him that we got it right and sometimes he couldn't see that we were doing the best we could. We weren't like other groups – as musicians we were completely unschooled – none of us had ever had a lesson, we did everything in our own entirely individual fashion.

The rehearsals really paid off – we had the backing track down in three or four takes. To make room for the overdubs we had to bounce the whole lot down to one track. I did the vocal and Ian overdubbed a couple of drum bits and then we realised the guitar was a bit low in the mix. There wasn't anything we could do about that because it was on a track with the bass on drums so I put another one on. Feeling a bit more confident now, I turned the amp up full to get some feedback, like on a Who record. It really took off. We made a rough mix and took it to Stiff for approval. Everybody loved it and we went back in one evening a couple of days later to mix it. We were a winning team.

It was a wonderful summer. I got very fit clipping hedges, mowing lawns and clearing overgrown gardens. Humphrey Ocean lived round the corner. He was the original bass player in Kilburn & The High Roads. One afternoon Humphrey came round to a rehearsal and bought Davey Payne with him. Davey played the saxophone in the Kilburns. It was a strange thing – I'd seen Davey make a guest appearance with a band called the Fabulous Poodles only a few days before. I thought at the time how fantastic it would be to have him in the band, and here he was. He listened to us crank out a few tunes and said, 'I'll be back tomorrow with my saxophones if that's all right.'

Ian was suddenly on Stiff Records too, and there was talk of a package tour – Nick Lowe, Elvis Costello, Larry Wallis, Ian and me. Whole Wide World came out as a single. It got a ridiculous amount of airplay. There were so many requests for it on Annie Nightingale's programme that the producer had to do an investigation to find out if we were sending them in ourselves. But we weren't. It was 'Single Of The Week' in all the music papers and number one in the *Time Out* Alternative Chart. It stayed there for weeks. Elton John reviewed it for *Record Mirror*. It was the only record he liked – he said it reminded him of The Troggs. I started getting fan mail from girls.

Ian was recording *New Boots & Panties*. Me and Denise went to see him at the studio and got dressed up in funny clothes to make him laugh. I went as a village idiot from Ohio – very small tartan jacket, large drip-dry shirt, braces, bow tie and a homemade haircut. There was a photo session the next morning because the package tour had become a reality. Nick, Elvis and Larry had a lot of trouble looking cool next to a couple of congenital English eccentrics – I was still wearing my village idiot outfit and Ian wore his mum's mac. The others all wore black and tried to look rock 'n' roll. I think we let the side down magnificently.

We had to rehearse properly in a rehearsal studio. I'd never been in one of these before and I thought we sounded better in my front room. They fixed up two warm-up gigs for my band before the tour started. The first was at Barbarellas in Birmingham, supporting The Damned. It was my first professional gig. We had roadies and everything. We weren't advertised but when Dave and Jake saw me and Denise carefully tuning up, obviously taking it very seriously, they sent instructions to the DJ to announce us as Wreckless Eric. The crowd were all young punk kids and they went bonkers. We had a great time and I even got a kid up from the audience to play the spoons.

The next night we played with the George Hatcher Band at Oxford Polytechnic. That wasn't so exciting because the George Hatcher Band all seemed to be blokes from the Midlands with little moustaches, feathered mullets, gold-topped Les Pauls and huge white flairs. I don't think Oxford Polytechnic was ready for us but Humphrey came along with Paul Tonkinson, the guy on the back cover of the Kilburns album, and while we played they danced all over the otherwise empty floor. Afterwards one of the George Hatcher Band asked me if Denise was available. I found that very offensive so I pointed to Fred Rowe and said, 'He'll fix you up.'

We did a John Peel session and the Stiffs Live Stiffs tour was announced with the village idiot pictures on the front of all the music papers. Sue made me a jacket out of candlewick bedspreads especially for the tour and I covered my Top Twenty guitar with Co-op stamps. The first night was at High Wycombe Town Hall. The second night was at Aberystwyth, and then it was Bristol. After that it's just a blur. Everybody got fifty pounds a week and the playing order changed every night. In the end it was a battle for supremacy between Ian and Elvis so the two of them alternated top billing.

I felt very insecure and started drinking too much. It was different now – on fifty pounds a week I was soon getting through whole bottles of gin and vodka. Something had changed. We were no longer a little family unit with our whacky clothes and funny, home-made music. The music business had bust in and run amok through what Ian later described as our 'good little bohemian thing'. And Ian changed into a person I didn't know, somebody I didn't like. The same thing was happening to me too.

Ten years later I rang Ian from the mental hospital where I was having my nervous breakdown.

'Do you want a visit?' he asked. And he was there the following afternoon. I loved Ian for that. He turned up in a Nissan Micra driven by the Sulphate Strangler, a seven-foot giant who used to be our roadie. They brought Ian's mum with them too and we all went for a walk round the hospital grounds. Ian said he'd seen it coming for years.

'I know when you stopped liking yourself,' he said, 'because it happened about the same time that I stopped liking myself.'

He told me to look after my talent and my talent would look after me. It's a piece of advice that I've never forgotten. He was absolutely right – Ian was always right in the end. I miss him terribly.

I can't really begin to describe the time I spent as a Stiff recording artist. If I got started on that I'd have to write a book about Stiff Records. There isn't room in this one, and in any case, this is a book about me – I get a bit tired of promoting the name and reputation of Stiff Records. It comes back to me at times in jagged flashbacks. It was like being picked up in a tornado and whirled around, violently.

When the tornado subsided, my whole existence dropped out of the sky and hit the earth in bits and pieces.

The Slippery Slope

JUNE, 1980. WE WERE IN LA, enjoying a few days off in the sunshine while the tour manager sorted out visas for New Zealand and Australia. My second US tour had gone very well, even though Epic Records hadn't done as much promotion as they should have. They thought I wouldn't want to be bothered with too much of that sort of thing – after all, I'd only come to America for the third time in eighteen months to have a good time – I think the word 'party' was used as a verb at this point.

I was also hanging out with a glamorous record company chick. Actually I think she was a glamorous booking agency chick – not our agency, another one. She lived in a condo with a swimming pool. I had my own room at the Tropicana Motel. She had bubbly, reddish-blonde hair with sunglasses in it, and her own sports car. I didn't seem to have any money but I was on every guest list in town, and people were falling over themselves to take me out to dinner, so I survived quite well, Better than the band – they hung around the pool at the Tropicana, subsisting on a diet of waffles with maple syrup from the coffee shop.

Even with the lack of ready cash I was beginning to feel successful. I wasn't doing coke, though I could have hoovered it up by the sack, and at no expense to myself – people wanted to get next to me.

It was my mum's birthday so I rang her from my room.

'Where are you?' she asked.

'I'm in Hollywood.'

'Ooh, are you making a film?'

The sun shone every day and there were palm trees. At night I went to the Whiskey A Go Go and the Roxy with a chick on my arm and a complicated drink in my hand. Not that I was even drinking that much – I didn't need it – I was in LA, and I was successful. Luckily we got our visas – another week and I would have been sucked in. When we left I felt as though I'd crawled out of that *Rumours* LP by Fleetwood Mac.

We'd gone to Fred Bundy's Rent-A-Wreck to do a photo session for an article in Cream magazine entitled 'Stars And Their Cars'. We hired one of his cars – a pink convertible Ford Mustang with a crumpled-in front wing and a white hood that came up automatically and got stuck halfway. We cruised Sunset Boulevard with the Beach Boys playing on the radio. Fred Bundy came to one of the gigs. He brought Patty Hearst with him though I didn't get to meet her. Kim Fowley was there too. He was very tall, and he was surrounded by dubious looking young chicks. The backstage area was full of people we didn't know – it even seemed to have its own waitresses. It was a full-on creepy experience and it was really quite boring. I felt as though the only reason I was there was to demonstrate to the music industry on the West Coast that I was capable of actually doing what I was doing. It was little more than a formality – there didn't seem to be much point to any of it. I'd been thoroughly sanitised. I'd even started wearing smart clothes. I was playing the game, and I'd totally lost touch with myself.

In New Zealand and Australia I turned into a professional rock-biz puppet. Big media attention. We left LA International Airport at nine o'clock on Thursday night and landed in Auckland at seven o'clock on Saturday morning after a fifteen-hour flight. That's my version of events anyway. I'd be glad if this wasn't so, because I'm down by one Friday, and I like Fridays. Friday means no school tomorrow.

Saturday in New Zealand started with a press conference. The journalists wanted to know what I thought of New Zealand. I didn't know yet, so we reached a bit of an impasse. After that the day was mine to do anything I liked. I wanted to go shopping, but New Zealand was shut for the weekend. So I went to the hotel instead and sat in my room, which was like a set from a '50s Ideal Home Exhibition.

New Zealand was a homespun sort of place. I had the impression that someone in a municipal building somewhere had pulled a giant lever and New Zealand had shuddered to a halt for the weekend. Everybody was at home, busy making raffia mats, arranging flowers, or pegging rugs. Outside there weren't many cars. It was eerie – every classic model in perfect condition – Austin A40, Hillman Super Minx, Singer Vogue, Ford Prefect, Ford Popular, Wolsely Hornet.... And in the distance a spouting geyser. It looked like the back cover of Meccano Magazine – every month there was an illustration of the latest Dinky car in some kind of setting. New Zealand was evidently modelled on this. The latest Dinky was quite often a disappointment when you saw it for the first time in die-cast aluminium reality. New Zealand, on the other hand, wasn't at all disappointing because I had no expectations of it. I had hardly any feelings left, I just wanted to go home and buy a car.

When I finally arrived home, a couple of months later, the first thing I had to do was move house. I obviously couldn't run a car if I lived on the corner of Oxford Street and Tottenham Court Road (Hanway Street – you could see Centre Point from the living room window) because I didn't know about resident parking. The building I lived in had a new owner, the Hare Krishna organisation. They wanted to double the rent. I said they couldn't consider any increase until they'd sorted out the sanitation. They started sending people round to see me.

There was a mysterious break-in earlier in the year while I was touring Germany. The intruders got away with a pair of boots and a broken Polaroid camera. They opened a case containing a 1955 Les Paul Junior but left that behind, even though that was the most valuable thing in the flat. I got the strong impression that I was being warned off.

It's traumatic dealing with that sort of thing, hysterical girlfriend and all, down the phone from a foreign country in the middle of a tour. We were doing some dates together with Lene Lovich – they'd been tacked on to the end of our tour as an afterthought. The promotion wasn't very good – the Germans just sat on the floor and stared at us because the New Wave hadn't broken there yet. A couple of months later and they tell me it would have all been different. As it was I just wanted to cancel and go home, but they wouldn't let us. Those dates ate up all the tour profits. The last gig was in Munich. There wasn't enough money for a hotel so we drove overnight to Calais and arrived home at lunchtime, frazzled, after another seven weeks away.

There hadn't been time to do anything then about moving because I had to go to America. But now I was back. I'd been on the road for the best part of eleven months and now there were no more gigs. I had all the time in the world to find another flat, buy a car, and write an album about it all.

I'd been happy in Wandsworth so it had to be South London. I was into down-to-earth rock 'n' roll now. Rock 'n' roll was people music, and that's where people lived – South London – down among the R 'n' B bands. Car, amplifier, guitar – drive to gig, play guitar, drink pints, say goodnight, drive home, twenty quid in pocket. An evening of cover versions – from Chuck Berry to Chuck Berry taking in a spot of Chuck Berry – and hey, what about a slow blues in E? Lawdy, mama!

Did I really want to be part of that? Probably not, but I'd almost convinced myself. I just wanted to be accepted somewhere. Anywhere. I wanted to belong. So I found a flat in Stockwell. It was sixty pounds a week and it was horrible. I was offered a cheaper flat next to Regents Park but I turned that down because it wasn't South London.

48 Stockwell Green was a bad conversion job on four floors. We had the ground floor and basement. The place had been completely gutted and reconstructed with hollow plasterboard walls. If you made a sound in the basement they heard it on the top floor.

On the day we moved in, my publishers sent me a royalty cheque for a huge amount of money – enough to half buy a flat. I could have had a mortgage but that never occurred to me because I was a musician – they didn't give mortgages to musicians. everybody knew that. Someone should have put me right.

I settled in and bought a Triumph Toledo. It was like an upholstered shopping trolley – dark blue paint and light blue plastic seats. Driving around in it I felt like a plain-clothes policeman. It was OK, but my heart wasn't in it. I think I only bought it because it was for sale. I had a vague idea that the car of my dreams was a Jaguar 3.4 or a Karmen Ghia. The Jaguar would have to be bright red. Ideally the Karman Ghia would be orange and black – like a Crawfords Cream Cracker packet. And it had to have a white steering wheel.

A couple of months later, strolling down the Stockwell Road past a second-hand car dealers, I saw a red two-seater with a hard top. It was a 1957 MGA coupe, on sale for twice what it was really worth. I took it for a test drive and bought it for just a little bit less than twice what it was worth. Now I had two cars, and it was going to stay that way, because although I was beginning to get the hang of buying cars, I had no idea how to go about selling them. After about twenty-five parking tickets I managed to fill in the form and get a resident's permit for the Toledo. I had to keep driving the MG round the block until I found a non-resident's space because you were only allowed one car per resident. Either that or I parked it on a meter. My life was fucking ridiculous.

It was time to make another album. This time it was going to be different – Dave Robinson had decided that I couldn't write tunes. We were going to get someone else in to do that. I'd always thought my tunes were quite good so this came as a bit of a surprise. Stiff Records just didn't know what to do with me. Success, in their terms, was hit singles. I didn't have hit singles therefore I was a failure. I was an embarrassment to them – Dave Robinson boasted that he could sell anything to the public, even a recording of total silence entitled: 'The Wit And Wisdom Of Ronald Reagan'. But he couldn't sell me. He once told me I was his Achilles heel. I had to have a hit. Nobody at Stiff cared a damn about me, or what it did to me in the process – the little fucker had to have a hit.

All the touring, the sell-out shows (for which Stiff took all the money), the loyal fan-base – none of that seemed to count for anything. I'd been away for too long. Most of the staff didn't even know who I was. Those that did hadn't got a clue where I'd been. They said things like, 'Hello stranger!' and, 'Where have you been hiding?' Nobody ever thanked me, patted me on the back and said well done. I've always suffered from low self-esteem. Right now I didn't have any – just an ego running out of control, an accelerating drink problem and enough money to fuel it. And though I didn't know it, I was confused and deeply unhappy.

I was still on a fifty pound a week retainer from Stiff. They never accounted to me or paid me any royalties. And now that I'd been relegated to lyric-writer, Robinson had to see at least five finished lyrics on Friday afternoon before I could pick up the cash. With all that publishing money in the bank it wasn't worth the humiliation. I still did it though. I wanted to be patted on the head like a loyal dog. I should have left long ago, but I didn't dare – who'd offered me another record deal? I couldn't even write tunes.

But I had a red sports car, Italian jeans and Mexican boots. I could go to the off-licence and buy a half bottle of whisky to drink in the afternoon. I could entertain my friends, tell them how great I was, and fall slobbering to the floor in a pool of piss at two o'clock in the morning when the people upstairs came down to complain about the noise.

Tunesmiths had been found for me. They were a song-writing team called Fairweather Page. They had a publishing deal and they were really going places. They were called Martin Page and Brian Fairweather, or it could have been the other way round. They wore matching American baseball jackets with

Fairweather Page

emblazoned on the back. They'd had them specially made.

They were extremely professional. Every morning they convened round at Martin's bedsitting room, just off the Essex Road, and put in a hard day perfecting their craft. Brian was a guitarist. Martin played slap bass. They were pretty excited about working with me – it was just the boost their career needed – a connection with a 'name' artist.

I drove round there with my half-baked lyrics and we set to work. The only bit I enjoyed was driving round there – it made me feel like a real person. I didn't feel comfortable about sharing the creative process. Songwriting is like other people's sex lives – shrouded in mystery. If ever anyone asked me how I went about writing a song I used to tell them that I didn't know – it always seemed like a bit of a fluke to me, a happy accident. I wasn't going to tell them about all the boxes of embarrassing cassettes full of random guitar chords and inane vocal wittering.

The creative process with Fairweather Page was a real drag. It wasn't all their fault – though when I tell you that they later shot to fame by penning a number for Jefferson Starship entitled: We Built This City On Rock 'n' Roll, you might well disagree. The raw material, as in my half-baked lyrics, scrawled out for beer money, couldn't have been the greatest inspiration, but they attacked the project with gusto. Martin wore slippers because it was his bedsitting room, but pretty soon, with the drum machine switched on, slap bass licks and funky chords were flying around the room, they were trading falsetto harmonies and scat singing all the way to the bank.

In between, they enthused about Boz Scaggs and the new Steely Dan album. What was going on had nothing whatsoever to do with me. I suggested a trip to the pub, or maybe I should just pop to the off-licence…

Bit by bit a collection of tunes was assembled and demoed on the Fairweather Page four-track. Stiff appointed yet another producer – this time it was Bob Andrews from the Rumour. Fairweather Page were taking care of guitar and bass, and surprise, surprise – they had a couple of session-playing mates waiting in the wings to do the drums and keyboards. Stiff made a block booking at Battery Studios and Dave Robinson told me he'd secured a very good deal, which I later found out was the full going rate. Fair enough, he probably had shares in the place. From the first day it was all complete crap.

And then it was 1981 and I was sharing a flat with a young man called Rupert. Rupert was tall and good-looking in a clichéd sort of way, and although I never met his mother I could tell what she looked like from looking at him: over-large brown eyes and a long horse's nose, out of which she'd blow cigarette smoke. She probably wore expensive silk scarves – the square ones that come from exclusive department stores. In her youth a crude gentleman might have remarked that she had legs that went all the way up to her bum. But they wouldn't say that now – they'd have more respect for a nice bit of vintage: mutton dressed up as lamb.

Rupert was our roadie. We met him through some Sloane Rangers who used to come to the gigs. The posh set liked us. We played in places like the Embassy Club where the girls thrilled to our rough edges. I don't think Robert particularly wanted to be a roadie. I think he would have preferred to be a pop svengali, but it gave him a purpose in life, and a focus for his aspiring socialite lifestyle.

Most of the job involved driving the van when I was too pissed-up to do it, and catching flying guitars with broken strings. We used to practise this at home (the throwing and catching of guitars, not the van driving). I used to break a lot of strings, and part of his job was to replace them, re-tune the guitar and throw it back to me. I had an Epiphone Coronet, a 1955 three-quarter scale Les Paul Junior, and my trusty Rickenbacker 330 as featured on the cover of my first album.

Actually the Rickenbacker wasn't at all trusty – it used to go out of tune because the neck was too thin. I had to play it standing very still and try not to breathe because the slightest movement could result in discord. The Rickenbacker came to a sticky end at Brunel University. We were in the middle of some bizarre, psychedelic hoedown when I noticed that my guitar strings were missing. I looked at the neck and there were shards of splintered wood where the machine heads should have been. I'd been executing some feedback, but I'd executed the guitar as well. As I turned round, the head had glanced off the corner of the amplifier and separated itself from the rest. It flew into the audience where it was caught by a fan who asked the drummer's girlfriend if she thought I'd mind if he kept it. 'Well, it's not much use to him now,' she said. I only got it back because the kid wanted it autographed. The two bits of guitar stayed in their case for over a year because I couldn't afford the repair.

Everything was falling to bits – guitars, cars, the flat, and me as well. I had to go to a doctor. He gave me a thorough examination and told me that unless I changed my ways I could reasonably expect to live for another two or three months. I needed stability – everybody said I should get back together with Philippa, the girlfriend I'd split up with three years after I split up with Sue. I rang her up and told her I was ill. She suggested a date. I can't imagine anybody wanting a date with me – I looked like a jellyfish. But she couldn't see that over the phone and we met that evening. I went back to her place and stayed the night. Eventually we became an item again.

On New Year's Eve we played at Dingwalls. At midnight the streamers went off and I reeled one in. It must have been twenty-five feet long but there was nobody on the other end of it. Anybody would have done, anybody who'd take care of a jellyfish, but there was nobody there. So I went home with the mother of one of the guitar players in the other band. She had *The Joy Of Sex* by the bedside, but we were too drunk to do anything about it.

The flat in Camberwell was a shithole. All of it faced the road except for the corridor and the bathroom, which had a door leading to what an estate agent might describe as 'a small roof terrace'. It was on the first floor above a travel agent's and a barber's shop. There was a bus stop outside, and it seemed as though every bus that crossed South London stopped there and revved its engine especially for us.

I carried on doing gigs but they were hardly worth while. Promoters would hand me twenty quid, effusive in their apologies, unable to understand why only ten people had showed up, but steadfast in their resolution

not to pay more. Sometimes there was a spot of unpleasantness. One promoter even burst into tears and
explained that he was getting married next week.

I got the drinking under control by giving up for two
weeks. Suddenly it was obvious to me that the way out of
the rut I was in was to move to New York. I didn't know
why I hadn't thought of it before.

I had to go somewhere where I was appreciated. The
British music press hated me. Actually I didn't know
whether it was me they hated or my association with the
once cool Stiff Records. I was sick of being described by
Time Out as 'Stiff's loveable small person' at a time when
they were ever so careful to not be fat-ist. Unfortunately
they were unable to apply this laudable ideal to the vertical dimension. And I wasn't even on Stiff Records any
more. The *NME* described me as 'a belligerent alcoholic
dwarf', and at Christmas they gave me a special 'dead but
won't lie down' award. My latest crappy manager com-
pounded this hatred by scoring an unexpected interview
with *Sounds*. I could hardly believe my luck. But I hadn't
been paying attention – the journalists were on strike.
The article was written by a scab.

The record labels were no better. I used to sit and listen
to my demos while A&R men twined themselves into exotic poses on expensive sofas, and then explained that, while
they could offer me a deal, they weren't going to. Others
just got up, left the room and got on with something else
while I listened to the demos on my own. Quite often they
said they liked them – 'But sorry, can't hear another Whole
Wide World in there.' I don't think they would have heard
Whole Wide World in the first place if it had jumped up and
pissed in their faces. Eventually I explained this to a young
time waster at Phonogram, and then I gave up.

I always acted on the advice of people who were less well informed, and quite often less intelligent than I was. It was a perverted massage to my fucked-up ego. All the losers and know-alls told me to go to the States where I was appreciated for the talent that I undoubtedly was. So I flew to New York on a very cheap standby ticket. I was very together, very sober. I had a horrible time. It was expensive, it was freezing cold, and I stayed with an American girl I knew in Brooklyn who turned out to be psychotic. Eventually I escaped with as many of my belongings as I could pick up as I ran out of the house. I was actually scared for my life. I met up with an English woman I'd known in London and spent the rest of the week drunk. Then I caught a plane home. The dream of a new life in New York was over.

When I got back the MG wouldn't start. The camshaft was buggered, the bottom end was on its way out, and it looked very much as though there was a crack in the cylinder head. I drove it very slowly to an MG specialist near Staines. He gave me a choice: I could buy a reconditioned engine or sell him the car for next to nothing. I couldn't be arsed with fitting an engine, and anyway, I didn't have any money on me and I needed a drink. So I sold off the remaining vestige of my success. He paid me by cheque and I had to jump the train and tube to get home. When I got back I borrowed a fiver from Rupert and shivered in a pub across the road called the Sun In Splendour. It had nothing to recommend it. I got pissed on Stones Bitter.

The next day I bought the *Exchange & Mart* and went through the car section looking for something affordable. There were two that caught my eye. Both were in West London, way out past the Hoover Factory, near that bit of the A40 with the stubby street lamps and the military airport.

The first affordable possibility was some sort of Citroen Estate. The bloke started it up, revved the engine and said, 'Sweet as a nut'. There was an enormous popping noise, and the engine died. He couldn't understand what it was, but when he opened the bonnet I was able to point out a large hole in the engine casing where one of the spark plugs should have been. The plug itself was still on the end of its lead, screwed into a chunk of hot, distressed metal. The man said that he would have been pig-sick if this had happened after I'd bought it.

The second car was in Hillingdon. It was an Austin 1300 Estate. I didn't know what one of these was, but the price was about right at two hundred and twenty pounds, and when I saw it I was absolutely charmed – it looked like the sort of car that someone who had once been successful might drive. It was sludge green, with green, sludgy plastic seats, and outside there was a strip of wooden plastic veneer running along each side. I was going to cut quite a dash driving around in that, so I bought it – even though it was quite obvious that the engine was loose on its mountings. It was the sort of car that old gits drive with the right-hand indicator permanently flashing. I drove it back to Camberwell, intent on starting a new life as a retired musician.

We were thrown out of Rupert's flat for omitting to pay the rent so I was sharing a 'hard to let' council flat in Nunhead with a prostitute who worked out of a massage parlour in Penge. She was a girl called Donna. We met when she was helping to run a rehearsal studio. The flat was in an old 1930s block – metal window frames, no lift, and no central heating. Official council tenants didn't want to live there, so the council used the estate as a dump for problem families, and let the remaining flats to the hopeless and desperate at very low rents.

A gang of kids hung out on the staircase. Some of them were only ten years old but they could roll joints better than I could. They took a dislike to a guy living in the opposite block so they turned his car upside down and set fire to it. But they never bothered me. I fitted right in. I was at one with the flotsom and jetsom, in perfect harmony with the tide of human scum. I drove a clapped-out car with three bald tyres and a bent MOT, and I didn't have a job.

In between administering topless hand relief in Penge, Donna sat on the bed in her room with the door wide open, throwing the I Ching for hours on end. She was short and voluptuous to the point of plump, with dark eyes, black hair and olive skin. I wouldn't have minded shagging her, but she was plainly mad, and anyway I don't think she was interested.

I was knackered from a year or so of sliding down the slippery slope that so many people had warned me about. I didn't really do much. I fucked around with the car, wrote the odd song with tired chords and dull sentiments, and tried not to drink until five thirty when the pubs opened for the evening session. By this time Donna's I Chinging was really getting on my nerves so I slobbed off over the road to the Old Nun's Head for a pint or two of draught Bass.

I don't know why I spent so much time in the pub – just looking at the furniture was like having the DTs. The carpet yawned up at you – thick red Axminster with a pattern like puke swirling down a plughole; and as you caught sight of them from the corner of your eye, the curtains and cushions twitched with hundreds of riders and horsemen. Horse brasses, beaten copper chimney cowls, hunting prints, cartwheel-backed chairs, and the fucking fruit machines, flashing, bleeping, and clunking out change for some lucky loser.

And yet I was compelled to spend time and money in this place. I would like to have been considered a regular – stopping just short of the personal tankard behind the bar. I wanted to blend in, to belong somewhere, but it wasn't easy to blend in with the regulars at the Old Nun's Head. For a start, they all seemed to be related to each other and probably had been for generations. They looked as though they spent their days converting houses into flats. They had a way of leaning on the bar, huge in their jeans and T-shirts, and even though they probably weren't, they gave the impression of having a carpenter's pencil tucked behind the ear. These were blokes, black and yellow Stanley tool-toting blokes – Black and Deckering their way through roofing timbers, lobbing up partition walls, and supporting whole houses on Acroes while they inserted an RSJ. They knew everything and they weren't scared to voice an opinion:

'That Pat Phoenix – Elsie Tanner – now she's what I call "a man's woman"…'

And I sat there, short and pasty, overweight but otherwise insignificant, getting slaughtered on five pints of Bass. I was the cunt in the Worthington E advert – only here for the beer – the retard that wanted to be Jack the Lad and couldn't make it, and this was my way of conforming to the norm. I didn't want to be like those fuckers but I bet that if they shagged Elsie Tanner they'd give her a right good seeing to, and she'd love it, and it wouldn't be like slopping a sausage around in an oven-ready chicken – oh no, they'd fill her right up and leave her begging for more (because they'd probably come too quick, but I hadn't figured that out back then).

I wasn't at my best in the mornings. I used to lie in bed, depressed and scared to get up. I used to stare at photos of the good old days, wondering if all that had really happened to me – live on stage in Chicago – fifteen hundred people. A total sell-out. After the show all the whisky, cocaine and foxy chicks in Chicago were mine for the abuse, if only I could have been bothered.

I'd spent the day with a journalist from *Rolling Stone*, nervous in case I put a foot wrong and came over like the boring, middle-class nerd I really was, instead of the cool, up-and-coming rock star that I felt I was expected to be.

We had to go to a radio station with Lou Mann, Epic Records' head of promotions in the Mid-West. He was everything you'd expect someone in that position to be. I was thrilled to bits. He was seven feet tall and, because it was summer, he was wearing a lightweight green safari suit, complete with the belt and patch pockets. He came at me in the hotel foyer with a handshake like a pound of Wall's Pork Sausages: 'Lou Mann, head of promotions in the Mid-West.' I'd met the *Rolling Stone* journalist minutes before and I knew he was a good guy because I could see that he was having trouble not laughing too.

We headed out for Lou's car, a green Lincoln Continental that matched his suit. Being a well brought up young man, and mindful of the dire warnings not to get arrogant with a *Rolling Stone* journalist, I made for the back seat so as to let him travel in comfort in the front. I don't think Americans could ever imagine the Morris Minor/Ford Anglia/Vauxhall Viva world that I came from. American cars of the late '70s and early '80s were big, ungainly box-like things with chromium, mock-Tudor fronts. There was a huge amount of space in the back. The journalist followed me in and Lou turned frosty as he drove us round Chicago, alone in the front. When he dropped us back at the hotel I asked him if he was coming to the show. 'Er... no,' came the answer, 'I have a er... er... family commitment...' I found out later that Lou Mann had been extremely put out at being treated like a chauffeur in his own car.

What's a poor English boy supposed to do? They didn't understand the pressure I was under – I wished they'd fuck off, but I wouldn't admit that, even to myself, because I was terrified of letting the side down. There were two guitar players, a bass player, drummer, lighting technician, backline roadie, and front-of-house sound-man (doubling as tour manager), and they were all dependent on me for nights in Ramada Inns and Best Western Hotels, and for dollar bills to pay for Rolling Rock and Pina Coladas. It was important that I did not rock the boat... don't tip the boat over... rock the boat...

I walked into the soundcheck. There was a band on-stage. They sounded massive. I realised it was my own band – we certainly didn't sound like that on the stage. Close up we sounded poxy – everything was going on in miniature in its own little space. The sound man padded the drums with gaffa and toilet paper until they were completely dead so that he could make them sound fabulous out front. On stage they didn't even sound like drums. They were almost unplayable and Dave the drummer was depressed. We were all depressed. The onstage sound was shit and we weren't even a band any more. The rhythm section had retreated into a private enclave of cosy habits – Space Invaders, joints, late-night TV, and a personal soundcheck formula that never varied – Dave did his funk bit, John the bassist did his disco riff, then the two of them played Reconnez Cherie using a riff that I never intended to be there. Night after night after night after fucking night...

We had a lead guitarist, an excellent musician. Reasonable, balding, mild-mannered... and boring. If someone said we were on in twenty minutes he'd say 'Yeah, time to skin one up,' and then he'd roll a '*jay*', because you had to be '*mellow*' when you hit the stage. He was working with a great songwriter: my great songs were a great vehicle for his fabulous guitar playing. I was being flattened blues-rock. None of them understood, not that I ever made it easy for them. I was detached, and musically I felt like the poor relation.

The day after that gig was a day off, which meant that we didn't have to get in the green Ford Econoline van and go somewhere, so I sat in my hotel room instead and stared out of the window.

The hotel appeared to be situated in the middle of a highway construction site. The view wasn't very inspiring – especially on a muggy, overcast day like today. Concrete drain sections, abandoned JCBs, expanses of dry mud, a distant highway intersection. My room was on the ground floor so I climbed out of the window and went for a two-hour stroll along a half-built highway. Then I climbed back in and carried on as before.

It was like a little hole in my life, a microcosmic holiday away from the tedium of being in a touring rock group. I should have been thrilled to bits with America but the reality was a van with plastic seats that you got stuck to in the heat as the Ohio State Turnpike, or some other such nonsense, rolled past the windows for twelve hours at a stretch. All we did was moan about things and create little routines for ourselves. I wanted to see America but all the band seemed to want was Ramada and Best Western. We took it in turns to choose the hotel. Once a week they'd have to give me a go and we'd end up in the worst Psycho motel I could find. In one of them the beds had an apparatus that was supposed to lull you to sleep. There was a metal box with a coin slot attached to the headboard. I shoved a nickel in the slot and laughed myself silly as the bed jiggered round the floor, vibrating itself to pieces.

One night we got back to the motel around midnight. I went into the room, picked up the phone and dialled reception. The guy took ages to answer, and when he did he wasn't very happy.

'Do you know what time it is?'

'Yeah, it's about half-past eleven. I'd like to put a call through to London, England.'

'I can't do that now, you'll have to wait 'til the morning.'

I suppose I was a bit uptight: 'Then what the hell did you answer the fucking phone for?'

'Phwhat did you say…'

'I said, what did you answer the phone for?' (Editing myself slightly.)

'Phwhat *exactly* did you say?'

'Oh, I said. "Then what the hell did you answer the fucking phone for."'

'That's what I thought you said – I WANT YOU AND YOUR LIMEY FRIENDS TO GET YOUR BAGS PACKED AND GET YOUR GODDAMNED ASSES OUT OF HERE RIGHT NOW.'

I put the phone down and lit a cigarette. Fuck it, the guy was obviously a nutter. The call could wait till tomorrow. A few minutes later the door crashed open and the tour manager stumbled in, white with rage, and fear as it turned out. He'd come round the corner, having parked the van, and collided with the motel owner who'd stormed out of reception armed with a large handgun. Somehow he convinced him that no offence had been meant, that it was just my eccentric British humour. But for an instant the guy had been intent on blowing my head off. At last, a taste of the real America...

Something had to happen. I obviously couldn't spend the rest of my life living like this but I was making no attempt to do anything about it. Philippa lost her bedsitting room in St Saviours Road, Brixton. The landlord threw her out. He didn't like the fact that I seemed to be living there, then he discovered the cat. And then the cat shit – or maybe the cat shit was what put him on to the cat in the first place. I never wanted to go back to the flat in Nunhead. It was violent and I only had a camp bed to sleep on.

But Philippa moved in and brought the bed with her, and the TV, and suddenly we were properly back together – holed up in a room on the fourth floor with a view of the car park and the opposite block.

The Austin 1300 fell to pieces. I left a few things in it overnight – a suitcase containing a few effect pedals and a small Fender amplifier. The car was broken into while I slept. They took everything, including a wicker picnic hamper containing most of my paperwork and receipts for the last five years. I'd been thinking about addressing my tax situation but with this huge loss of paperwork I put it on hold.

They got in by breaking the quarterlight. I patched it up with gaffa tape. It was a complete mess anyway. When I let the clutch out the whole car jerked and jiggled as though the parts were all trying to catch up with each other.

Then one day the car came to a standstill outside a florist's shop in Peckham. Smoke started to pour out of the engine compartment. When I lifted the bonnet the wiring loom was on fire so I emptied several bunches of chrysanthemums out of a bucket and chucked the water over the fire. I immediately regretted this action because I was insured third party, fire and theft. If I'd left well alone I could have made an insurance claim – the car was, after all, insured for two hundred pounds and burning cars were a commonplace event round there.

I had to get a new car with my latest PRS cheque. It was going to have to be something cheap because the royalties were definitely dwindling. But it had to have style. It came to me in a flash – I wanted an Austin Cambridge, a powder-blue one with a white stripe down the side, just like the one that the dentist's wife used to take us to school in.

There were quite a few Austin Cambridges in the *Exchange & Mart*, and though most of them were a little pricey I found a likely contender.

I had to be in Hammersmith at seven o'clock that evening. I was the first person to ring and the first to see the car. It was a 1968 A60, dark grey with red leather seats and a printed metal dashboard made to look like real wood. I took it for a drive round the block, came back and offered the full asking price. We went back to the house, which was pink and wallpapery. The man's wife said another potential buyer had rung up and it was only fair to let him have a look at it. I didn't think this was at all fair. When he arrived he was a young black man. The wife immediately told him that the car was sold, which it was as far as I was concerned. When he'd gone she said, 'I couldn't see it go to one of his sort,' and her husband agreed. I didn't feel good about that, but I paid the money and the man gave me back a tenner to get a tank of petrol.

The summer rolled around and Joe Strummer went missing. Some people said it was because the tickets weren't selling for the Combat Rock tour. I can quite imagine that he was just pissed off with it all. I know that I was. The only record I ever seemed to hear was Goody Two Shoes by Adam & The Ants – *you don't drink, don't smoke, what do you do?*

Strummer reappeared looking mean and lean, sporting a mohican and camouflage fatigues. It was a great look, I wished I could do it but I was too fat.

I ran into our old lighting man, Harry MacDonald. He was working for the Mervyn Conn Organisation who organise the Wembley Country Music Festivals. He asked me if I'd be interested in a couple of weeks' work driving a truck with some backline equipment in it.

Harry wouldn't tell me who I was going to be working for in case it put me off. We picked up some gear in a transit and took it to the White House Hotel where the mysterious artiste was staying. As we parked up outside the hotel, a tall, middle-aged man wearing a toupee strolled round the corner. Harry said, 'That's your new boss.' It was George Hamilton IV, the International Ambassador Of Country Music with the late-night TV show.

As I got out of the van preparing to meet the new boss, a woman popped her head over some railings and asked if we could help her climb over because the gate was locked. By this time George was in our midst. He took command of the situation, ordering (or rather requesting, because George was nothing if not a perfect gentleman) that Harry (pronounced Hairy) got a speaker cabinet out of the van so that he could stand on it and assist the lady to safety. The lady was surprised and delighted, if slightly nonplussed, that her gallant rescuer was that nice American from the telly.

'A couple of weeks' turned out to be a sixty-date tour sponsored by Volkswagen Trucks & Vans. I had to go to Milton Keynes to pick up a large blue Volkswagen Van with the legend:

VW George Hamilton IV **VW**
Volkswagen Trucks & Vans
On Tour

emblazoned on the sides and back of it. The band were presented with a Volkswagen Caravelle Delux with similar logos plastered all over it. There was a little champagne celebration for everybody, hosted by VW, but I wasn't invited.

Harry drove the band, I drove the van with the equipment in it. I had to set up the amplifiers and help rig the PA. During the gig I had to watch the stage in case anything went wrong. It never did. Harry took care of the sound.

It was a middle-of-the-road show for a middle-of-the-road, middle-aged audience. As George said, 'We're a *nice* band playing *nice* music for *nice* people.'

The guitar player and Musical Director came from Heckmondwike, West Yorkshire. (I knew this because George made a point of saying it every night in the course of his band introduction. It's one of the rules of country music – everybody has to *hail all the way from* somewhere.) He stood behind a music stand with his musical charts, 'the dots', perched on it. At the end of every number he'd turn the pages and look self-important. I was almost convinced until I saw 'the dots' at close quarters. Normally he whisked them away and locked them up in a cheap attache case, but one night he forgot and left them out. They were just the words of the songs, typed out with the chord names written in above each line. I found it quite heartening – he was one of us after all, a self-trained musician, a busker.

The band came on in the first half wearing checked shirts with red piping and a Roman numeral 'IV' on the top pocket. They wore these over black suit trousers – the sort that come with a free plastic belt. In the second half they wore sports jackets. I have an enduring memory of shiny black fabric stretched tight over large bottoms like those of the lady bus conductors of my youth. Between sets the backstage resembled a CID locker room.

The band were called The Numbers (get it?). Every night they struck up and George came rushing on, businesslike in grey flannels, blue double-breasted blazer (also with a 'IV' on the top pocket) and a blue gingham check shirt worn with a cravat. They'd whiz through Canadian Pacific and George would shout into the applause: 'Let's hear it for my backing band – The Numbers!'

When the applause finally died away he'd thank everybody for coming, say it was good to be in wherever we happened to be, and get on to what we were up to now. It was like a newsletter:

'We're at the beginning of a marathon tour, we're gonna be doing around sixty dates UK-wide, so *(chuckle)* I guess you'll be seeing us up and down the highways and byways in a lotta Lil' Chefs, which are our favourite places to hang out between shows…

'Before that we were performing shows in Boodapest – guess you could call that *(chuckle)* country and *Eastern* music…'

It was exactly the same every night. Halfway through

the tour I had a word with him and he changed the first line to: 'We're *midway* through a marathon tour...' and similarly in the last week I suggested a change to: 'We're on *the final furlong* of a marathon tour...' I think he may have re-edited that because I'm not sure that Americans have furlongs.

After a few drinks he said to me, 'You know, a lot of people think I wear a toupee, but I don't.' Then he invited me to pull his hair to prove it. He was telling the truth. His musical taste was quite unexpected. One night he asked me, 'Do you know a band called Doctor Feelgood? They're ma favourite group.' Him and Lady Di. He wanted me to take him to see them if they were playing when we had a night off, but sadly they never coincided. I would love to have introduced Lee Brilleau to George Hamilton IV.

He only did two soundchecks in the whole tour – he surprised everybody by running through a few mid-period Dylan numbers – Like A Rolling Stone, Subterranean Homesick Blues, Highway 61 Revisited... He knew all the words.

About fifteen dates into the tour the keyboard player announced that he'd had enough and headed back to the States. Harry got the gig playing the piano. He was still going to be the tour manager but now I had to do the sound.

Harry was a belligerent Scotsman, and now that he was on double wages he turned the full force of his belligerence on me – it was my fault that one of the cables hadn't been coiled correctly by a stagehand the previous night, or that the piano supplied by the venue was a heap of shit. When he was my lighting man I never gave him a hard time so I couldn't understand why he was doing it to me. Now I can see that it was his own problem – Harry was at odds with the entire world.

He used to give me the money to go to the bar and get him a drink in the intermission, and when I came back he didn't say thank you, just counted the change. He shouted at me, and for me, constantly. It was like a touring production of Tom Brown's Schooldays. I was expecting at any moment to be required to warm up a toilet seat.

He always insisted on us going for a drink together before the gig because we were the crew, even though he was in the band too. It was a real drag going for a drink with Harry. He used to swagger into a pub murmuring, 'I'll just piss off the locals by emptying that fruit machine.' And then he'd do exactly that. You couldn't really hold a conversation with him because most of his mind was on the fruit machine, which would be emitting a succession of bleeps, beeps and arpeggios. Suddenly his whole attention would be distracted by a line of oranges, and anger would turn briefly to happiness as the machine went *kerchunka kerchunka kerchunka* and vomited half a ton of two-pence pieces. Sometimes he didn't go straight for the fruit machine, lurking instead like some predatory bird with half a pint of bitter while a hapless local filled the machine up for him. And then he'd go and empty it.

The bassist came from a different planet – Planet Cabaret. His bass playing was a quasi-melodic mess. He was a rotund sort of person with black hair and a thick black beard. He addressed the bass carefully, legs together and feet at right angles. He had his own featured song – a ballad from Planet Cabaret – and because he had to concentrate on the singing, his bass playing got even weirder. Before every show he would politely remind me to put his vocal level up in the monitors during his number. I always did, but he was always fearful that I might forget, so every night during George's introduction, he would fix the area in the theatrical blackness where he thought the sound desk might be, form his mouth into an 'O' shape, draw a circle around it, point to the monitor and perform a discreet flapping movement with his other hand. Nicely done. A nicety from Planet Cabaret.

The drummer was an English bloke from Kent called Luce Langridge. It's down to him that I wound up in the Medway Towns. When I told him halfway through the tour that I was looking for somewhere to live he hardly looked up from his drink as he said, 'What you need is a mortgage – I can fix you up if you don't mind living in the Medway Towns.' I didn't really take him seriously, but a few days later I got quite a good publishing cheque. I mentioned it and he said: 'Got enough for a deposit?'

The next time we had a day off Luce, arranged for me and Philippa to see a man called Simon who was overseeing the renovation of a terraced house in Gillingham. When I say renovation what I mean is woodchip wallpaper, acrylic carpets and Artex. Luce warned me that Simon was quite posh. When I met him I couldn't immediately figure out whether he was a yob who'd been to charm school or a toff that was slumming it. He wore a camel-hair coat that was dusted with cement and drove a black Ford Capri that was evidently used to fetch supplies from the Texas Homecare. He spoke in a squawky voice with an upper-class accent that slipped from time to time.

He showed us round the Gillingham house, a bijou three-bedroomed residence arranged on three floors with an unnegotiable asking price of twenty-one thousand pounds. It was horrible. The bathroom had a brown plastic concertina door – the sort that never opens or closes properly and eventually gets permanently stuck halfway. He could see we weren't keen so he loaded us into the Capri and drove us round to Chatham where he had a couple of slightly less desirable properties.

We chose 75 Gordon Road because it'd had the least amount of renovation work done to it. We agreed on a price of seventeen thousand pounds and extracted a promise from Simon that his lads would do the minimum in order to make the place mortgageable. They had to put in a bathroom. We didn't trust them to build an extension so they put it in the third bedroom, which opened off the back bedroom. The bathroom suite came in a choice of colours: shell pink, jade, pampas or azure. We could have a low-level WC with silent flush or a standard one. We chose the standard one in jade because white was apparently out of the question. The bath was made of plastic and it wobbled when you got in it. It was fixed hard up against some original tongue and groove, which slowly went rotten as it got splashed with bath water. They put the toilet next to an almost floor-to-ceiling window, and although they replaced the panes with obscure glass it still meant that the neighbours were treated to a perfect silhouette of anybody using it.

The way the mortgage scam worked was through a friendly building society manager who was part of a consortium that bought up old terraced properties. They got the places for next to nothing, did the necessary work as cheaply as possible, and operated a quick turn-over by selling them to people like me who normally hadn't a hope in hell of getting a mortgage. The building society manager was there to steer me through the proceedings. He organised clandestine meetings in the Farthing Corner Services on the M2 in order to go through the paperwork. I had to open an account with the building society to make it look good, and invent a profession for myself. I became an audio engineer working for Crandon Electronics, and when the letter from the building society came addressed to Crandon Electronics at a friend's house, asking for a reference, I wrote one myself and signed it Dave Crandon.

The tour ended during a cold spell in early December. I went home to the flat in Nunhead where Donna was still desperately throwing the I Ching. Now she was convinced that her ex-boss was obsessed with her. 'Look,' she'd say, pointing down at the car park, 'he's been there all day just staring at my window. He really loves me.' I looked but I couldn't see anybody.

She lived on dry Ryvitas. She'd take a couple of bites, her mind would be drawn to something else, and she'd absent-mindedly drop the redundant cracker on the floor where she stood. The kitchen was just about unusable, a dark hole off the empty living room. Philippa and I used to flit in there to make mugs of tea and hurried bacon sandwiches. We threw the debris from our takeaways onto the overflowing rubbish.

One day some hippy friends of Donna's came round with a floor sander. They divested Donna's bedroom of its clock radio, pile of clothes and single divan bed, and sanded the floor. She was going to do the flat up – it was going to be sophisticated.

They were so thrilled with Donna's bedroom that they decided to do the living room. The dust got everywhere and Donna strutted about talking of new beginnings and special varnishes.

But the floors never did get varnished. The divan bed, the clock radio and the pile of clothes went back into

Donna's room, and the living room carried on as before – except that a trail of grubby footmarks was beaten into the sanded pine expanse between the door and the rubbish. By the time we left, the floor in Donna's room looked exactly the same as it had before it was sanded.

A couple of nights before we were due to move out she brought a man home. He was bulky and middle-aged. They spent the night in a screaming, shagging frenzy.

In the morning the I Ching spoke to her. It was imperative that we moved out immediately – there was some *heavy shit* going down. She couldn't say what it was but we would be in grave danger if we stayed for the final night. We must leave immediately and take all our belongings with us. She looked dark and threatening, and we were so scared of her by this time that we did what she said.

We loaded our belongings into a transit from Dial-A-Van and spent the night on somebody's floor.

2 Up
Too Down
in the
Medway
Towns

I DROVE THE VAN DOWN to Chatham, and picked up the keys to our new house. By the time I got there night had fallen. It was very cold. The electricity was turned off so I stumbled around and found the meter in a cupboard under the stairs. I threw the main switch and the place was flooded with a naked forty-watt glow.

I couldn't even remember what it looked like – we'd only been there the once.

It was smaller than I thought. A tiny front room with enough space for a settee, one armchair and a TV set. And possibly a cabinet for trophies. It had fiddle-some pink and grey wallpaper that was difficult to look at. There weren't any curtains so I turned my attention to the back room.

No carpet, just bare, grubby floorboards. It was fucking freezing. There was no heating although we could have had central heating at no extra cost – the improvement grant would have covered it but I was suspicious of such things. Proper heating, government grants – they belonged to a world that I didn't think I had any right to inhabit.

I bought a small bag of coal, firelighters and a bottle of milk from the corner shop. Then I went to the nearest pub. (Beaten copper table tops and a copper cowl over a decorative fireplace feature. Bench-style seating round the walls with green vinyl upholstery. Green and gold wallpaper with a design like ovaries and fallopian tubes.) The beer was sour. It tasted of cleaning fluid.

Philippa arrived from work clutching a couple of bottles of Black Tower. I was working my way through a six-pack of Ind Coope Long Life, having come back from the pub three or four pints to the good. We unloaded the van and lit the fire. There was a knock at the door.

It was Linda and Keith, the neighbours whose kitchen we could see into from ours. They were just on their way out but they'd come round to see if there was anything we needed. Like hell they had – they'd come round to have a fucking good look at us. They were all togged up for a Friday night out – a slap-up dinner followed by a spangled evening at some hideous local niterie. They were hardly going to go back into their place to fetch us a cup of butter and a trowel, though I was tempted to ask. Everybody knows that game – you give them time to unpack so that you can see what they've got, and then you pop round on the pretext of being neighbourly. But really it's just being nosey. I know – I've done it myself.

Linda and Keith were younger than us but they looked older and they didn't want a drink. Linda may have accepted a small glass of wine, meaning a normal-sized glass of wine, given that Philippa used to drink it in half pints, but Keith abstained because he was driving. He had on casual, driving-a-car shoes that just covered his toes, leaving an expanse of white sock between the shoe and the bottom of his peg-leg slacks (this was the '80s). Keith was an accountant. Linda was a voluptuous Jewess with bubbly brown hair. She wore a coat with a fun fur collar, and shaggy black leg-warmers. Her voice was a husky adenoidal croak that spoke of forty cigarettes a day.

They were my first experience of neighbours. In the fly-by-night world of rented accommodation, I never had neighbours – just people living above, below and on either side who complained about the noise. I'd never had people coming round to ask if there was anything I needed, people of whom you could ask: *'What day do the bin men come round?'* in the certainty of a correct reply. I was almost charmed.

Linda and Keith beat a hasty retreat – left us to get settled in. We were probably a bit lairy by then because we were running out of essential supplies. It was time to go back to the pub.

By the following night, with the aid of a couple of flagons of cider and four bottles of Black Tower, we were well and truly settled in. There was knock at the door – the second in the space of two nights. It was Linda. This time she was wearing a figure-hugging brown tracksuit. They wanted to invite us into their house the next afternoon for a drink and some *'nibbles'* so that we could *get to know one another*.

We scrabbled around for some smart-looking clothes so that we wouldn't create too bad an impression. We needn't have bothered. Linda was wearing another tracksuit, a purple velour effort, and Keith was wearing the same sort of thing in beige.

They'd had their house knocked through into one – the downstairs was a big indoor playground and leisure zone with an open-tread staircase and a kitchen off the back. The room was carpeted in brown shagpile. It crossed my mind that it was lucky Linda wasn't wearing yesterday's brown tracksuit or we wouldn't have been able to see her.

Today Linda and Keith were *relaxing*. They had a huge four-seater settee that curved around like an ox-bow lake in front of a plastic stone-finish hearth and a giant TV set. They parked Philippa in an armchair and me on the ox-bow sofa, and offered us a cup of tea or coffee – or maybe we'd like to join them in a *drink drink*.

Linda parked herself on the opposite end of the ox-bow, with a massive velour flank angled towards me ever so slightly provocatively. Having ascertained that I was in the music business, she fixed me with a gimlet eye: 'So Eric, what area of *the business* are you actually *in*?'

I WASN'T GOING TO TELL HER THAT MY REAL NAME WAS WRECKLESS ERIC, THAT I WAS A WELL-KNOWN ROCK 'N' ROLL LUNATIC WITH A STRING OF INDIE HITS TO MY NAME, THAT I HAD A REPUTATION FOR DRUNKENNESS AND CHAOS AND THAT, MUCH TO MY SHAME, CLIFF RICHARD HAD COVERED ONE OF MY SONGS, AND THAT FURTHERMORE I'D NEARLY BROKEN THROUGH INTO THE BIG TIME IN THE US OF A BUT I'D SORT OF FUCKED-UP A BIT AND WAS HAVING A REST NOW.

No, I was a sound engineer working for a country 'n' western singer they may have seen on their enormous television set. It was fairly shameful but it was better than telling the whole truth.

Linda did most of the talking. Keith didn't say much, he was obviously the weak and silent type. We had a chat about cars that fizzled out, while Linda failed to engage Philippa in some girlie talk about the *'menfolk'*. We limped onto the subject of the *US of A*. Linda had never *made the trip* herself though she'd always wanted to. She'd seen it on Dallas – she was a big, big Dallas fan. 'It's such a sophisticated lifestyle,' she said, holding aloft a long-stemmed goblet of Chateau Collapso. 'The way they pour a drink and then they just don't finish it.'

We lumbered into silences. I drained my can of Tesco lager. We discovered that Alan, next door on the other side, was the neighbourhood hunk and eligible bachelor; that Linda's ambition, and this went for Keith too, because he nodded, was to move to Eltham. Philippa and I had never been to Eltham so we couldn't comment. It was time to go home.

On New Year's Eve I played at the Strood Community Centre in a band that had been assembled especially for the occasion. A friend of mine came down from London with a lot of coke. I wasn't really into the stuff but the festive spirit had got hold of him and he insisted that we shared it. So, in a dark corner of the parquet dance floor in the otherwise strip-lit Community Centre, we hoovered up a gram or two of cocaine in between hits from my bottle of Teacher's.

The evening ended in a magnificent fight shortly after Auld Lang Syne, during a dullard version of Me And Bobby McGhee. I viewed it from the stage, standing behind my guitar in detached cocaine arrogance. The fight started at the front and spread through the mutant Strood audience like a Mexican Wave. The power to the amps was turned off, more fluorescent lights were turned on, and a leading light from the Strood Community Centre Committee took the stage – 'That's it – if you can't behave you can all go home.'

Happy New Year 1983.

Since then I've always held that the way you spend New Year's Eve influences the kind of year you're going to have.

We met a god-awful couple called Mel and Lee. They

sang in a duo called Denim 'n' Lace. Everybody was going back to their council house in Gillingham. When we got there it was only us – we were newcomers so we didn't know that nobody else liked them. Mel thought it would be a beautiful thing if we wrote a song together but fortunately the cab we ordered finally arrived.

The Austin Cambridge was in a sorry state. I took it to a garage on the old Chatham navel dock run by a non-original member of the top '60s pop group Vanity Fayre *(a thumb goes up a car goes by it's nearly one a.m. and here am I hitching a ride…)* He did what he could with it. The alternator was gone so he replaced it with one from the scrap yard. But the prognosis wasn't good – the oil pressure gauge was showing a reading of next to nothing because the big end was on its way out. Time to start searching for another car.

I bought the local paper, the *Chatham Standard*, and had a look at what was on offer. Second-hand cars were really cheap. Not surprising – the dockyard had just shut down. It was slowly dawning on me that we'd moved to a depressed area. Every week another shop in the High Street was closed down and boarded up. It was turning into a ghost town.

I'd always wanted a Jaguar 2.4 so I bought a Daimler 4.2. It was a D registration 1966 model. Old, dilapidated and uncared for, and the paintwork had turned matt. It was gun-metal grey – the same as James Bond's Bentley (in the books at any rate). It was huge, low, sleek and coach-built. It had blue leather upholstery and walnut interior trim with the varnish flaking off like psoriasis. It had two petrol gauges, a rev counter, speedometer, oil-pressure gauge, a small clock, and a sign that lit up and said O V E R D R I V E when you lifted a lever on the steering column.

It was an absolute bargain. I figured that what I spent on insurance and increased petrol consumption would be more than offset by all-round reliability. These cars were built to last.

There's one born every minute. The man I bought it off probably couldn't believe his luck. After I'd left I can imagine him dancing around the lounge – 'I got rid of the fucker! I got rid of the fucker!' I know I would. I can imagine his wife throwing a little caution into the mix: 'Let's just hope it doesn't break down too soon, dear – let's hope the engine-oil treatment that you popped in does the trick...'

They would have salted the money away ready to spend on a nice weekend break when they were sure I wasn't going to come back. A trip somewhere in the sensible Vauxhall Chevette they bought after hubby got over his midlife crisis.

I could only fill up one petrol tank because there didn't seem to be a key for the other. It took six gallons. I drove round town, out to a country pub and back again. It had done three-quarters of a tank. I planned a trip to London – to show off a bit. I filled up before I left and stopped in New Cross to fill up again. I drove around London, went to see some friends in Notting Hill Gate, filled up again in Shepherds Bush and set off back. As a precautionary measure I popped in another two or three gallons in New Cross, which saw me most of the way home. I finally ran out of petrol on the hill going down into Strood from the A2.

It was a very fast car. One afternoon after the pub shut I did a hundred and thirty miles an hour in it on the M2 motorway bridge across the Medway. I think that's what unseated or caused three or four of the valves to stick. After that it only did eighty and I seemed to run out of petrol more frequently. It became difficult to start, and even though I pumped in three tins of that stuff that un-gums your engine – the stuff that turns the exhaust blue and blots out the entire street, causing the neighbours to shout at you and slam their replacement windows – there wasn't much improvement.

I found a specialist, a large man in a woolly hat and oily dungarees whose great passion was Daimler Sovereigns of a certain vintage. I found myself imagining him actually making love to one, taking it to bed with him and kissing it...

...he pulled the car towards him, chassis first, one hand under her ample windscreen, the other caressing her roof, wings and mudguards... mouth suckered onto her differential, moaning sweet nothings into her brake linings, he worked himself into her oil sump drain and pushed a finger up her less than pliant dipstick hole...

But usually I'd manage to put the brakes on before he got his dungarees off. He fixed it up and charged me about three hundred quid. I had burned-out valves, like metal mushrooms, lined up on the mantelpiece, but the car really wasn't much better.

Every two weeks I cashed my giro, put a pound's worth of petrol in the tank and drove the thing round town. Then I parked it up until the next giro came. A royalty cheque coincided with an advert in the paper for a 1964 Vauxhall Viva. It was only ninety quid and it had an MOT. My mind was made up before I even saw it.

After the Daimler it was refreshingly tinny. It had a youthful vibe about it. The previous owner had 'souped it up' by putting black and white chequered tape along the sides from front to back – from the headlights to the tail lights. He'd obviously spent time and money in the

sticker department of Halfords. There were several chequered flag stickers dotted about on the metalwork, and
on the back there was a Grateful Dead sticker – the one
with the skull – and a sign that said DEAN, KENT with a
Kentish crest next to it.

It spoke to me of new hope in the '60s and even
though I was twenty-eight going on twenty-nine, I felt
young again. It didn't break down very often, but little
puffs of exhaust came from the engine compartment, and
if I drove fast with the window down I tended to turn
blue. I'd get that feeling like my face was turning into a
spider's web and I'd have to quickly wind the window up
before I died.

We shivered through the murky winter of 1983, burning
small, overpriced bags of coal from the local petrol
station. Some kind of routine imposed itself. I'd wake up
with a hangover at about half-past six or seven o'clock in
the morning, cold light from white street lamps leaking
through the cheap, unlined Superman curtains that we'd
got from God knows where. My first thought was that
soon they'd find out that we weren't legit and then they'd
take the house away from us. There was little pleasure in
home ownership. The dawn chorus round here was sung
by starter motors – the sound of other people going to
work. I didn't have a job.

We'd get up and have a cup of tea, and then I'd take
Philippa to the station in the Daimler, or the Vauxhall
Viva, unless neither of them would start, and then she'd
get a taxi. And after that the day was my own to do whatever I wanted.

I did the crossword in the *Sun* or the *Daily Mirror*. I
went for long, solitary walks, came back and wrote yards
of lyrics. Once a fortnight I signed on. In the afternoons I

watched TV. Then I went to the pub for an early evening drink.

Just like other people do. At the end of the working day (that's a laugh for a start) they take themselves off to the pub for a nice pint. Unwind. Relax. They set their pint (preferably a pint of real ale) on a beermat and spend a moment in quiet contemplation. Some of them hold it up to the light, the better to appreciate it. Then they start on it with sluppery, slubbery sips. They make a sighing noise. 'Aaaah.' The Good Life.

I hadn't got time for any of that bollocks. As soon as the bubbles had risen to the surface I was pouring it in. I'd learned all about drinking at an early age by watching *Coronation Street*. The Rover's Return. Len Fairclough and Ken Barlow hoisting up foaming tankards that looked quite delicious to a seven-year-old. They seemed so happy when they'd poured the stuff into themselves. After I stopped drinking I realised that I'd never actually liked the taste of beer, it put me in mind of earwax.

Word had got around that a punk rock star had come to live in the Medway Towns, and I met all the desperate local musicians. I don't think that most of them knew who I was in the first place, but the fact that I'd once made records, been on the TV, the radio, and the cover of the *NME* was enough – I might be some use to them. So I met loads of gits that had once nearly made it, done demos for the Pye label, backed Brian Poole of the Tremeloes, been in a band with someone who'd been in a band with a founder member of Dire Straits. Fat-arsed no-hopers playing adequate cover versions in adequate local groups. The worst of it was that I loved the attention, and soon I was getting up and doing guest spots with some of these groups, singing puerile versions of rock 'n' roll numbers like Boney Maronie, Slippin' and Slidin' and Bye Bye Johnny. I was losing my grip.

Duran Duran were the new thing. The pop world was all about youth, vitality, money and success – all the things that I hadn't got any more. I was almost beginning to feel sorry for myself.

One morning my routine was broken into by the arrival of a solicitor's letter. A demand for payment of a bill left over from the days of my creepy ex-manager, a man called Vernon Rossiter. Vernon took over around 1981. Before that I didn't have a manager, just Dave Robinson. Vernon had been the Stiff Records' accountant. Now he was moving into artist management. He offered to manage me – he could get me off Stiff Records and set up with a new deal in no time at all.

Vernon was quite unfortunate in every way – he was tall and thin and had a face that crossed a weasel with a bambi. He had a ratty little moustache, carried a plastic briefcase and wore a grey polyester-flannel three-piece suit that had gone out of fashion ten years previously – high-waisted, massively flared trousers, a crisp white shirt and tie, waistcoat done up to the very top button, and a shaped jacket, double-breasted with extremely wide lapels.

He wasn't wearing this get-up for bizarre effect, the fact is that he didn't know any better. He was a callow youth grown old, and in his thirties he'd somehow stumbled into the music business.

He thought he was razor sharp. Witty and sarcastic. But his wit was sour, like the after-stench of old toilet cleaner. He had the most obsequious turn of phrase – he would say things like: *'I can come and visit you at your home'*. He promised that if I formed an alliance with him

I'd *'come up smelling of roses and violets in next to no time'*.

I'd gone to see Dave Robinson. I told him I wanted to knock it on the head. I said I wanted to go to teacher training college. Not surprisingly, he didn't believe me. I wanted to know where we stood financially and pointed out that I'd never actually received a royalty statement in the four years I'd been with Stiff. Dave growled at me in his transatlantic accent, 'The situation is that you owe me about ninety thousand quid – if you'd care to pop a cheque in the post.'

I still can't understand how this could be – I was on a retainer of fifty pounds a week. Most of my records were recorded on the cheap – the musicians were paid a pittance and I was paid fuck all. I was never given an advance. The tours were done on a low budget – apart from the second Stiff Tour, the Route 78 Be Stiff train tour. But the cost of that one was spread between five artists and, hopefully, the record company, because God knows it had done more to put Stiff on the map than it had for me.

We used to share hotel rooms on the road. In the end I got my own room by behaving so obnoxiously that the rest of the band refused to share with me. I was the focus, the centre of attention – I had to deal constantly with journalists, record company people, fans, well-wishers, lunatics, and even the staff of the local record shop. And every fucker I met wanted something from me – an interview, an autograph, a photo for a friend, a free drink or maybe just a quick fuck. I felt that the least I could expect was a bit of privacy for five or six hours a night. My wages went up to seventy-five pounds a week on tour.

But I was in the dark, blissfully unaware that I was running up a ninety thousand pound bill. I was selling records and filling venues. In the back of my mind I had this idea that one day there'd be a big share-out.

I told Dave that I wasn't enjoying it any more. Dave told me that it wasn't me that was supposed to enjoy it – it was for the punters to do that. That's what it was all about now, punters – bums on seats, units shifted. Strange, four years ago he'd been emphatic that there was no money in it but we were all going to have a lot of fun. Now here I was, thoroughly compromised, and it seemed that it had cost me ninety thousand quid to end up having no fun whatsoever. In the beginning it had been huge fun, but most of the fun fell away when Jake Riviera left.

I'd developed another idea of 'fun'. 'Fun' was when you drank half a bottle of cheap red wine, four pints of best bitter, a couple of large gin and tonics, two cans of Red Stripe, and rounded it off by being rude to somebody that worked for a record company, before chucking up outside Dingwalls and walking home in the rain.

I'd been going off the rails since I started in this business. I'd lost touch with the kid that had the vision – a band that crossed the Monkees with the Velvet Underground. Upstairs at the Bull in Hull on a summer night in 1976. Playing my new song, Whole Wide World. The light from the taxi office flashing on and off outside the window next to the stage. Short-wave radio cutting into the sound over our trashy equipment. Graham Beck's cheap, overdriven electric piano rattling round and round through a Roland Space Echo. My psycho guitar-playing – the same psychotic playing that moved Allan Jones to compare me with Syd Barratt in the *Melody Maker* in 1977. I knew what I was doing then. And I was pretty.

By the time Vernon took me on I was in a disgusting

state. I found a photo the other day. For a minute I couldn't think who it was, then I realised it was me. I could hardly bear to look at it. It's a photo of me, a pasty looking fat boy. There's nobody at home – the eyes are dead. I look as though I've been kept underwater for a long time. Which is about right – I was out of my depth.

But disgusting state or not, this was going to be a rebirth. A new band and a new beginning. I was approached by a large agency – they thought that before I put a band together I should have a new record deal, and they were willing to help me get one. I thought this was good news but Vernon was appalled. I was off Stiff Records, the world was my oyster, and just as I was about to come up smelling of roses and violets – if I would just allow that to happen – here I was willing to throw it all away by signing with a major agency who were obviously going to fuck me up. I'd end up being just another artist on their roster.

I felt such a fool – Vernon had a better plan than that. We were going to keep it all *'In House'*. Vernon and his business partner were starting their own agency. I'd soon have a string of dates and I'd be assured of their best attentions at all times. The business partner, who looked like he lived on cold baked beans, worked from a living room floor in Thornton Heath, endlessly arranging and rearranging sheets of lined foolscap paper with the names of clubs, bands and promoters written on them.

I got a band together with my old bass player, John Brown, and two ex-members of the Lew Lewis Reformer, Buzz Barwell on drums and Rick Taylor on guitar. We rehearsed a lot and drank a lot too. We soon had the promised string of dates, starting with a big relaunch in my home town.

Brighton Polytechnic – what a fucking great idea.

There was a preview of the gig in the *Evening Argus* – the partner drove us down in his Cortina and we had our photo taken standing in a line, holding our guitars, outside the railway station. It was a real traffic-stopper.

There were only about twenty people at the gig. I don't think I'd ever played to such a small audience – not even when I was in Addis & The Flip Tops. Hiring a hall at the polytechnic in the first week of the holidays was not a shrewd move on the part of Vernon and his partner.

But we played a lot better than Vernon expected – he'd been to some rehearsals and quite frankly, he told me later, he'd been appalled. In the rehearsals we were out of tune and 'untogether'. He said it was a shame there weren't more people at the gig, but assured me that from little apples acorns will grow. Afterwards, when everybody had gone home, I signed a management contract with him.

The year that followed was a blurred mess of dates in pubs and clubs that led absolutely nowhere. They took their commission – fifteen per cent for management – and because we were *in house* as it were, only ten per cent for agency. That rounded up to a nice twenty-five per cent – twenty-five per cent of gross that is – a quarter of everything we earned before such things as PA rental, van hire, rehearsal costs and petrol came off. I footed the bill for all that. I also had to arrange the PA and van hire. One night we were stuck without transport at Kingston Polytechnic so I rang Vernon. 'Am I to believe,' he said, 'that I am expected to be used as a taxi service?' I told him to forget it – we made our own arrangements and I paid for them as usual.

We made some demos at Wessex Studios. Vernon had blagged the time – it wasn't going to cost us anything.

Then the news came through – nothing to get too excited about yet, but it looked like we'd got a record deal. A company called Camouflage wanted to try us out for a single. I'd never heard of Camouflage and neither had anybody else – they were an up-and-coming 'indie' off-shoot of DJM.

We went into a studio with Camouflage's chosen producer, Nick Tauber, who'd produced hits for Toyah. It didn't work out. The Camouflage boss, Nick Raymonde (son of Ivor, the Dusty Springfield arranger), tried to rescue the sessions alone with me in the DJM studio. I did my best but somehow my heart wasn't in it. It had been so long since I'd had a record out that I couldn't imagine a record becoming a reality. It was a waste of time. Valuable drinking time.

I ditched the band and activated a get-out clause in the management contract. I've never seen Vernon Rossiter again and I'd like to keep it that way. He rang me a couple of times demanding payment for the Wessex sessions. He wanted to know just exactly what he should do with the tapes that were now sitting in his living room. I told him to use them as a coffee table. I've never spoken to him since.

Two years on, here I was with an outstanding legal bill for fifteen hundred pounds incurred on my behalf by Vernon Rossiter during my extrication from Stiff Records. I nearly flipped. It was a massive amount of money. I couldn't imagine what I was going to do now. I left the house in a panic and woke up in a food factory.

They gave me some green overalls, a pair of welling-ton boots, the key to a locker, a hairnet, and a hat to cover up at least some of the humiliation caused by the hairnet. They made faggots. A woman with no teeth was in charge of the operation in my section. Having ascertained that I could read and write she gave me a job on the end of the conveyer belt, chalking numbers on the boxes.

The noise was deafening. Sometimes the woman with no teeth held her hands up with the forefingers crossed and this meant that I had to chalk an X on each box before I stacked it up on the pallet. At lunchtime I went to the canteen – no going to the pub for me, this was real life now and I was in serious debt. I was going to have to work, work, work.

At four thirty the production line shuddered to a halt. A life sentence at the food factory was over for the day. I wouldn't be going back. I'd been doing sums in my head in between chalking up numbers. At two pounds fifty an hour I'd earned just fifteen pounds. When you took away the stoppages it was fuck all. I got in the minibus that took the temporary part of the workforce back to the Medway Towns. When we got there I went to the pub – I might be in serious debt but I'd just earned some money – so I spent half of it getting drunk.

The debt was reduced to half what they originally asked for and the court gave me time to pay, so I saw some of it off in instalments until it was forgotten about. It had shaken me up. I was on a downward spiral and I knew it.

The Clash's old road manager, Johnny Green, rang. He was back in the Medway Towns. He'd had some tragedy in his life that left him with a young son to bring up on his own so he'd moved in with his parents in Gillingham. I hadn't seen him for years. It was a relief to meet somebody in the Medway Towns that I could relate to at last – somebody who could understand what I'd been through.

Johnny cuts a menacing figure – six foot eight tall and built like a wardrobe, pale myopic eyes behind thick black lenses. He speaks with a deep, crunching voice with a Medway Towns accent.

We started hanging out together. We had shattered lives that needed rebuilding so we decided to relaunch my career, yet again, with Johnny as my manager. I had nothing to lose, at least we could have a laugh. We met every day in a café in Rochester High Street – Andy Snacks. We revelled in anything that was 'Towns' (Johnny still maintains that you can tell you're in Strood by the number of people pushing old cars). Andy Snacks was very 'Towns' – it had yellowing transparent perspex screwed to the wall up to dado-rail height in case anyone spilt anything. We wanted to set up our office in there. We dreamed of the day the payphone would ring and I'd say, 'If that's Detroit it's for us.' We were a couple of classic small-town layabouts.

We stumbled into BBC Radio Kent. The receptionist gave us an imperious look.

'Can I help you?'

'Got any stickers?' Johnny asked.

'There are plenty there, you can help yourselves.'

We helped ourselves to a few handfuls and then I started wandering towards the door leading to the studios. The woman said, 'You can't go through there,' and I said, 'Cor, is that where they do the programmes? I've never been in a radio station before.'

She looked at me in a patronising way. 'No, I don't expect you have…' I was starting to have fun again.

The stickers were very useful. I'd bought another car, a Morris Marina. The Daimler was all right for occasions when a bit of flash was required but it was uneconomical.

It tended to break down a lot too. The Morris Marina wasn't much better but it was cheaper to run. We covered it with stickers – George Hamilton Trucks & Vans, If It Ain't Country It Ain't Music, BBC Radio Kent… and hung fluffy dice from the rearview mirror. On our trips to London, with all this crap hanging off the car, plus our puzzled expressions and the *A to Z* open at the wrong page, we could take a short cut the full length of Oxford Street. It took hours off our journey times.

Johnny put me on a diet and fitness regime. Every morning I had to go for a run while Johnny sat in the Marina and smoked a cigarette. I lost a stone and a half in weight – I looked fucking great. Johnny drank lots of Special Brew. I only drank beer on special occasions, the rest of the time I was limited to large gin and tonics.

We started trying people out with a view to forming a band. Candidates had to come down to Strood and meet us in a pub called The Three Crutches. It gave them a foretaste of the Towns before we took them to whichever church hall, community hall, or on one occasion even a Masonic hall, we'd rented to conduct the audition in.

Johnny's behaviour was increasingly erratic. I should have twigged that there was something more than Special Brew going on when a Methodist church hall in Gillingham cost thirty pounds for an afternoon's hire – Johnny kept coming back and saying that the woman in charge of the hire, who was under the impression that Johnny was a show-business entrepreneur called Jeffrey Halcyon, needed more money. I had to come up with it because I had the giro that week. People I knew kept telling me he was 'on something'. I didn't believe them.

One night, after an over-the-limit drive back from London, we headed straight for a pub called the Tam

O'Shanter at the top of Chatham Hill. It was run by a smarmy thug from London. He liked Johnny, who he regarded as a fellow thug, and he more than tolerated me because I'd once sung with a local band in his pub. Apparently I'd given it *plenty of bollocks*.

The exact steps that led to a lock-in – Johnny on pints of Special Brew with whisky chasers and me on pints of best bitter topped up with a double gin – elude me. Eventually we had to leave. The smarmy thug had made his money out of us and was intent on fleecing some local builders in a game of poker. We were almost falling asleep on the bar.

The cold air woke me up a bit. It was an icy night and I remember Johnny saying we should drive home. I wanted to say that we couldn't possibly do that in our condition. I came to in the passenger seat of the Marina as it hurtled up Castle Road, which ran parallel to my street.

There was a lot of crashing and scraping and screeching. We were swaying around everywhere. The car came to rest with a lurch. Johnny turned to me with his big face, his eyes were almost translucent. He looked quite pleased with himself. 'Boof!' he said, with a smile. 'Where are my glasses?' I picked them up off the back seat where they'd landed, having flown off his face with the force of the impact, and reinstated them. Together we surveyed the scene.

Castle Road was a street of terraced houses with the front doors opening straight off the pavement. It was lined on both sides with parked cars, and behind us, although I didn't yet know this, most of these cars were seriously damaged. We'd done a good job. Lights were going on, front doors were opening. The first residents were beginning to appear on the scene.

Castle Road holds a special place in Chatham folk-lore. A few weeks previously the police had been called to an incident involving feuding families who had taken to fighting in the street with ornamental swords plucked from above the mantelpieces of their catalogue homes. These were the kind of people that were coming out of the adjacent houses.

It was like *The Night Of The Living Dead*. In the dim light of the street lamps they were coming towards us in their pyjamas. A moaning and groaning sound filled the air and, even though my vision was impaired by excessive alcohol intake, I could see that one of them was eating somebody's liver.

They didn't look at all pleased. I didn't know how we were going to talk our way out of this one. Insurance details would have to be exchanged. I didn't really want to get out of the car, it was warm and comfortable. Johnny thought differently. He said, 'Fuck this, let's get out of here,' and dragged me by the collar of my coat across the car and out of the driver's door.

'Fucking run!' he shouted.

As luck would have it, the final throes of the collision had happened next to a wide alleyway with steps leading up to my street. Johnny grabbed me and we ran, fell and stumbled up the steps over broken glass, weeds and litter. If we could just make it to the top we were four houses from my front door and sanctuary.

There were flashing blue lights everywhere. Uniformed policemen in front of me like rugby players. One of them said, 'Right you!' I took a swing at him. Luckily I missed. I was smacked face down on the bonnet of my neighbour's Ford Granada. Then I was in a van, accompanied by a policeman who warned me that there was only him and me in the back. As we pulled away I saw Johnny blowing up a balloon so I gave him a regal wave.

Inside the police station there appeared to be a reception committee – large, uniformed officers in their shirtsleeves, baying for blood. I was getting very nervous. I knew what was coming up – I'd been arrested once before, in Hull, for being drunk and disorderly. I gave them a bit of lip and they gave me the treatment. This time was sure to be worse – I'd tried to hit a policeman. They were going to have some fun with me.

They catalogued my belongings and took the belt out of my trousers. And then, even though I didn't resist, it took a lot of policemen to get me down to the cells. There were so many of them that there wasn't enough room for us all in the corridor and we kept falling over one another. They kept up some kind of rugby or beer-drinking chant, punching and kicking me in time with it.

At the cell door they picked me up bodily, and with a great roar, threw me inside. I landed face down on a brown stone floor. There was a smell of disinfectant. This was it, I was going to die in police custody. I covered my head and waited for the inevitable.

It never came. I was aware of some commotion – running feet and a voice: 'Lads! Lads!...' The serge trousers and Doc Martens that surrounded me melted away and a different, almost kindly voice said, 'Yes, well, you just get a bit of sleep and then we'll take a statement and you can probably go home.' I couldn't believe it. I sat on the bench and stared at the wall for a very long time.

It turned out that Johnny had arrived just as I was being taken to the cells. Seeing what was going on he thought it was a good idea to inform them that his father was a local magistrate and headmaster. It blew a hole in his credibility but he probably saved my life. The

Chatham police had a reputation for this sort of thing – Chatham was apparently a training ground for the Met.

I was charged with being drunk and disorderly and let out at seven o'clock in the morning. When I got home Johnny was already crashed out on the floor. He'd been charged with drunken driving, failing to report an accident, leaving the scene of an accident, and possession of a small amount of heroin. The Morris Marina was a write-off. I had to find out which scrapyard it had been sent to and retrieve my bits and pieces from it.

Philippa was pregnant. I tried hard to be thrilled to bits but I was terrified. I could hardly look after my self so I didn't know how I was going to deal with a new life. I felt incapable of earning a living, of leading what I imagined would be a normal life. I'd lost contact with reality years ago but here it was, trampling all over my insecurities and trying to bust in on me. I didn't know what I was going to do – I'd have to get a record deal now. Philippa had been supporting us both since we'd moved to Chatham.

But now she'd had enough. She decided to leave the job shortly before the baby was due and dedicate herself to motherhood. That was going to be it – there was going to be no turning back, no maternity leave, it was over. 'It's your turn now,' she said.

I quite understood. I decided to put an end to all the silliness – hanging around in cafes, getting drunk in the afternoon, watching daytime TV, that sort of thing. I was still drinking but I was focused on my songwriting. The Medway Towns was a great inspiration. I wrote about the place, about the banality of it all, about living in England on a low income in 1983. I never moaned about it in those songs, I wrote as an observer. As a songwriter I was right back on track and better than I'd ever been.

I had a phone call from Billy Bragg. His first album, the great *Spy v Spy,* had just come out on the Go! Disc label. His big gimmick, as I'm sure everybody knows, was that he didn't have a band – it was just him and an electric guitar. He was doing a series of gigs in the upstairs room of a pub called the Captain's Cabin, just off Regent Street. He wanted other songwriters to come along and do solo sets too. He was a fan of mine so he asked me.

It was a huge success. The Go! Discs boss, Andy MacDonald, was all over me. He almost offered me a contract on the spot. I felt valued and when I went on stage I was on top of the situation. Some people said that I completely eclipsed Billy Bragg. I think they were right.

The gig was reviewed in the *NME.* The review was all about me – it hardly mentioned anybody else. It was the best review I'd had since I started out. The spell was finally broken.

I was forming a new group, the Captains Of Industry. We made demos on a Teac 3242 tape recorder. I bought it back in 1979 with the first royalty cheque from my publishers, Zomba Music. I've still got it and Zomba still own the publishing rights to the stuff I wrote when I was on Stiff. We've had our ups and downs in the past, but the way things are now I wouldn't have it any other way. Since 1979 they've sent me a royalty statement and a cheque every six months and they haven't missed once.

I recorded the demo for Hit 'n' Miss Judy (my Belgian Number One) on a four-track Teac at the producer Nick Garvey's house. Then I bought one myself. I made some demos, learning how to work the machine as I went along, and took them to Stiff. They gave them to the office boy to listen to. I've never known if that was a

measure of the value in which they held me or an attempt
at loveable record company whackiness – if the office boy
can whistle the tune it's a hit. All he had to say was that
they were better quality than the last lot I'd given them,
which I'd recorded on a cassette player. I never gave them
any more, I kept my demos private.

By 1984 I knew what I was doing with the Teac. The
Captains Of Industry demos were great. Andy
MacDonald at Go! Discs was very keen. The trouble was
he only wanted to sign me – he wasn't interested in
signing a band with me in it. I wasn't sure about this but
he got me on my own in his office, wrote out a cheque for
five thousand quid and I capitulated. I never felt very
good about that but something had to give.

By now Philippa was huge. I couldn't afford to fuck
about. I had to make a success of this. I got Norman Watt
Roy to play the bass and we spent a week rehearsing the
songs while Go! Discs looked round for a studio for us to
record them in. I had this idea that I wanted it to sound
like American bubblegum pop, like the Ohio Express. I
wanted it to have a trashy edge, like the Standells or the
Shadows Of Night, with a sarcastic touch of easy listening. And I wanted to get back to the thick sound of the
early Stiff records. I was going to produce it myself. I
would have liked to have recorded it in Pathway.

I was sick and tired of producers. My recording career
went wrong in 1978 the day Robinson called me into the
office to meet the man who was going to produce my
second album.

It was a sunny day and through the open door I saw
my new producer silhouetted in the sunshine. He was
wearing flares and stack-heeled shoes – *flares and stack
heels in 1978?* He had bubbly hair too – it looked like a

perm. He spun round in the office chair as I came through the door –

'Hi! I'm Pete Solley. You must be Eric... I've heard your demos and there're a couple of good little songs in there – I think there's an album in it.'

Yuk. His shirt collar spanned the lapels of his jacket, with the tips touching the shoulders. He was the keyboard player from the death throes of Procol Harum. He found us a studio where he'd be comfortable working and a week later there I was in Brittania Row, Pink Floyd's place, knee-deep in the shagpile.

The album was called *The Wonderful World Of Wreckless Eric*. The title wasn't my idea and neither was the cover. When I listen to the record I can hear that it had once had something to do with me, but my musical input ended with writing the songs. I wasn't even allowed to play the guitar on that record – Solley said I wasn't good enough. Apparently when he soloed my guitar in the control room you could hear my fingers moving across the strings, fumbling the changes. I played the guitar on my first album, all of it except for a solo by Larry Wallis, but now I felt as though I hadn't existed until Pete Solley got hold of me. Later on it became obvious that I couldn't sing either. He suggested that I should just talk my way through the lyrics – 'Like your mate, Ian Dury – how badly crippled is he? Can he fuck?'

He even played my organ part on The Final Taxi. I suggested that I could do it but he insisted on doing it himself. I asked him what difference it made and he said, 'The difference is, I'm a keyboard player, you're not.' I had to show him how it went and then I stood by and watched while he did it wrong. There were already embarrassing bits of cod reggae on the song so it didn't really matter any more. But what really takes the biscuit is that dreadful, syrupy version of Tommy Roe's Dizzy. I wanted to do it like the Troggs doing Wild Thing but Solley couldn't get his head round that idea. I think he saw the song as a vehicle for his production skills and a chance to get in some of his session player mates. He put some synthesised flutes on it and when he'd finished he turned round, looking pleased with himself, and said, 'Yeah, I think that sounds pretty.' And pretty had two Ds in it.

Go! Discs were fine about me producing, in fact it was Andy MacDonald who suggested it, but they wanted me to do it in a bigger studio than Pathway. We ended up in a studio in Soho called Gooseberry.

I was in a rush to get it finished because Philippa was due to give birth at any moment. We'd even been to an open day at the maternity unit so that we'd know what to expect when the time came. It was all very matey. Mums To Be were left in the care of Matron while the expectant fathers were taken on a tour of the unit. I sort of tagged along behind.

I hadn't a hope in hell of measuring up. They were tall and solid looking with a self-assured swagger that spoke of Ford Cortinas, regular hours in a proper job and baby conceived quite deliberately in the master bedroom of a Bovis home. I was a thirty-year-old pop star with a drink problem. I felt quite inadequate. I didn't fit in.

At the end of the tour Matron addressed the assembled company, finishing off with: 'Fathers – if you're going to faint, for heaven's sake get out of our way, we haven't got time to be dealing with you.' She looked straight at me as she said it. They developed a sense for these things – she could tell.

We didn't really make any preparations. Philippa just about gave up smoking and limited herself to one glass of wine occasionally. We bought a second-hand pram and people kept giving us baby clothes. We got a cot from somewhere too.

Philippa went into labour on a night I stayed in London. When I got to the studio there was a message – if I hurried I might just get there in time.

The drive back to Chatham was terrifying. I had a Morris Traveller – a Morris Minor 1000 with a wooden back. It did eighty miles an hour if you pushed it but today it did ninety. I saw faces in a horrified blur as I shot past. The car was badly in need of a service and halfway down the A2 I noticed that the brakes weren't working any more.

I arrived with hours to spare so we made a list of all the things Philippa had forgotten to bring with her and I went off to phone the expectant grandparents. Even though I was sure I was going to faint I was determined to get everything else right. At six o'clock I was back, fortified by an early dinner and a quick one in the pub.

Things were hotting up. Suddenly the contractions were coming thick and fast and we were bluffing our way through the breathing exercises – we'd stopped going to the ante-natal classes because we didn't like the other couples.

Philippa asked for an injection of Pethedine. I can't stand injections. They're one of my phobias. But I had to hold her still while the nurse pumped up a vein and stuck the needle in. They left us alone and I had to hold a cardboard sick tray while Philippa threw up into it. I can't stand people being sick – it's my other phobia.

But I'd gone through two of my phobias without fainting. I was quite possibly going to get away with it. I had a new resolve.

The contractions were getting more and more dramatic. The midwife said it was time to start. I really wanted to help, I wanted to show that I was enthusiastic. I shouldered my way into the white gown, feeling like Doctor Kildare, and said: 'Great! Can I do the gas and air?'

The midwife gave me a disdainful look. 'No,' she said. 'You can start by standing over there and putting the gown on the right way round.'

Philippa looked pained and slightly embarrassed but it didn't matter because soon it was all screaming and shouting and people yelling 'Push!' and Philippa swearing even more than I do on a normal day. First her foot was pushing against my hip, then my shoulder, then it was in my face. I kept wiping her forehead with a damp cloth because she asked me to, then she told me to fuck off with the cloth, which I thought was a bit much, so when another midwife came in and started yelling instructions that had nothing to do with us, I turned round and told her to fuck off, as a sort of reprisal. (Later on she apologised – she'd got the wrong room apparently.)

There was a baby's head and then there was a baby, a wriggling purple thing, covered in slime and connected to an umbilical cord that looked like a string of badly made sausages. The midwife said, 'It's a girl.' She cut the umbilical cord, wrapped the girl in a blanket and gave her to me. The girl had dark, almond-shaped eyes. She opened them, looked at me, then she looked round the room, closed her eyes and went to sleep. For a moment she looked as though she knew everything there was to know. Here she was for the first time – my daughter, Luci. She's eighteen now.

I've never had the chromosome that makes people go soppy over babies – it must have gone the same way as the football one. I've never understood the fascination. They leave behind a smell of mother's milk, Johnson's baby products and over-ripe Camembert. Dribble, vomit, and equipment – light blue and lemon yellow plastic equipment.

I was terribly proud of us all – I still am. Later on things went wrong. I'm really sorry that I fucked-up later and became a long-distance dad. But for now there were three of us. Philippa was knackered and Luci was asleep so I didn't hang around for too long. I had a laugh with the midwives – I made them all a cup of tea. And when I saw the other dads sitting in the waiting room looking shaken up, I felt rather good about myself. Some of those big men had their heads between their knees because they were feeling faint.

The next day Philippa's parents came. They seemed to have brought the entire family along. We crowded into the hospital room and they passed Luci round and goo-gooed and said she had the Thomas nose, the Thomas mouth, the Thomas ears... They even detected musical talent and attributed that to the Thomas side of the family. I stood at the back wondering when I was going to get a go. They didn't really like me – they thought I was a simpleton – I was a runt, I was a bit of a disappointment. I felt surplus to requirements in the maternity ward so I fucked off to the studio to carry on with the album.

That was a mistake. As soon as Philippa was out of hospital her mother came to stay. Somebody had to look after Philippa while I carried on with my recording commitment. I was starting to lose it in the studio. The situation at home was making me insecure, and when I felt insecure I drank. The record company thought it would be best if I had some time off so we stopped recording and I stayed home. With the family. There wasn't much to do except the shopping. Philippa's mother had it all under control. So I drank.

One night she gave us the benefit of her opinions on art schools. They didn't teach us how to draw, we had no grasp of the basics, and that's why modern art was such rubbish. I thought about the hard year of life-drawing I put in on the foundation course in Bristol I was furious. I was also three quarters of the way through a bottle of gin, so I told her to shut the fuck up and not to open her mouth again until she knew what she was talking about.

There wasn't so much a row as an atmosphere. Her mother left the following day.

We finished the album and mixed it with the help of a woman from the record company who had attended a sound-engineering course. There's an unfortunate point you can reach in recording where you think that you might have a success on your hands, so everybody starts being very careful. That's what happened to the Captain's album – we got careful, we got precious, we blanded out. I still think it's a good record up to a point, and I think it deserved a lot better than the reception it got. Andy MacDonald was pretty pissed off with me by the time it came out – he was probably wondering why he'd signed a drunken egomaniac. I was a has-been because I was acting like one.

The album came out the following year, April 19th 1985. By then Go! Discs were heavily into the Red Wedge thing with Billy Bragg, demonstrating that unlike other labels

they held good Socialist principles. I was a forgotten
cause, I was broke and back on the dole.

I was bitterly disappointed at the reception of the
Captains Of Industry album. Nobody liked it. It was the
right thing at the wrong time. The ideals of the Thatcher
regime had found their way into pop. It was one great big
glorious pop-star party – the Belle Stars, Duran Duran,
Wham!, Madness. Everybody was young, fresh-faced
and enthusiastic. My album was about the banal, the
mundane and the commonplace. One reviewer wrote
about 'this horrible record populated with misfits and
morons...' It was just what nobody wanted to hear.

If we'd gone with my original plan to record it in
Pathway it would have had a trashier sound, but as it
was, it sounded like a low-budget attempt at sophistica-
tion. As an indie record it didn't have much credibility. It
should have been great but it wasn't, and as a result I was
plumbing new depths of serious depressive drinking. The
record company had had enough of me, I'd had enough
of them, and I hadn't even got a band any more. It was
time to jack it all in and get a job.

So I went down to the Oxfam shop and got a set of the
sort of clothes that I thought blokes that were in work
might wear. Then I hit the Job Centre. It was harder than
I thought. It hadn't occurred to me that I'd be expected to
account for the last ten years of my adult life. It hadn't
actually occurred to me that I was an adult. At least I
could play at being one. I could only get to grips with real
life by pretending to be someone else anyway, and as I
was beginning to get an idea of the kind of tax bill I'd be
facing once the high street accountant had finished
pissing about with the woefully inadequate paperwork

from my days as a success, I could see that it was no use pretending to be one of the proletariat. A salt-of-the-earth-chalking-numbers-on-the-boxes-as-they-came-off-the-conveyer-belt-and-throwing-them-onto-the-trolley sort of job was not going to do it.

What I needed was an executive position – company car, fifteen Gs a year plus commission and bonuses... something involving a briefcase. I'd developed an image of myself in a shirt, tie and golfing jacket – terylene trousers and tidy hair, zipping around in a white Ford Escort with a plastic briefcase in the role of an insurance salesman or something.

The woman at the Job Centre obviously didn't share my vision. I suppose what she saw sitting in front of her was a hung-over bum in a frayed shirt, second-hand tie and polyester windcheater. You've got to be convincing – I couldn't even say my name without fucking-up. I didn't create a good impression. There was an interview. It was in Gillingham, in the heart of shirt, tie and golfing jacket land. It ended in unpleasantness because they didn't believe that I'd ever been round the world as a pop star. I don't think they were going to offer me the job anyway.

It was utterly hopeless. And in the middle of it all there was the tax problem. I had no paperwork. What I hadn't given to Vernon had gone missing when the Austin 1300 got broken into. The tax people got onto me because of the day I worked in the food factory. They couldn't find my P45. I didn't know what a P45 was so I rang the tax office in Chatham and bit by bit the story came out. I told the woman on the other end of the phone that I hadn't paid tax since 1976. She said I'd have to make a declaration. I asked her what would happen then. She laughed and said, 'I expect we'll hang you from the highest yardarm.'

Somebody suggested that I should find myself an accountant – Mr Grayson looked like marine life. He would have been at home in an aquarium. He was everything you'd imagine an accountant would be – boring, devoid of any personality whatsoever, with thick wet lips and opaque eyes behind glasses that looked like goggles. He had hands like lumps of meat and yet he was an effete and over-particular sort of man. He wore a matching shirt and tie. The firm he worked for had their offices above a parade of shops. It was all very shabby and the walls were covered in blue painted woodchip.

He gave me some photocopied forms on which I could fill in details of my professional outgoings. He looked through the paperwork I'd supplied in a dismal and dejected manner. He asked on what date I'd left 'Stiffs' and had they given me a P45. He always said 'Stiffs' with an S on the end, as though they were an engineering firm. I don't think he understood what was needed any more than I did, but somehow, after a lot of boring trips to his office, a tax declaration was made on my behalf.

And then we were invited into the tax office to try and explain it.

The tax inspector was a vicious-looking, middle-aged woman. She asked all kinds of bizarre questions – how much did I spend *per annum* on Christmas presents, birthday presents, petrol, socks, shoes, holidays... She consulted the figures supplied by Mr Grayson. The figures didn't add up. She asked if I could explain but I couldn't so we asked Mr Grayson to have a look. He prepared the accounts after all.

Mr Grayson was nodding off in the corner, rocking backwards and forwards in his gabardine mac with his briefcase on his knees. He pursed his big fat lips and gave the accounts the briefest glance.

I said: 'The figures don't add up, can you explain them?'

'Mmmm... no, not really.'

The inquisition carried on: Do you smoke, Mr Goulden? And do you drink?

'Like a fucking fish,' I said.

The accounts had to be prepared and presented again. A bit of a money-spinner for Mr Grayson, though I had no intention of ever paying him. In the meantime the tax office sent an estimate of what they thought I owed them. It was an inconceivably large amount of money – I'd have to cover the walls with gold records to get near to it, and then I'd have to pay the tax on that too. I found the best way to deal with it was to forget about it. I sent them a ten-pound postal order.

I tried not to care, but the fear of eviction, foreclosure, bankruptcy, imprisonment, and abstract fears that were even worse, hung over me. I was desperate. I felt useless. I could only sleep at night if I got drunk. When I woke up I couldn't remember going to bed. And always, my first thought was where was I going to get the money for the drink I'd need later on.

Our finances were a complete mess. With Philippa at home looking after Luci, our only income was supplementary benefit. We had two county court settlements and the mortgage was in arrears. We cut back and cut back. I started drinking at home. It was cheaper. We both liked a drink but Philippa was a lot more restrained about it since the pregnancy. Home drinking was a far more sensible option for me because I was getting to the point where I couldn't go to a pub without fucking-up. I'd fall off a bar stool or get into an argument. The landlord or landlady would have a quiet word, tell me to go home and sleep it off. So I'd try another pub and when I ran out of pubs I'd weave my way home via the off-licence and finish myself off with a bottle of cider.

It suited me to drink at home because I couldn't stand the music that accompanied drinking in the pub. I was depressed enough without having to hear I Know Him So Well by Elaine Page & Barbara Dickson, or Bat Out Of Hell. It seemed like such a long time ago (early 1978 in fact) that Dave Robinson took me along to meet a guy called Steve Popowitz who managed a singer called Meatloaf. Meatloaf was going to be a hot property and Popowitz had a film clip to prove it. We picked him up at his hotel and took him to a preview theatre in Soho. The film was the famous video of Bat Out Of Hell. Dave and I were the first people in the country to see it. Meatloaf was on offer and Stiff had got first refusal. Dave looked amused and turned it down. I thought it was hilarious. We were much too cool for that sort of thing.

And now I didn't want to hear about Paradise By The Dashboard Light or The Power Of Love or the highway crammed with broken heroes. This gun's for hire – even though we're just dancing in the dark. They were about to cut the electricity off.

For a while some kind of sense prevailed. I've always had strong survival instincts. I rationed myself to one bottle of supermarket cider a night and took our finances in hand. Cider was the most cost-effective form of drink-ing. That and the occasional bottle of Don Cortez, which I usually had to open by pushing the remainder of the crumbling cork into the bottle with a screwdriver. I hadn't got a problem – I just liked a drink. I needed a drink but it wasn't a problem. We had to itemise every-thing we bought in a 1985 Boots Scribbling Diary.

Typical entries read:

29 Wednesday   **May**
   Cigarettes   1.20
   Cider and nappies   4.38
   Newspaper   0.20

30 Thursday   **May**
   Shopping + cider   4.10
   Newspaper   0.20
   Cigarettes   1.20

As long as we had our cigarettes and cider, and a newspaper for the TV guide, we could function. The regime lasted for about five weeks and then it sort of petered out. We were over the worst of the debt by then.

There was an uneasy truce between me and Go! Discs. I decided to play solo. It seemed like the best way to promote the album, even though I couldn't really go out on my own as Captains Of Industry. I didn't want to be like Billy Bragg but at least I wouldn't have to pay a band. It was just going to be me and my guitar.

I was offered a twenty-minute solo set at a festival while some roadies set up a drum kit behind me. The festival was part of a GLC campaign to give everybody a job. It was called 'Jobs For Cowboys' and it happened in Battersea Park in July 1985. The Men They Couldn't Hang, the Boothill Foottappers and some group called the Shrieking Shillelagh Sister or something were coming up in the wake of The Pogues and Billy Bragg. They played electric skiffle and demonstrated a marked lack of feeling for country music. They were politically motivated in a woolly sort of way – socialist by virtue of wearing checked shirts, having heard of Woodie Guthrie and being, for the most part, on the dole. The music papers were calling it Cow Punk. I didn't fit into this scene at all. But for an afternoon I was a jobbing cowboy in between The Boothill Foottappers and Hank Wangford.

The concert was organised by Peter Jenner's company, Sincere Management. I got the gig on the understanding that I didn't get drunk – apparently I had a reputation. As long as I didn't fuck-up I'd be paid fifty quid.

I didn't fuck-up because the booze didn't arrive until after I'd played, so I got paid, then the booze arrived, and I got drunk for free and used the fifty quid as a down payment to stop them cutting off the electricity.

My performance wasn't very good but I hadn't got drunk so they offered me another titbit as a reward. A real cracker this time – two nights at the Edinburgh Fringe Festival. Half an hour per night for two nights with accommodation and food thrown in – and although I wouldn't actually be getting paid *as such*, the eyes of the world would apparently be upon me, and the 'knock-on' effects could be considerable. How right they were.

After the Unemployed Cowboys fiasco I couldn't face going on stage alone again. I couldn't be bothered with it all any more. I only accepted the Edinburgh Festival job because it was a trip out, a break from the routine and I thought that there might be some free booze in it. Apart from that, there were a couple of Captains Of Industry commitments that I was going to honour because there was a guaranteed fee attached to them. And that was going to be it.

But for some reason I started listening to the Velvet Underground again, and that coincided with seeing a film of the Violent Femmes playing live on the telly. Something clicked. Suddenly I knew that I had to have a very simple group playing with me. We'd be a group in a

suitcase – two small amplifiers, one for the bass and one
for my guitar, and a minimal drum kit. We'd be a cool
little combo, bizarre and uncomplicated, and we'd drive
up to Edinburgh in my Chrysler Avenger Estate. It was
really quite simple.

I remembered a character called Russ Wilkins who used
to be in a Medway band called The Milkshakes. When I
moved to the Medway Towns, The Milkshakes were on
the verge of becoming more than just a local group. I saw
them play at the MIC (Medway Indian Club) but we
didn't meet at the time. One afternoon I went into an
electrical shop on the corner of Chatham High Street and
the bright young assistant behind the counter was Russ
Wilkins, the famed ex-Milkshakes' bass player. He said,
''Ere, you're Wreckless Eric – you've seen us play at the
MIC.' I thought he was fucking big-headed – if he'd been
a real fan he would have talked about seeing me play, not
me seeing him. But I'd yet to understand Russ Wilkins'
arrogant attitude. I don't mean that unkindly – this arrogance had a lot to do with the good things that happened
subsequently. We had a chat and discovered a mutual
admiration for Dusty Springfield. He showed me round
the shed at the back of shop where he'd masterminded
the recording of several Milkshakes albums and said that
if I ever needed a bass guitarist I should give him a shout.

But that was a couple of years ago. In the interim I'd
recorded the Captains album and the Milkshakes had
split up. So I rang Russ and asked him if he'd like to play
at the Edinburgh Festival for no money whatsoever and
he said he would. He suggested that Bruce Brand, the
Milkshakes' drummer, could play too. I was a bit
nervous about all this but Bruce made me laugh – he only
lived down the road so he popped up to my house and

made me autograph a copy of my first album. I found this excruciatingly embarrassing because I was convinced that nothing I'd done before the Captains album was any good. When I played him the Captains album I got quite a shock – he didn't like it. He didn't like the production, it wasn't rough and tough enough. He even said that I should have done it in Pathway like Whole Wide World.

We cobbled a set together in a damp archway under Rochester Bridge, which was shared by several groups. It was a disgusting place, full of redundant equipment, speaker cabinets, amplifiers, shopping trolleys, old car tyres, that sort of thing. Everything seemed to be covered in encrusted vomit and there was a smell of piss. The place was as long as the bridge was wide and I could just about stand up in the middle of it. It was lit by one forty-watt light bulb.

In the hour and a half that we rehearsed we managed to get six numbers together. It was a bit rough. It was primitive. I hadn't heard anybody play like Russ and Bruce did for years. I was a bit worried that it was too rough, but as I was already finished – as I'd already made some of The Worst Records In The Whole History Of Pop Music Ever and fallen out with a record label due to being an obnoxious drunk, as I was a washed-up waste of space and I was going to jack it all in anyway – well, it didn't really matter. And it sounded so fucking exciting – it was like being in Addis & The Flip Tops all over again – it was like the old days in Melody Road.

Russ went up to Scotland a day or two early with his wife, who had some business there. I drove up with Bruce. We got there without any problem – we listened to the radio, laughed a lot, stopped at a pub for lunch and still managed to arrive sober.

The venue was a draughty old church, deconsecrated and turned into a community centre. We were sharing the bill with a band called Design For Living. They'd finished their soundcheck and were getting on very well with the promoter, who was one of the Sincere Management gang. They gave me the creeps, especially the promoter, he was like a scoutmaster. After we'd done our soundcheck he clapped his hands together and said: 'OK everybody, it's time to eat – walk this way, people.' Russ looked at the big scoutmaster's arse and said, 'I'd have to stick cushions down me trousers to walk like that!' And then I knew that we were going to be all right. I felt like I was in a group for the first time in years.

Design For Living were getting on my nerves. They spoke with that self-assured North London transatlantic accent that a lot of would-be successful musicians of the '80s adopted. It was about seven o'clock in the evening and I'd had an almost dry day. I was beginning to feel VERY twitchy. But the nearest pub or off-licence might as well have been miles away because I hadn't got any money. And although I knew that I presented a somewhat seedy and shabby spectacle – a podge dressed in grubby, second-hand clothes – I was beginning to resent the disapproving, sidelong glances that The Scoutmaster kept giving me.

Eventually we got our drink ration – two cans of Heineken each. Then we did our set. We played really well, and the twenty or so people in the audience clapped themselves silly. The Scoutmaster was quite impressed, despite himself. He was very patronising but we hit him up for some expenses and got drunk.

Design For Living started with a pre-recorded cassette. They crept out of the corners of the hall and made their way to the stage singing in harmony. The rest of it is just a misty beer-stained memory to me, though I do remember the flute player wearing a Tibetan hat.

I woke up in the morning between white sheets in a clean white room. I had the usual hangover. I went into the kitchen where the Design team were busy having breakfast. They were enthusing about the night before. They said 'Morning!' It was obvious that none of them had a hangover. I wasn't going to let them see I was suffering so I refused the offer of a mug of Nescafé and opened one of the cans of Strongbow cider that I had leftover from last night. I poured it down and the heat behind my eyeballs subsided to a low throb. I could almost risk a cigarette. I found myself sitting next to the drummer. He was eating his breakfast. I was drinking mine. He felt obliged to strike up conversation: 'Heard it went pretty well for you last night...didn't catch your set...hoping to catch it tonight...heard a lot of good things...didn't you used to be in a name band or something?'

In the time it had taken to consume two large cans of Strongbow I'd heard a lot of talk about record companies – *it looked like Ariola were going to bite so it was time to tell Virgin to either shit or get off the pot* – that sort of thing. They sounded like office colleagues in a pub at lunchtime. I wanted to know what was motivating them – why they were playing music and not marketing some product like Cornflakes. So I asked the drummer. He obviously thought I was a moron. He explained: 'It's a career like any other, and we're just like any other group – we're looking for the big one.'

And I thought we were doing it because we believed in something. I could understand now why the music scene was in such a mess with cunts like these knocking about. I was furious, I was depressed, and I was drunk. I had a pocketful of expenses and the pubs were just opening. I rounded up Bruce and we went into town to have a drink. One drink led to another and, what with one thing and another – like another round of drinks – I didn't get around to eating anything. I was feeling insecure so I couldn't eat, and there was plenty of time to kill before the evening's gig, and it was raining, and anyway, I needed another drink.

When the landlord refused to serve us any more we went to the venue. We had an altercation with the Brighton Bottle Orchestra, and when they left, between sets, we pissed in their bottles. The next time they went on they were out of tune and faintly disgusted. I can't remember much more – that is, I can but you don't really need to know it. I tried to order a vodka and tonic in the bar before we went on stage – to freshen up – but they wouldn't serve me.

When we went on I was at pains to point out that I hated everybody, including myself, and I wished that I'd never been born. The first song was over before I'd finished singing the first verse to my complete satisfaction. The second petered out in a silent guitar solo after my finger got stuck under the strings. I fell on the floor, off the stage, into my amplifier. Bruce threw drumsticks at people in the audience and shouted belligerent comments. He'd painted his face with make-up stolen from the Brighton Bottle Orchestra. Russ was a bit surprised because he hadn't spent the day with us. He tried to keep the whole thing together at the start with a few slick announcements and amused observations. But he soon gave up and got stuck into a bottle of scotch. The set ended in a free-form free-for-all with everything turned up full. A blaring mess of feedback with me telling the whole world to fuck off.

I could tell that The Scoutmaster wasn't very pleased. It was an obscenely drunken mess. We upset a lot of people but I think some of them deserved it. A few years ago I met someone who was working at the venue that night. The Scoutmaster ordered us to be removed from his presence so this guy took us back to the house in a black cab. He had to prevent us from jumping out of the speeding taxi when we thought we saw an off-licence. We were crazed with drink.

It should have been the end of my career. As far as Sincere Management and Go! Discs were concerned, it was. I was secretly ashamed because I had a rule – I would never go on stage in a paralytic drunk condition. I used to do that on the first Stiff Tour and when my first album came out, but I learnt not to. It was too humiliating. I used to like a drink or two before I went on but I drew the line at noticeably slurring the words and falling over. I used to have a certain amount of professional pride.

I stumbled through another week of drinking but something had changed – I knew that I was in hell. It was a god-awful existence. The following Saturday I got so drunk that I came round full circle, and in the early hours of Sunday morning I had a sober realisation: I didn't want to drink any more. I couldn't carry on living like this. It was a problem and the problem was me. I had a drink problem. Philippa agreed that I should cool it. She tried to cheer me up, saying that I could be back on the white wine by Christmas. But I knew it was more serious than that.

In the morning I got up, had a cup of tea and rang Alcoholics Anonymous. The enormity of this action didn't escape me; I felt like a pervert. A woman answered and I said, 'I think I might be an alcoholic.' She asked a lot of questions – did I ever drink in the morning? Had I ever stolen money to get a drink? Did I ever have black-outs (did I ever)? I answered yes to every question. There was no doubt about it, I was an alcoholic.

I felt a bit better now that I knew what I was.

We had a gig that night in Medway's cool music venue, the Nag's Head in Rochester. It was a surprise guest appearance with Thee Mighty Caesars, darlings of the Medway garage scene. Word had got around – Wreckless Eric and two Milkshakes in a local group – that sort of thing. The place was packed.

I was in a dreadful condition, ill beyond belief, shaking and sweating, and on the edge of panic. A drink would have sorted that out but I wasn't going to have one. If I could get through tonight, I could deal with it tomorrow. I didn't tell anybody what was going on, I just said I was going on the wagon for a while because I had a hangover. Everybody was very nice to me – they pressed me to have a shandy or something, but I was steadfast. When we got on the stage somebody passed me a glass of orange juice. I was shaking so much that I splashed it all over myself in plain view of the audience.

I played and sang staring at the light fitting in the middle of the bar. I didn't dare take my eyes off it, didn't dare look elsewhere. Paranoia was creeping in now – what were people thinking about me. It was like going on stage with no clothes on. I had the worst withdrawal symptoms I'd ever had. My guitar was running away from me – I could hardly keep it under control, and the space between the light fitting and my eyes was crowded with birds, insects, shooting stars and sudden beams of light. I had the DTs. This was the worst it had ever been.

I was still alive when we finished playing and I felt

slightly better. Everybody liked the band – they thought we were psychotic. I was soaked in sweat and dying for a drink so I got a pint of lemonade and forced that down instead. I just had to get through until half-past ten – after that there was nowhere I could get a drink on a Sunday night in the Medway Towns.

I went to an AA meeting. Everybody was very discreet: 'Are you here for the meeting?' I hadn't had a drink for forty-six hours but I still felt rough. I thought I was going to die from it. They gave me a cup of tea in a Snoopy mug. We sat on chairs in rows and listened while a woman with a face like a brick described her life with alcohol. She'd been a sergeant in the army. When she was in the sergeants' mess, surrounded by male sergeants in their uniforms, all chucking down pints of lager, she felt like the girl in the Martini ad. I nearly cried.

A suave looking middle-aged man got up and described how he went from being a success to sleeping in a storm drain. As I slopped my mug of tea over myself I was thinking, 'Have these people got no self-respect?' But their stories were exactly the same as mine.

They told me it would get easier. The only way was to take it one day at a time. I'd been taking it one minute at a time. If a minute could turn into an hour without a drink I could face the following minute. I couldn't think in the long term – the future only seemed to hold devastation and ruin.

I never admitted to anybody outside Alcoholics Anonymous that I had a drink problem. As far as they were concerned I was on a health kick. I was too ashamed to tell the truth and anyway, I'd gone through that scenario before – turned over a new leaf, told everybody I'd change, how I'd started a new life, and the next time they saw me I was crawling around the floor, blind drunk. If I was going to get this right I was going to have to do it quietly, on my own.

It was probably a mistake in some ways to turn away from Alcoholics Anonymous. I spent fifteen years learning what they might have shown me in two. I could have made life easier for myself but their insistence that there was no other way than theirs put me off. I wanted to learn how to live in a world that contains alcohol and people that drink the stuff. They told me I must never go in a pub again. They trotted out little homilies. Arch-warnings – if you sit in the barber's long enough you'll eventually get a haircut – if you walk across a ploughed field you'll get mud on your boots. If you keep your mouth open you'll probably say something stupid.

The physical addiction wore off very quickly. I started to feel better and lost a lot of weight. Eventually I started to sleep at night. My nerves were shot to pieces and quite often, as I was about to fall asleep, my back would arch in a spasm and nearly catapult me off the bed.

I was amazed at how much time there was to do things – drinking takes up a lot of time and energy – it's hard work. Now I could even read in bed without having to hold one eye shut, and in the morning I could remember what I'd read.

A lot of people exchange one addiction for another – they become dependent on AA meetings. I didn't want that to happen to me; I hadn't got time because I'd got work to do. I got addicted to my new group instead. I suppose you could say I became a workaholic except that I've got an appalling work ethic.

We had a gig at the Cricketers in Kennington Oval, just a couple of doors down from Ian's old flat. We were shambolic but I was three days into being sober. We did our set, all six or seven numbers, and when it wasn't anywhere near long enough we just did it all again as an encore. David Quantick came along and reviewed it for the *NME*. The review took up a whole column. He compered us to The Troggs fronted by Ray Davies. We didn't even have a name – the piece was headed 'The Mighty Wah!' with 'Eric Goulden' underneath. I'd left the Captains Of Industry behind. The promoter offered us another gig on the proviso that we gave the group a name.

Bruce arrived at the next gig with The Len Bright Combo carefully painted on the front of his bass drum. Around it were the names of various styles of music, each with its own exclamation mark: 'Pops!', 'Ballads!', 'Country!', 'Olde Tyme!', 'Modern!', 'Rhythm 'n' Blues!', 'Latin American!', 'New Romantic!'.

We desperately needed a name for the group. The promoter phoned one day demanding to know what we were called. I thought of the bass drum and said, 'We're called the Len Bright Combo.' There was a pause and he said, 'Not in my pub you're not.' And that was it, we were the Len Bright Combo.

I rang every promoter I knew, and some I didn't. I booked us into clubs, colleges and universities all over the place. I asked for outlandish fees and sometimes got them. I wrote a set of songs for us to play – it took about a week and those songs formed the basis of our first album, *The Len Bright Combo Present The Len Bright Combo By The Len Bright Combo*. We recorded most of it in a village hall on a borrowed eight-track Tascam. We finished it off in my bathroom and Bruce's attic and put it out on a label Russ had started, called Empire. It was a complete DIY job and it cost eighty-six pounds to make, including hire of the village hall and artwork.

It was a perfect union. Between us we were rude, arrogant and eccentric. And none of us wanted anything to do with the music business. At one gig at the 100 Club we stopped playing because I'd recognised an A&R man from EMI. I told him to fuck off. We wouldn't start playing again until he'd left. Russ said, 'We don't need you, we've got our own label and it's got more letters in it than yours.'

We may have been deluded to think that we could do it without the music business but it was a brave attempt. We were a truly independent group with a genuine punk DIY ethic.

I was starting to have fun again, even though I was haunted by twelve years of hard drinking – ashamed of some of the things I'd done. Memories crowded in on me and I wanted to go and hide. They used to stop me in my tracks, literally. One day when I was walking down the street I found myself cowering on the floor in somebody's gateway with my jacket over my head. But most of the time I could keep that sort of thing at bay. Life was a lot better now. And I hadn't had a letter from the Inland Revenue for months.

I never started drinking again – it's been eighteen years now. In the aftermath my life fell to bits, then it slowly got better. There isn't time to talk about that because this is the end of the book. I wasn't sure how to finish but somebody told me you just have to stop.